Pelican Books
Crime and Industrial Society
in the Nineteenth Century

John J. Tobias was educated at Lindisfarne College,
Westcliff-on-Sea, and Leeds College of Commerce.
He joined the Civil Service as a clerk in the
Colonial Office, subsequently serving in the Department
of Scientific and Industrial Research. Studies during a
long illness resulted in an External degree from London
University in 1958. In 1959 he was appointed a tutor
in the Department of General Studies at the Police
College, Bramshill House (where he is now Director of
General Studies of the Special Course), and this post led
him to choose the history of crime as his research subject
at the London School of Economics, where he was a
part-time student from 1960 to 1965. He was awarded
the degree of Ph.D in 1965 for the thesis on which
this book is based.

Dr Tobias has written two illustrated textbooks –
Against the Peace (a history of crime and policing)
and *A History of Local Government* – has contributed
to the *British Journal of Criminology*, the *Police
Journal* and other publications, and has given broadcast
talks on nineteenth-century criminals.

Crime and Industrial Society in the Nineteenth Century

J. J. Tobias

 Penguin Books

Penguin Books Ltd, Harmondsworth,
Middlesex, England
Penguin Books Australia Ltd, Ringwood,
Victoria, Australia

First published by B. T. Batsford 1967
Published in Pelican Books 1972
Copyright © J. J. Tobias, 1967

Made and printed in Great Britain by
Cox & Wyman Ltd,
London, Reading and Fakenham
Set in Intertype Times

To my mother and to the memory of my father

Contents

Part Four: Conclusion

Preface

This book is based upon a Ph.D. thesis accepted by the University of London in 1965. I owe a great debt to my two supervisors at the London School of Economics, Professor A. H. John and Mr J. E. Hall Williams, respectively Professor of Economic History and Reader in Criminology in the University of London, whose guidance and criticism have over a number of years been of the utmost value to me. I have also had advice and assistance from Dr A. N. Little and Dr D. M. Downes of the London School of Economics. I have had the benefit of discussions with Professor L. Radzinowicz, Director of the Institute of Criminology at Cambridge. Mr P. Macnaughton Smith, late of the Home Office Research Unit, advised me on statistical aspects of my work.

Members of the Police College have given me much assistance. It has been a great help to be able to discuss the crime and police of the past with police officers of the present day, who have often been able to put things in perspective and clear up obscurities. Among those who have helped have been Mr J. C. Bliss (now National Coordinator of the Regional Crime Squads), Mr A. F. C. Clissitt (now Assistant Chief Constable of Leeds) and Mr R. G. Fenwick (now Chief Constable of Shropshire); but many other members of the staff and student body have allowed me to draw on their experience. I am also grateful to my colleagues in the Department of General Studies and to the College Librarian, Mr D. T. Brett, F.L.A., and his staff.

Finally, I have received much assistance from members of my family, in reading and commenting on successive texts, in typing and map-drawing and in many other ways.

It hardly needs to be said that the opinions expressed in this

Preface

book are my own, and do not in any way represent the views of
the Commandant of the Police College or of the Home
Office.

J. J. TOBIAS

The Police College,
Bramshill House
July, 1967.

Note to the Pelican Edition

The only difference between this edition and the original is the
addition of material on the criminal areas of London (pp. 144–
58) and Liverpool (pp. 166–9).

Note on Sources

Volumes in the annual series of Parliamentary Papers have
been cited by the abbreviation 'P.P.' followed by the year and
the volume number. 'S.C.' is used in the footnotes for 'Select
Committee', and 'R.C.' for 'Royal Commission'.

Books for which no place of publication is indicated after the
title were published in London.

Part One
Introduction

1. The objective and the difficulties

This book sets out to study crime in the nineteenth century as part of social history, and to see what conclusions can be reached about the influence on crime and criminals of the various changes taking place in that period. It must be recognized at the start that this subject is not one in which anything approaching certainty is attainable; we are dealing at best with probabilities and possibilities. Even today we find it difficult to decide the course of crime or its causes, and the problems are of course intensified when we are dealing with the past.

The difficulty is not that evidence about the subject is lacking. Crime was a popular topic in the nineteenth century as it is today, and there is a wealth of material to be found in parliamentary papers and in books, pamphlets, journals and newspapers. This material is, however, of uncertain and uneven reliability. Much of it is based on the criminal statistics; but it will later be argued that no reliance can be placed on nineteenth-century statistics of crime, whether produced at the time or assembled later by investigation of court records and so forth. If this is accepted we must discard also nineteenth-century discussions of the statistics, and are thus left with contemporary descriptions and assessments of crime and criminals. Some of these can be seen to be merely a restatement in words of the story told by the statistics. Others may fall into the same category without the fact being obvious, and we might thus unwittingly be examining statistics at second-hand.

Moreover, when dealing with this material we are faced with an acute form of a general problem of historical research. Even if contemporaries are agreed on something, we cannot be sure that they were right. In this field we learn at best the opinions of those who themselves did not possess the information we seek; and we must be careful not to accept an opinion merely because it is held by a number of people. We are dealing with intangible, unmeasurable evidence which is very difficult to assess. Nevertheless, it is suggested that something of value has been gained from the sifting of the evidence, and that the accumulation of general impressions here presented does add up to something worth-while.

Another limitation which must be recognized is that the terms used in this book cannot be defined with any precision. What do we mean by 'crime', by 'criminals'? Can we be sure what was meant by those terms in our source-material, and did our witnesses always mean the same thing when they used them? To deal with the latter, double, question first, the answer is not so uncompromising a negative as might at first sight be expected. To be sure, the terms were bandied about in the nineteenth century just as loosely as they are today. Seldom do we have a precise definition. And yet the people of the nineteenth century had a fairly definite picture in their minds of what they were talking about. When they spoke of 'criminals' they meant the class which lived a life of its own separate from the rest of the community, members of which were usually easily distinguished by their clothing and habits and lived wholly or largely on the proceeds of crime. Assaults and drunken misbehaviour, etc., were not usually included in the term 'crime'. What is now called 'white-collar crime', criminal activity carried on at the margin of a respectable trade or profession, seldom entered into the matter – though it was of course prevalent. The 'criminals' were Fagin and the Artful Dodger and their like, and 'crime' was what they did and what they lived by. Members of the 'criminal class' were not the only ones who committed crimes, but they had adopted a way of life in which crime played an important part. Whether or not we today regard these ideas as valid, the contemporary evidence has to be considered in its own terms, and the nineteenth-century concepts are the ones denoted when the terms 'crime' and 'criminal' are used.

The chapters which follow frequently discuss the effect of the topic under consideration 'on crime'. This expression and similar ones may be thought to betray an attitude to crime and its causation which is far too naïve and simple. Indeed, the very idea of the 'causation of crime' – of crime of all kinds as a single entity – is scouted by modern criminologists. Phrases of the kind referred to are used as a rapid means of denoting the criminal class just defined, and of considering whether whatever is being studied has in some way affected the ease with which this criminal class could operate, has altered the pattern of recruitment to it, or in some other way has had an effect on its operations.

There is a further word which appears frequently in this book and which requires consideration here. The term 'juvenile' cannot be given a precise definition. The people of the nineteenth century can be forgiven for using it loosely, for it can seldom have been possible to prove the age of any youngster who sought to obscure the facts. Compulsory registration of births was not introduced until 1836, and thus it was not until the 1850s that birth certificates would have been available for the purpose of determining whether someone qualified as a juvenile. Registration was not complete until the second half of the century, and even then it must often have been difficult to prove the identity of a person appearing before the courts and to trace his birth certificate.

Thus, nineteenth-century observers usually had to rely on appearance or on the frail reed of the criminal's own declaration of his age. Yet once again they had a fairly clear picture in mind, a picture of a group of youngsters, of ages ranging from about eight to about eighteen to twenty, who had certain well-known habits and who formed a reasonably clear-cut group. 'Juveniles', 'youngsters' and similar expressions are in this book used in the same way.

A further problem of definition arises in connection with observers' references to particular places, especially when estimates of numbers are being given. The exact area to which the description or the figure relates is not always certain. Thus,

Introduction

'London' may mean the whole of the metropolis or just the City of London proper; and sometimes people added to the confusion by talking about the 'City', with the capital letter, when they meant (or seem to have meant) the former rather than the latter. The distinction is not mere pedantry, for the City has for centuries had a separate system of policing and a separate system of courts, and these differences affected the pattern of crime. Another difficulty is that, though the City has just been contrasted with 'the whole of the metropolis', there is no clear meaning to this latter term. Before 1829, references to this larger London should probably be related to the area within the Bills of Mortality, the weekly statements of deaths issued by the parish clerks and covering the Cities of London and Westminster and a number of other parishes in the central part of modern London. After 1829 such references may have had in mind the Metropolitan Police District, a much wider area, and one which was still further extended in 1839. Other interpretations are, however, possible and their number increases as the century progresses.

Some other place-names present difficulties. Remarks made about 'Manchester' probably had reference to both Manchester and Salford – much of what is said about Manchester later in this book probably relates to the combined area. Most town names used by the people of the nineteenth century probably referred to the area of the municipality, but sometimes towns had different limits for different purposes and one cannot be sure which boundary was in mind. No real difficulty is presented in these cases, however, nor need we be troubled by the ambiguity presented by phrases such as 'the country' or 'the whole country'. These have been taken to mean England rather than the United Kingdom, for the problems of Scotland and Ireland in criminal matters were well known to be very different from those of England. Wales might or might not have been included in the term, but this does not make much difference.

These qualifications about the nature of the evidence and the meanings of the terms used must be borne in mind when reading this book. None the less, a general picture has emerged which, however provisional, is suggested to be worth keeping until something better can be put in its place. No doubt more detailed studies of particular places or particular aspects of the problem will enable corrections to be made to the general view here presented; but until that can be done, what follows is offered as a contribution to the understanding of a period not long past and a problem which is still very much with us.

2.   The statistics of crime

Before the study of past crime can commence, one problem of method must be tackled. It is necessary to consider whether anything would be gained by a study of the criminal statistics. Material for such a study is not lacking, for there is an abundant supply of nineteenth-century criminal statistics. Though the present series of Judicial Statistics commenced only in 1856–7, there were earlier criminal statistics stretching back before 1815, and in addition there were many other sets of figures, official or unofficial, for particular years, places or categories of crime or criminal. These statistics are to be found in returns to the House of Commons, in Select Committee reports, in books, pamphlets and journals, and in manuscripts. Patrick Colquhoun, a magistrate and reformer active at the beginning of the century, was an indefatigable counter and comparer. There was much attention to the criminal statistics during the early years of the Statistical Society of London, which was founded in 1834. The first dozen volumes of its *Journal* contained frequent discussions of the topic, and the Society's first two secretaries, R. W. Rawson and Joseph Fletcher, and the Continental pioneers, A. M. Guerry and A. Quetelet, were active at this time.[1] Henry Mayhew, a journalist who produced a study of the criminals of the 1850s, was again a great man for hard figures, and F. G. P. Neison produced a most elaborate study of the criminal statistics in 1857. By this time the *Journal of the Statistical Society* carried fewer articles on the subject, and the revision of the Judicial Statistics in

1. The work of the pioneers is described in T. P. Morris, *The Criminal Area*, 1958, ch. 3; see also W. A. Bonger, *Criminality and Economic Conditions*, American edition, Boston, 1916.

1856–7 did not touch off an outpouring of discussion like that of the 1830s. However, each volume of the new series was, as hitherto, preceded by a detailed analysis by the Home Office Statistician. In 1892 a discussion based on the Judicial Statistics commenced in the columns of the *Nineteenth Century*. The Chaplain of Wandsworth Prison argued that crime had increased, the Chairman of the Prison Commissioners argued that it had decreased, and the Chief Constable of Staffordshire argued that it was substantially unchanged in amount. The statistics provided ammunition impartially for all three, and the welter of figures leaves us none the wiser.[2]

Those mentioned were not, of course, the only ones to use or analyse statistics. It was quite common for an assertion on the topic of crime to be backed up with statistics, either taken from official or other publications or drawn from personal investigations. However, not everyone was prepared to take the mass of figures at face-value.

As early as 1816 Colquhoun's habit of giving estimates of criminal activities with a laughable degree of precision was pointed out:

The great foible of Dr C, which excites distrust in all his statements, is the assumption of accurate calculation upon subjects that do not admit of any calculation at all. He can have no possible data on which to found the conclusion to which he has . . . come, as to the number of houses open for the reception of stolen goods. . . . How indeed can it be imagined that men who have the strongest of all motives for eluding observation, can be so open to it as to have their numbers as accurately defined as those of a regiment of foot?[3]

Many contemporaries were no more inclined to pay heed to

2. W. D. Morrison, 'The Increase of Crime', *Nineteenth Century*, vol. xxxi, June 1892, pp. 950–57; E. Du Cane, 'The Decrease of Crime', ibid., vol. xxxiii, March 1893, pp. 480–92; G. A. Anson, *The Fluctuations of Crime*, Stafford 1895. See also G. D. Robin, 'Pioneers in Criminology: William Douglas Morrison', *Journal of Criminal Law, Criminology and Police Science*, vol. lv, March 1964, no. 1, pp. 55–6.

3. *Minutes of Evidence . . . before a Select Committee . . . into the State of Police of the Metropolis, with Notes . . . by a Magistrate . . . of Middlesex*, 1816, pp. 63–4.

official returns, and throughout the century there was a vigorous chorus of critics of the statistics of crime. People knew that many crimes went undetected and unrecorded. They knew that changes in the law or in the practice of the courts often made comparison pointless. Examples were given. In 1835 offences which had formerly been tried at assizes as burglary and which still in law belonged to that category were at the judges' request being tried at sessions as simple larceny. In 1833 the judges had decided that when prisoners were being tried for non-capital felonies as second offenders (which made them liable to heavier penalties) proof of the first conviction was to be given to the jury before they considered their verdict. This practice was three years later prohibited by statute (6 & 7 Will. IV, c. 111), but even then it was not always possible to prevent the jury hearing the arraignment, which mentioned the previous conviction.[4]

Another source of error was the variable use which magistrates and judges made of their powers. There was a steady trend to shorter sentences over the century, and this would make comparison difficult. Moreover, heavy sentences were at times passed for trivial offences in order to have boys sent to one of the reformatory institutions of the day, rather than confined for a brief period in a local prison and then released to mix again with their old companions.[5] On the other hand, magistrates were in the 1830s punishing offenders summarily to avoid the delays involved in sending them for trial – and to do this, one admitted, 'we contrive to bend the laws ... out of their line to bring these cases within them'.[6] One way of doing this was to convict a youngster as a 'suspected person' when there was full proof of a substantive offence which could only be tried by a superior court. The magistrates were later spared the

4. S.C. on County Rates, P.P. 1835, xiv, p. 77; S.C. on Gaols, P.P. 1835, xi, pp. 188–9; W. O. Russell, *A Treatise on Crimes and Misdemeanours*, 3rd ed., 1843, vol. ii, p. 129n.

5. Letter from J. Park, dated 12 April 1831, H.O. 6/16, Public Record Office; H. Mayhew and J. Binny, *The Criminal Prisons of London . . .* , 1862, p. 432.

6. S.C. on Police, P.P. 1837, xii. p. 368 (q. 571); cf. ibid., pp. 353–4 (q. 437), 495; ibid., P.P. 1838, xv, pp. 577–9.

necessity of finding loopholes of this kind by an extension of their powers of summary jurisdiction, but this in its turn of course made comparison more difficult.

Some of the reasons put forward for the unreliability of statistics have a familiar ring to twentieth-century ears. As early as 1820 it was said that more attention was being paid to crime than had hitherto been the case: offences which in former times would have been ignored or dealt with on the spot by a ducking or a thrashing, administered by victim or police officer, were now, it was said, being brought before the courts.[7]

Criticisms of statistics about prisoners were particularly severe. In the absence of adequate means of identification, prisoners' declarations regarding their age and background had to be accepted – unless a policeman or a gaoler recognized the person concerned as an old acquaintance, or unless a fellow-prisoner 'split'. Policemen and gaolers frequently had in their care people who for want of evidence had to be treated as first offenders but who obviously were no strangers to courts or prisons. Elaborate arrangements were made for police officers and gaolers to see new prisoners, in the hope that they would be able to recognize them, and photography was used for this purpose on an increasing scale in and after the 1850s. None the less, in 1887 the Chaplain of Clerkenwell Gaol, the Rev. J. W. Horsley, could still write:

We take very little notice of names and ages in prison, as from various reasons they are apt to alter with each entrance. Thus Frederick Lane, aged 15, has just been sentenced to eighteen months' imprisonment. He has previously been in custody as Alfred Miller, aged 15, John Smith, aged 16, John Collins, aged 16, John Kate, aged 17, John Klythe, aged 17, and John Keytes, aged 17. In 1883 he is 15; in 1881 he was 17. But lads and lasses are usually over 16 while there is a chance of their being sent to a Reformatory.[8]

He does, however, refer to aliases as the 'most futile of disguises', and the fact that he can list the various identities the lad

7. J. E. Eardley-Wilmot, *A Letter to the Magistrates of Warwickshire on the Increase of Crime* ... , 1820, pp. 9–10; M. D. Hill, *Suggestions for the Repression of Crime* ... , 1857, p. 110.

8. J. W. Horsley, *Jottings from Jail* ... , 1887, p. 59.

assumed perhaps suggests that the authorities were not deceived.

As Horsley noted, prisoners would overstate or understate their age. They would make their choice in the light of the advantages and disadvantages in a particular town or a particular prison of being classed as a juvenile. This might mean weighing a better diet against the unpleasantness of the treadmill, or balancing the latter against solitude. Henry Mayhew in 1862 described conversations with London youngsters who claimed to have arranged to be sent to the prison of their choice by declaring themselves to be of the appropriate age.[9]

The statistics of prisoners' religions were as unreliable as the rest. A prisoner might declare himself to be a Roman Catholic in order to avoid the daily service in the chapel; in one case a prisoner who had done this was said to have used the opportunity to steal other boys' picked oakum to make up his daily quota. A Roman Catholic might forswear that faith and claim to be a Protestant for the sake of the relief from monotony represented by the daily trip from his cell to the chapel; he might do it because he feared discrimination. Fear of discrimination is probably the reason why there were only 'one or two' avowed Roman Catholics in a total of 388 prisoners in Cold Bath Fields Gaol, London, in 1818, and it was given in 1847 as the reason why there were never more than twenty acknowledged Roman Catholics in the 500 or so prisoners in Pentonville.[10]

A new arrival in prison would describe himself as of whatever occupation was most convenient for the particular prison. Many would declare themselves to be painters, in order to have a chance of the most favoured work. In Dartmoor in the 1870s prisoners claimed to be shoe-makers in order to avoid the outdoor working-parties; it was said that most of them had acquired an elementary acquaintanceship with the trade in the

9. Mayhew and Binny, op. cit., pp. 412, 423.

10. M. Hill and C. F. Cornwallis, *Two Prize Essays on Juvenile Delinquency*, London 1853, p. 400; s.c. on Police, P.P. 1818, viii, p. 160; s.c. on Juvenile Offenders, P.P. 1847, vii, p. 230 (qq. 1968–9).

local gaols whilst qualifying for a sentence of penal servitude and earning a trip to Dartmoor.[11]

Prisoners were said often to pretend to be completely illiterate for the sake of the softer life of the prison school, and because good progress in learning gained one a good character. This accusation may, however, not always have been justified. Contemporaries grounded the charge on the fact that prisoners who said that they could not read would sometimes prove to have already passed through a prison school and to have attained some degree of proficiency. However, modern experience of a similar phenomenon with both prisoners and soldiers suggests that in fact reading skills may be lost when they are not used. No doubt there were times when prisoners did claim to be more ignorant than they really were, just as there were times when they made false claims to superior education – or indeed superior birth. Some prisoners, like some criminals and prostitutes outside the gaol walls, would lay claim to gentility or claim to be orphans or tell affecting stories of ill treatment and misfortune, if they could find a guileless listener. Many of them were incurable romancers, and the statements of prisoners could not be relied upon.

Thus many people of the nineteenth century were contemptuous of attempts to argue from the criminal statistics. Many modern writers have analysed in more stringent fashion the defects of such figures,[12] and the strictures passed on the modern statistics of course apply with even greater force to those of the nineteenth century. None the less, the statistics are there. They form part of the evidence about the period, and they demand examination. It would be improper to reject them without due consideration.

This consideration can best begin by a discussion of the series of Judicial Statistics commenced in 1856, for this series is much more elaborate than earlier sets of figures and has some claim

11. A. Morrison, *A Child of the Jago*, Penguin ed., 1946, pp. 143–4; Horsley, op. cit., pp. 162–3; *Convict Life . . . by a Ticket-of-Leave Man*, 1879, pp. 48–9.
12. For example, L. T. Wilkins, *Social Deviance . . .*, 1964, pp. 142–76.

to be regarded as more trustworthy. If the post-1856 statistics are, as will be suggested, of little value, we need not bother to examine the earlier figures.

The Judicial Statistics have been subjected to a certain amount of analysis, apart of course from the summary which preceded each return.[13] Most earlier work, however, has used the national totals, and this is sufficient in itself to invalidate the results. The national totals are made up of totals for individual police forces, and for much of the century many individual returns were unreliable – newly reorganized borough forces might not have high standards in this respect. (The Appendix on statistics casts doubt on the figures produced by a force with twenty years of successful operation behind it.) If national totals were used, it would be necessary to discard the returns for a number of years after 1856, for it was only in that year that the establishment of a police force became obligatory in all districts. Furthermore, the Home Office statisticians were bedevilled by differences of practice amongst forces. For instance, some forces reckoned one prisoner with two offences as two persons. In Yorkshire no man known to do honest work was classified as a 'known thief', while in Gloucestershire all men ever known to steal were so classified. Some series were discontinued from time to time as unreliable, and a Departmental Committee in 1895 expressed in strong terms its doubts as to the validity of many of the principal series. Thus any national totals may be made up of figures which mean very different things.[14]

These considerations are enough to rule out any use of national totals. Nor is it possible to aggregate the figures for the larger towns. Police forces were in existence in all of them before 1856, so one difficulty is avoided, but the improvement in the general policing of the country probably had an effect on

13. For modern use of the nineteenth-century statistics, see D. S. Thomas, *Social Aspects of the Business Cycle*, London 1925; K. K. Macnab, *Aspects of the History of Crime in England and Wales between 1805–1860*, PH.D. thesis, University of Sussex, 1965.

14. *Journal of the Statistical Society*, vol. xx, March 1857, pp. 22–3, vol. xxiii, Dec. 1860, p. 437, and vol. xxxi, Sept. 1868, pp. 350–52; Departmental Committee on Judicial Statistics, P.P. 1895, cviii, pp. 11, 19–21, 23–4, 32–3.

crime in the larger towns.[15] This effect may at first have acted to increase crime in the towns by inducing criminals whose former happy hunting grounds were now better policed, to seek the obscurity of the large centres of population; later on, it probably led to a decrease as more criminals were caught. It is certainly unmeasurable. In any event, terms and definitions, as already pointed out, may well have meant different things at different places.

Thus at best it is only possible to take the statistics for each town in turn and consider them over time. The comparability of the figures cannot even then be expected to be high; we are at the mercy of changes in practice. There is no reason to suppose that the superintendents of the various Metropolitan Police divisions compiled their returns on a standard pattern even when they all bore the same date. Indeed, there is some evidence to suggest that they did not. In the papers of the Royal Commission on a Constabulary Force there is a long return made in reply to a questionnaire sent to the various divisions, probably in 1837 or 1838.[16] The replies from the superintendents make it clear that the questions have been very differently interpreted and the answers very differently prepared. The Metropolitan Police was of course the largest force, and at the time in question it was less than ten years old, so we could reasonably expect greater comparability later on and in other forces. But, whatever the date and whatever the size of the force, we are unable to exclude deliberate adjustment of the figures.

Despite these doubts, a study has as an experiment been made of the statistics for Leeds for the period 1857–75. This study is described in detail in the Appendix on statistics.[17] It is sufficient to give here its conclusions: the only firm relationship which emerges is that changes in chief constable produce changes in one series of figures; other series present no discernible pattern. It is suggested therefore that criminal statistics have little to tell us about crime and criminals in the nineteenth century.

15. See p. 273.
16. Chadwick Papers, box 130, University College, London.
17. See p. 295.

3. Crime and industrial society from the eighteenth century to the present day

The lawlessness of London in the first half of the eighteenth century has often been described. Mrs M. D. George, in her *London Life in the XVIIIth Century*, observes that at the beginning of the century 'the forces of disorder and crime had the upper hand in London'; she quotes the City Marshal's remarks of 1718:

Now it is the general complaint of the taverns, the coffee-houses, the shop-keepers and others, that their customers are afraid when it is dark to come to their houses and shops for fear that their hats and wigs should be snitched from their heads or their swords taken from their sides, or that they may be blinded, knocked down, cut or stabbed; nay, the coaches cannot secure them, but they are likewise cut and robbed in the public streets, &c. by which means the traffic of the City is much interrupted.[1]

These remarks, moreover, apply to the area within the jurisdiction of the City, then better policed than the growing portion of the metropolis outside the City limits.

Over thirty years later, Henry Fielding, the pioneer Bow Street magistrate, took an equally gloomy view; his famous and often-quoted work, *An Enquiry into the Causes of the Late Increase of Robbers* ..., leaves us in no doubt of his views about the crime of London in 1751, three years after his appointment. Fielding can be left to speak for himself:

There is not a Street in [Westminster] which doth not swarm all Day with Beggars, and all Night with Thieves. Stop your Coach at what Shop you will, however expeditious the Tradesman is to attend you, a Beggar is commonly beforehand with him; and if you should not directly face his Door, the Tradesman must often turn his Head

1. 2nd ed., 1930, pp. 16, 10–11.

while you are talking to him, or the same Beggar, or some other Thief at hand, will pay a Visit to his Shop! I omit to speak of the more open and violent Insults which are every Day committed on his Majesty's Subjects in the Streets and Highways. They are enough known, and enough spoken of. The Depredations on Property are less noticed, particularly those in the Parishes within ten Miles of London. ... These are however grown to the most deplorable Height, insomuch that the Gentleman is daily, or rather nightly, plundered of his Pleasure, and the Farmer of his Livelihood ...

The Innocent are put in Terror, affronted and alarmed with Threats and Execrations, endangered with loaded Pistols, beat with Bludgeons and hacked with Cutlasses, of which the Loss of Health, of Limbs, and often of Life, is the Consequence; and all this without any Respect to Age, or Dignity, or Sex ...

Street Robberies are generally committed in the dark, the Persons on whom they are committed are often in Chairs and Coaches, and if on Foot, the Attack is usually begun by knocking the Party down, and for the Time depriving him of his Sense. But if the Thief should be less barbarous, he is seldom so incautious as to omit taking every Method to prevent his being known, by flapping the Party's Hat over his Face, and by every other Method which he can invent to avoid Discovery ...

How long have we known Highwaymen reign in this Kingdom after they have been publicly known for such? Have not some of these committed Robberies in open Day-light, in the Sight of many People, and have afterward rode solemnly and triumphantly through the neighbouring Towns without any Danger or Molestation. ... Great and numerous Gangs ... have for a long time committed the most open Outrages in Defiance of the Law ...

There are at this Time a great Gang of Rogues, whose Number falls little short of a Hundred, who are incorporated in one Body, have Officers and a Treasury; and have reduced Theft and Robbery into a regular System. There are [members] of this Society of Men who appear in all Disguises, and mix in most Companies. Nor are they better versed in every Art of cheating, thieving, and robbing, than they are armed with every Method of evading the Law. ... If they fail in rescuing the Prisoner, or (which seldom happens) in bribing or deterring the Prosecutor, they have for their last Resource some rotten Members of the Law to forge a Defence for them, and a great Number of false Witnesses ready to support it ...

Introduction

[Among the beggars in the streets] I myself have discovered some notorious Cheats, and my good Friend Mr Welch, the worthy High Constable of Holborn Division, many more. Nothing, as I have been well informed, is more common among these Wretches, than for the Lame, when provoked, to use their Crutches as Weapons instead of Supporters; and for the Blind, if they should have the Beadle at their Heels, to outrun the Dogs which guided them before.[2]

It is possible that one or two of Fielding's remarks would not stand up to investigation, but that the substance of them is correct is not in doubt. Jonas Hanway in 1775 wrote:

I sup with my friend; I cannot return to my home, not even in my chariot, without danger of a pistol being clapt to my breast. I build an elegant villa, ten or twenty miles distant from the capital: I am obliged to provide an armed force to convey me thither, lest I should be attacked on the road with fire and ball.[3]

There is much similar evidence, which has been described by other authors.[4]

Indeed, so powerful were the criminals that parts of the town were wholly given over to them: it was not until well into the eighteenth century that the Alsatia, or area of sanctuary, disappeared from London. Such places, by the end of the seventeenth century,

in theory ... had no existence, or existed on sufferance only to secure ... the protection of the debtor against imprisonment for debt; in practice they were criminal quarters where the officers of justice were set at defiance, and where no man's life was safe unless he had the privilege of being an inhabitant.[5]

2. The first paragraph is in fact from Fielding's *A Proposal for Making an Effectual Provision for the Poor* ... , 1753, p. 10; the others are from *An Enquiry* ... , 1751, pp. 2–3, 45, 94, 109, 111–12.
3. J. Hanway, *The Defects of Police, the Cause of Immorality, and the Continual Robberies committed, particularly in and about the Metropolis* ... , 1775, p. 224.
4. e.g. P. Pringle, *Hue and Cry* ... , 1955, pp. 81–90.
5. L. O. Pike, *A History of Crime in England* ... , 1876, vol. ii, p. 252.

They were a survival of the medieval sanctuaries, where criminals could take refuge prior to appearing before the coroner to
admit their guilt and abjure the realm. The comment that the
sanctuaries had in theory ceased to exist was justified, for an act
of 1623 (21 Jac. i, c. 28) had provided that 'no Sanctuary or
Privilege of Sanctuary shall be hereafter admitted or allowed in
any Case'. But, as was so often the case, Parliament did not at
its first attempt succeed in achieving its objective. Sanctuaries
continued to exist, and in the last decade of the seventeenth
century there were several in London. The Southwark Mint is
said to have been the most notorious of them all, but the one
which gave its name to the others was Alsatia (otherwise known
as Whitefriars), an area between Fleet Street and the Thames.
The Minories and Baldwin's Gardens, Gray's Inn Lane, were
other convenient refuges for hard-pressed thieves. A statute of
1696 (8 & 9 Will. iii, c. 27) made it an offence to resist the
execution of any legal process in any of the 'several pretended
Privileged Places' it named, and this seems in most cases to have
been successful. But not even this act managed to eliminate the
Mint. In 1722 the preamble to yet another act (9 Geo. i, c. 28)
declared:

It is notorious, that many evil-disposed and wicked Persons have,
in Defiance of the known Laws of this Realm, and to the great
Dishonour thereof, unlawfully assembled and associated themselves
in and about a certain Place in the Parish of St George in the
County of Surrey, commonly called or known by the name of
Suffolk-Place, or the Mint, and have assured to themselves (by unlawful Combinations and Confederacies) pretended Privileges, altogether scandalous and unwarrantable, and have committed great
Frauds and Abuses upon many of his Majesty's good Subjects, and
by Force and Violence protected themselves, and their wicked Accomplices, against Law and Justice.

It was made an offence punishable by transportation to resist
officers proceeding in accordance with the act, and justices of
the peace were given powers to order the sheriff to put the act
into execution – which may give us a clue as to the reasons why
a further act had been needed. The act relieved debtors owing

29

less than £50 from arrest for debt, and the scene when it came into force was described:

> The exodus of the refugee-felons and debtors, in July, 1723 . . . is described as having been like one of the Jewish tribes going out of Egypt, for the train of 'Minters' is said to have included some thousands in its ranks, and the road towards Guildford (whither they were journeying to be cleared at the Quarter Sessions, of their debts and penalties) to have been positively covered with the cavalcade of caravans, carts, horsemen, and foot-travellers.[6]

However, some of the residents of the Mint seem to have gone not to Guildford but to Wapping and Stepney. Those places had not been mentioned in the list of sanctuaries in the act of 1696, but a further act two years after the elimination of the Mint (11 Geo. i, c. 22) denounced the 'evil-disposed and wicked Persons' who had associated themselves in the 'Hamlet of Wapping-Stepney, and Places adjacent in the County of Middlesex' and who had committed 'great Violences and Outrages'. As it was 'absolutely necessary that Provision should be made for effectually preventing such Violences and Outrages for the future', it was made a transportable offence for any three persons to assemble for protection against the collection of debt in Wapping-Stepney – or anywhere else in the metropolis. The law-makers had learnt their lesson.

This act of 1724 seems to have been successful. However, even after elimination of the Alsatias, there remained areas wholly given over to the occupation of criminals, where a confused tangle of courts and alleys afforded endless opportunities of escape, where peace-officers penetrated only rarely and in force, and whence unwary strangers were unlikely to escape unharmed. We may turn to Fielding[7] once again:

> Whoever indeed considers the Cities of London and Westminster, with the last vast Addition of their Suburbs; the great irregularity of their Buildings, the immense Number of Lanes, Alleys, Courts and

6. H. Mayhew and J. Binny, *The Criminal Prisons of London* . . . , 1862, p. 355n.

7. op. cit., pp. 76, 94.

Bye-places; must think, that, had they been intended for the very purpose of Concealment, they could scarce have been better contrived. Upon such a View, the whole appears as a vast Wood or Forest, in which a Thief may harbour with as great Security, as wild Beasts do in the Desarts [sic] of Africa or Arabia. ... It is a melancholy Truth that, at this very Day, a Rogue no sooner gives the Alarm, within certain Purlieus, than twenty or thirty armed Villains are found ready to come to his Assistance.

During the course of the eighteenth century, says Mrs George,[8] 'many courts, alleys and crumbling houses inhabited by thieves and beggars ... succumbed to Improvement Acts and gradual rebuilding'. To improve the streets was, however, easier than to improve the inhabitants, and there were parts of London, and of the other large towns, to which Fielding's comments could well have been applied a hundred years later. Criminal areas, or rookeries, as they came to be known, formed an important part of the nineteenth-century scene.

Fielding[9] called attention to another evil of his day, to the

new Kind of Drunkenness, unknown to our Ancestors, [which] is lately sprung up amongst us, and which, if not put a stop to, will infallibly destroy a great Part of the inferiour People.

The Drunkenness I here intend, is that acquired by the strongest intoxicating Liquors, and particularly by that Poison called *Gin*; which, I have great reason to think, is the principal Sustenance (if it may be so called) of more than a hundred thousand People in this Metropolis. Many of these Wretches there are, who swallow Pints of this Poison within the Twenty-four Hours; the dreadful Effects of which I have the Misfortune every Day to see, and to smell too ...

However cheap this vile Potion may be, the poorer Sort will not easily be able to supply themselves with the Quantities they desire; for the intoxicating Draught itself disqualifies them from using any honest Means to acquire it, at the same time that it removes all Sense of Fear and Shame, and emboldens them to commit every wicked and desperate Enterprize. Many Instances of this I see daily: Wretches are often brought before me, charged with Theft and

8. op. cit., p. 106 (cf. p. 99).
9· op. cit., pp. 18–19.

Introduction

Robbery, whom I am forced to confine before they are in a Condition to be examined; and when they have afterwards become sober, I have plainly perceived, from the State of the Case, that the *Gin* alone was the Cause of the Transgression, and have been sometimes sorry that I was obliged to commit them to Prison.

This is not the place to describe the horrors of the Gin Era, details of which have often been given by modern writers. A brief summary of one writer's account will suffice. There was an

orgy of spirit-drinking which was at its worst between 1720 and 1751, due to the very cheap and very intoxicating liquors, which were retailed indiscriminately and in the most brutalizing and demoralizing conditions. . . . Distilling was a new trade in England and one which received special favours from the Government. . . . The cheapness of British spirits caused a new demand and altered the tastes and habits of the people. Brandy shops and geneva shops multiplied in the poorer parts of London. Almost every shop daily resorted to by the poorer classes also embarked upon the selling of spirits. Employers . . . sold gin to their work-people. The result was an orgy of spirit-drinking whose effects were seen in the streets of London, in the workhouses, in the growing misery of the poor, in an increase of crimes of violence.[10]

The high death-rate and low birth-rate of the period 1720–50 are ascribed to gin, and even if Fielding's strictures would not today be accepted in their entirety we need not challenge his view, which was indeed shared by many other justices, that the unrestricted sale of gin was an evil and that it can only have aggravated the crime problem.

The poor were not of course the only ones to cause trouble in the eighteenth century. As L. O. Pike observed:

Fielding might with quite as much justice have moralized upon the misdeeds of the 'better sort' . . . the roysterers who made night hideous in the eighteenth century.

The 'Mohocks', the 'Nickers', the 'Tumblers', the 'Dancing-masters', and the various bully-captains were not the 'dregs of the

10. George, op. cit., pp. 27–43; cf. Pringle, op. cit., pp. 26–8, 80–81, 93–4; C. Hibbert, *The Roots of Evil*, 1963, pp. 43–4.

people', but were in the habit of doing quite as much injury as thieves and robbers to their neighbours. If they met an unprotected woman, they showed they had no sense of decency; if they met a man who was unarmed or weaker than themselves, they assaulted, and, perhaps, killed him.[11]

Though it is possible that the activities of the Mohocks have been exaggerated, there are accounts of their amusements:

They employed their ample leisure in forcing prostitutes and old women to stand on their heads in tar barrels so that they could prick their legs with their swords; or in making them jump up and down to avoid the swinging blades; in disfiguring their victims by boring out their eyes or flattening their noses; in waylaying servants and . . . beating them and slashing their faces. To work themselves up to the necessary pitch of enthusiasm for their ferocious games, they first drank so much that they were quite 'beyond the possibility of attending to any notions of reason or humanity'.[12]

Such was London in the reigns of the first two Georges. Our concern in this book, however, is not with acts of riot and disorder but with crimes of a more mercenary nature, and it is unfortunate that there is little detailed information about such offences. We do indeed know something about some outstanding criminals of the first half of the eighteenth century, and their careers are worthy of examination.

The most colourful character of all the eighteenth-century criminals was Jonathan Wild. He adopted and developed the system of Mary Frith – otherwise known as Moll Cutpurse – a receiver of stolen goods who had dominated the criminals of Restoration London. Moll Cutpurse attracted the custom of a large circle of thieves by paying prices above those offered by other receivers, and adopted the policy of giving the rightful owner of the stolen goods first refusal of them. To buy back one's own property in this way, with 'no questions asked', was not uncommon at the time, and going straight to Moll's place of business saved the usual bother of advertising.[13] Jonathan

11. Pike, op. cit., pp. 340–41.
12. Hibbert, op. cit., p. 45.
13. H. Scott (ed.), *The Concise Encyclopedia of Crime and Criminals*, London 1961, p. 155.

Wild improved on Moll Cutpurse's system in two ways. First, he adopted the guise of a private thief-taker, one of those who sought out and prosecuted offenders for the sake of the reward which could thus be obtained. (This was the much-criticized Parliamentary Reward system, which survived into the nineteenth century.) Secondly, he showed the thieves how to manage their affairs more successfully, and indeed eventually had a number of gangs under his control. (Economists will recognize here the familiar case of a growing business finding it desirable to control the sources of supply of its raw materials – 'backward integration'.) He maintained discipline in his organization, and indeed over criminals not in his organization, by arranging the arrest and execution of the recalcitrant, and of any criminal who for one reason or another was in his way. He invented for himself the title of 'Thief-Taker General of Great Britain and Ireland', and for about ten years, from 1715 to 1725, dominated the criminal scene. Pike in 1876 summed up his career:

From small beginnings he became, in London at least, the receiver-in-chief of all stolen goods. He acquired and maintained this position by the persistent application of two simple principles; he did his best to aid the law in convicting all those misdoers who would not recognize his authority, and he did his best to repair the losses of all who had been plundered and who took him into their confidence. By degrees he set up an office for the recovery of missing property, at which the government must, for a time, have connived. Here the robbed sought an audience of the only man who could promise them restitution; here the robbers congregated like workmen at a workshop, to receive the pay for the work they had done.[14]

Wild's prosperity was unchecked by the act (4 Geo. I, c. 11) passed in 1717 specially to prevent his activities. The act, popularly known as 'Jonathan Wild's act', made his principal method a capital offence: it declared that whereas

there are several Persons who have secret Acquaintance with

14. Pike, op. cit., p. 256. The authority on Wild is now G. Howson, *Thief-Taker General, The Rise and Fall of Jonathan Wild*, 1970.

Felons, and who make it their Business to help Persons to their stolen Goods, and by that Means gain Money from them, which is divided between them and the Felons, whereby they greatly encourage such Offenders ... where-ever any Person taketh Money or Reward, directly or indirectly, under Pretence or upon Account of helping any Person or Persons to any stolen Goods or Chattels, every such person ... (unless [he] doth apprehend, or cause to be apprehended, such Felon who stole the same ... and give Evidence against him) shall be guilty of Felony, and suffer the Pains and Penalties of Felony ... as if [he] had himself stole such Goods and Chattels.

Despite the clear words of the act, no prosecution was launched against Wild, though everyone in London knew what he was doing. It is said that officers of the law were content to let him continue to operate because of the assistance he could give them (and indeed one foreign visitor thought his eventual execution a mistake for the same reason). Perhaps a more important reason was the efficiency with which he compromised all those who seemed likely to be dangerous, and the fear of giving evidence against him which he thus engendered. However, in the end Wild was executed, despite the fact that at his trial he produced a list of criminals for whose conviction he had, he claimed, been responsible. He was arrested for helping a highwayman to escape from custody, and whilst he was held powerless in Newgate witness after witness, removed from their fears, came forward to give testimony against him in relation to several more serious charges. In 1725, seven years after its passage, 'Jonathan Wild's act' achieved its immediate purpose.

The act was not entirely successful, however, for the victims of theft continued to buy back their property. Fielding wrote in 1751:

The Thief disposes of his Goods with almost as much Safety as the honestest Tradesman: For first, if he hath made a Booty of any Value, he is almost sure of seeing it advertised within a Day or two, directing him *to bring the Goods to a certain Place where he is to receive a Reward* (sometimes the full Value of the Booty) *and no Questions asked.*[15]

15. Fielding, op. cit., pp. 68-9.

Introduction

Despite Wild's importance in his own day, another criminal of the epoch had more influence in the long run. This was Jack Sheppard,[16] who was hanged in 1724 at the age of twenty-two – as a result, it is said, of falling foul of Jonathan Wild – but who had by then acquired notoriety as the result of a series of amazing escapes from custody. His adventures captured the popular imagination, and a series of plays and books – among them Harrison Ainsworth's *Jack Sheppard* of 1839 – kept his memory alive well into the nineteenth century. Over a hundred years after his death youngsters were still entertaining one another in lodging-house and gaol with tales of Jack Sheppard, and commentators on the criminal scene were still deploring the part which such tales played in creating new criminals.

The first half of the eighteenth century was the heyday of the highwayman. Dick Turpin was of course the most famous of them all, and was successful enough for many years, despite the fact that, as Barrows put it, 'many of the exploits put down to him are obviously imaginary, and, sad to relate, he did not even make that glorious ride to York'.[17] He, too, was the subject of a book by Harrison Ainsworth (*Rookwood*, published in 1834) and was a hero of the petty criminals of the early nineteenth century. He, Claude Duval and many others were active in and around London, and though many of them (like the two named) died on the gallows, there were enough unhanged at any one time to make travel an expensive business. Highwaymen of course continued to exist throughout the eighteenth century, but after mid-century the glamour had somehow begun to fade; as Pike observed, 'the highwaymen were continually falling lower and lower in social position', and no longer did fine ladies flock to see them in their cells in Newgate.[18]

It is not the purpose of this book to recount the exploits of the notorious, and hence the exceptional, criminals of the past. However, the careers of some leading criminals of the first half of the eighteenth century have been outlined because their ac-

16. Howson, op. cit., pp. 207–26.
17. J. Barrows, *Knights of the High Toby* . . . , 1962, p. 108.
18. Pike, op. cit., pp. 274–8, 384; cf. Scott, op. cit., pp. 135–6, 183, 326–7.

tivities enable us to snatch a glimpse of what was going on beneath the surface. Not all the criminals of the period were so colourful or so successful (for a time) as those mentioned. Wild, Sheppard, Turpin and the rest were the outstanding members of a large group – even if we cannot attach a numerical value to the word 'large'. For every petty thief who developed into a Wild or a Turpin, a Sheppard or a Duval, there must have been many who remained petty thieves. The careers of the men named, and of the others described in the Newgate Calendar or in modern accounts of the great criminals of the past are at present the only clues we have to give us a picture of a mass of criminal activity. It would be satisfactory if we could analyse the amount of this lesser crime and provide descriptions of the ordinary criminals, and if we could extend the inquiry to include the crime of the large towns other than London; but the necessary information has not yet been assembled. We must content ourselves with guesses. It seems probable, however, that only in the largest of the provincial towns was there anything approaching the crime of London.

Mrs George, after taking stock of the crime situation in London in the early part of the eighteenth century, suggests that things were at their worst in the 1740s and 50s, and that thereafter an improvement took place. Though some contemporaries raised the 'cry of national deterioration', she sides with Francis Place, the Radical tailor of Charing Cross, who claimed that the 'crimes and vices' of the days of his youth greatly exceeded those of the early nineteenth century. 'By the end of the [eighteenth] century,' she sums up, 'we are in a different world.'[19]

While Mrs George quotes testimony to the good order in London at the end of the eighteenth century – a guidebook of 1802 claimed that 'no city in proportion to its trade and luxury is more free from danger to those who pass the streets at all hours, or from depredations, open or concealed, on property'[20] – other modern writers take a more pessimistic view. Dr E. O'Brien quotes the Solicitor-General in 1785 – 'nobody

19. George, op. cit., pp. 10–17, 120.
20. ibid., p. 10.

could feel himself unapprehensive of danger to his person or property if he walked in the street after dark, nor could any man promise himself security in his bed'.[21] Professor A. G. L. Shaw quotes advice of 1790 to visitors to London 'never to stop in a crowd or look at the windows of a print-shop, if you would not have your pocket picked'.[22] Patrick Colquhoun's well-known *Treatise on the Police of the Metropolis . . .*, which went through several editions between 1795 and 1806, has often been used to show the level of criminality that existed at the time he wrote. He spoke of 'the outrages and acts of violence continually committed, more particularly in and near the Metropolis by lawless ravagers of property, and destroyers of lives, in disturbing the peaceful mansion, *the Castle of every Englishman*, and also in abridging the liberty of travelling upon the Public Highways'. In Cheapside, he said,

a multitude of thieves and pickpockets, exhibiting often in their dress and exterior, the appearance of gentlemen and men of business, assemble every evening in gangs, watching at the corners of every street, ready to *hustle* and *rob,* or to trip up the heels of the *warehouse-porters and the servants of shopkeepers carrying goods;* or at the doors of warehouses, at dusk and at the time they are locked, to be ready to seize loose parcels when unperceived; by all which means, aided by a number of other tricks and fraudulent pretences, they are but too successful in obtaining considerable booty. In short, there is no device or artifice to which these vigilant plunderers do not resort: of which an example appeared in an instance, where almost in the twinkling of an eye, while the servants of an eminent silk-dyer had crossed a narrow street, his horse and cart, containing raw silk to the value of *twelve hundred pounds,* were driven clear off. Many of these atrocious villains, are also constantly waiting at the inns, disguised in different ways, personating *travellers, coach-office clerks, porters and coachmen,* for the purpose of plundering every thing that is portable; which, with the assistance of two or three associates if necessary, is carried to a coach called for the purpose, and immediately conveyed to the receiver.

21. E. O'Brien, *The Foundation of Australia (1786–1800),* Sydney 1950, p. 47.
22. A. G. L. Shaw, *Convicts and the Colonies . . . ,* 1966, p. 40.

He described in great detail the various river thieves who preyed on the shipping in the Port of London, though he had the satisfaction in the later editions of the work of recording that the Marine Police – of which he was the originator – 'may truly be said to have worked wonders in reforming the shocking abuses which prevailed'.[23]

There is thus a conflict of views. Those who consider conditions around the end of the eighteenth century are struck with the level of crime and violence then prevalent, while Mrs George, surveying the century as a whole, sees an improvement. Others indeed have shared her opinion.[24] Crime of course still abounded, and criminals were often violent; but things, it seems, were probably better than they had been earlier. The changes appear to be associated with the Industrial Revolution, and before discussing them further it is desirable to say something of the Industrial Revolution and its consequences.

In the hundred years from the middle of the eighteenth century to the middle of the nineteenth century, writes Miss P. Deane in her *The First Industrial Revolution*,[25] 'a revolution took place in the social and economic life of Britain which ... established a totally different way of living and working for the mass of its people'. This revolution can be seen as an acceleration of the rate of change in economic activities. A series of technological changes in different industries acted to reinforce one another and to inaugurate further change. (To say this is not to ascribe the origin of the Industrial Revolution to technological change – economic historians are still arguing about the causes of the Industrial Revolution.[26]) Agricultural improvement had begun before 1750. It was now matched and surpassed by improvements in transport – the development of the canal system after 1760 – and in the techniques of industrial

23. I have used the 6th ed., 1800, pp. 93–4, 106–7nn., 242.

24. Pike, op. cit., pp. 370–71; Pringle, op. cit., pp. 110, 131, 136–7, 160, 196.

25. Cambridge 1965, p. 4.

26. On the vexed question of the origins of the Industrial Revolution, see R. M. Hartwell, *The Industrial Revolution in England*, 1965 (Historical Association pamphlet).

production. The cotton industry was transformed by the water-frame, the iron-making industry by the use of coke and the puddling process, and the coal-mining industry first, and next the other two industries already mentioned, and then on an increasing scale all others, by the steam engine. The water-wheel and the steam engine – that is to say, mechanical power – brought about another great change, the coming of the factory. There had of course been factories before the use of mechanical power, but water-power and steam-power made it necessary to introduce factories into industries where work had until that time been carried on in the homes of the workers. The coming of the factory in its turn led to the growth of the towns, for the workers had now to cluster round the factory so as to be within easy reach, so as to be able to start work on time when the factory bell rang and to get home quickly when, many weary hours later, the bell rang again.

Certain features of the Industrial Revolution are of particular importance for the present study. The population of England began to grow. The movement probably began in the 1740s and was at first largely a consequence of a fall in death-rates. The rate of change increased, and by the end of the eighteenth century a rise in birth-rates was playing its part as well. The population of England and Wales 'seems to have been virtually stagnant at between 5·8 million and about six million people' between about 1700 and about 1741. By 1751 it had probably grown to something between six and 6·5 million. By 1851 it was nearly eighteen million.[27]

More significant for our present purpose was the growth in the size of the towns. In the middle of the eighteenth century less than one fifth of the population lived in towns of 5,000 people or more; by the middle of the nineteenth century the corresponding fraction was over three fifths. In 1750 London had, according to one estimate, a population of about 676,000; the corresponding figure for 1820 is 1,274,000. In 1851 only

27. The discussion of population growth is largely based on Deane, op.cit., pp. 22, 32, 146–7, 260, 270; the London population estimates are from George, op. cit., pp. 24–5, 329.

about a third of the population of London and the main towns of England and Wales had been born where they were then living. In the first forty years of the nineteenth century all the large towns were growing more rapidly than the total population of the country, at a time when that total population was increasing at the rate of over ten per cent every ten years. In the decade 1821–31, Liverpool, Manchester, Birmingham and Leeds all had increases of population of forty per cent or more. Population figures of any accuracy are available only from 1801, when the first census was taken, so that it is not possible to make precise statements of this kind about the growth of the towns in the latter part of the eighteenth century; but it is clear that something of the same sort was going on.

Growth-rates of the order of magnitude of those given in the previous paragraph cannot be achieved without strain. Miss Deane remarks that 'the towns had been outgrowing the existing technology of urban living . . . it is fair to say that in most urban areas the human environment was deteriorating perceptibly through the first half of the nineteenth century'. Miss D. Marshall called attention to the impact on one part of the administrative machine of the changes taking place:

The original structure of the Poor Laws had been contrived to meet the needs of a very different England, an England that was rural rather than urban. . . . As the industrial changes of the eighteenth century gathered momentum, so the strain on this out-of-date structure increased.[28]

Her remarks can be applied to other aspects of town and indeed national government.

It was not merely population growth which was placing strain on the country's institutions, of course. All the changes mentioned earlier, and the many others which are important to a full understanding of the Industrial Revolution, even though they are omitted from this brief summary, had profound consequences. By the 1820s, says Miss Deane, Britain

28. Deane, op. cit., pp. 242–3; D. Marshall, *English People in the 18th Century*, 1956, p. 191.

was a changing, growing industrial complex in which the old moulds of economic and social behaviour were being rapidly broken before the new moulds had begun to set. ... Although a substantial proportion of the inhabitants of mid-Victorian England were pursuing traditional occupations with traditional techniques and methods of organization, there were few of them whose way of life had not been changed radically by the industrial revolution and its associated developments. ... An industrial revolution entails profound social as well as economic changes, and the first industrial revolution found society unprepared for the problems that emerged during the upheaval. ... There was a loss of leisure and a building up of tension.[29]

In the last half of the eighteenth century and the first half of the nineteenth century, then, society was in violent transition. The towns were growing rapidly, and the facilities available to their rulers were very limited and their knowledge of how to use them even more limited. Their population, ever increasing, was predominantly a young one, and the young town-dwellers were faced with a whole host of unfamiliar problems, problems for which their background and training provided them with no answer. The towns, and especially London, had always had a criminal problem different from and larger than that of other areas, and there were groups of people, living in distinctive areas, who had evolved a way of life of their own based on crime. Many young town-dwellers, faced with these problems and receiving no assistance from their families or their employers (if they had families or employers) or from the municipal authorities, found solutions by adopting the techniques, the habits and the attitudes of the criminals. There was thus, in London and the other large towns in the latter part of the eighteenth century and the earlier part of the nineteenth century, an upsurge of crime which was the fruit of a society in rapid transition.

We now return to the question of the course of crime at the end of the eighteenth century. It was seen earlier that the weight of evidence is in favour of the view that the level of crime about the year 1800 was lower than it had been earlier in the century.

29. Deane, op. cit., pp. 212, 259, 260, 268.

However, if the analysis just made were correct it would be expected that crime should by then have increased somewhat as a result of the first decades of the Industrial Revolution. The contradiction can, it seems, be resolved. First, it is necessary to make a distinction between qualitative change and quantitative change. There seems no reason to doubt the view that crime was becoming less violent in its nature in the eighteenth century – there is considerable evidence that such a trend existed throughout the nineteenth century. Such a change can be ascribed to the more civilized way of life and the reduction in the violence of life in general which is attested by historians of the eighteenth century. Mrs George, for example, speaks of the

change in the attitude towards social questions which was the outcome of the new spirit of humanity, the new command of material resources, and the new belief in environment rather than Providence as the cause of many human ills. ... There had been a number of obscure reforms, whose cumulative effect was very great ... an increasing realization of evils and a growing intolerance of hardships. ... The improvements in medicine and sanitation had bettered conditions ... in London.[30]

It is perhaps not irrelevant to note here that by the end of the century a much lower proportion of those condemned to death was actually being executed than had been the case earlier. For example, in the period 1749–58 two in three of the offenders sentenced to death in London and Middlesex were executed, but by the end of the century the ratio had dropped to less than one in three.[31] There are thus grounds for accepting that there was a reduction in the amount of violent crime. However, such a reduction could very well have accompanied an increase in the amount of non-violent crime. Indeed, as violent crimes are the spectacular and eye-catching crimes, a decrease in their number could well have blinded contemporaries to an increase in the total amount of crime. Some contemporary observers were in the early nineteenth century able to insist that crime was

30. George, op. cit., pp. 321–2.
31. L. Radzinowicz, *History of the English Criminal Law*, London 1948–56, vol. i, p. 151.

increasing in quantity at the same time that they agreed that it was decreasing in violence; but a lesser increase in non-violent crime might well be masked from view. However, it is not necessary to adopt this line of reasoning, for it seems probable that other special factors were operating at the end of the eighteenth century.

A number of changes had taken place in the latter part of the eighteenth century which may well have offset the effects of the movement to the towns. Mrs George attributes the reduction of crime which she notices, in part at any rate, to the various improvements in the lighting and policing of London, and she regards Henry Fielding's magistracy at Bow Street (1748–54) as 'a turning-point in the social history of London'.[32] The street-lighting of London had indeed improved considerably during the eighteenth century. The City authorities took over the lighting of streets within their jurisdiction in 1736, providing 5,000 lamps where there had previously been 1,000, and soon increased the number to 15,000. The level of street-lighting was good outside the City limits too, by contemporary standards; Oxford Street alone had more lamps than the whole of Paris, it is said. Towards the end of the eighteenth century commissioners of sewers became responsible for the street-lamps and brought about further improvements.[33] The provision of better lighting would undoubtedly have made crime more difficult.

Equally certainly the life of the London criminals was made more difficult by improved machinery for enforcing the law. From the time of Henry Fielding's appointment, there was in London a magistrate who was both honest and zealous in the prosecution of crime. (Thomas de Veil has some claim to have anticipated Fielding: appointed a magistrate in 1729, he is described by Pringle as 'the first London magistrate of the century to make a serious attempt to suppress crime' and as 'the first of the Bow Street police-magistrates'; but unlike Fielding he did not live on his pay from government but took fees and other

32. George, op. cit., pp. 6, 120.
33. W. T. O'Dea, *The Social History of Lighting*, 1958, pp. 97–8.

profits where he could.) After a time there was more than one magistrate at Bow Street, and in 1792 seven more police offices, each manned by three paid magistrates, were established. One of Henry Fielding's achievements was the establishment of a small group of detectives, 'Mr Fielding's People', who eventually became the Bow Street Runners; and when the seven police offices were established in 1792 each of them had a group of detective police officers of their own. The reform of the parochial watches had commenced in 1735, and continual improvement occurred during the remainder of the century. There was also, from about 1782, a Foot Patrole of 68 men attached to the Bow Street Office and patrolling the streets at night. The changes thus made in the policing of London were to prove inadequate before long; but their impact might well have been sufficient to account for the improvement in the crime situation detected by some observers.[34]

Together with these permanent changes there was in the years around the end of the eighteenth century a temporary change, an improvement in employment in London. The industrial expansion since 1760 had done something to increase the demand for labour, and in addition the generation-long war with France (1793–1815, with only brief intermissions) did much to stimulate industry and led to an increase in the chances of getting a job. Even Patrick Colquhoun thought that some of the decrease in crime on the river was due not to his Marine Police but to the employment possibilities created by the war – 'the resource afforded by the present war, gives employment, for a time only, to many depraved characters and mischievous members of the community'. It may well have been more important that employment was available more readily for youngsters who had not yet become 'depraved' or – in the sense intended – 'mischievous'.[35]

The argument that wartime conditions were operating to

34. Pringle, op. cit., pp. 61, 75, 198 and passim; D. G. Browne, *The Rise of Scotland Yard* ..., 1956, pp. 21–8, 43–5. See also my forthcoming *Policing before Peel*.
35. Colquhoun, op. cit., pp. 100, 220.

reduce the level of crime gains support from what happened when peace came, or rather, when the end came to wartime prosperity. There was a change in conditions about 1811–12, arising from the checks to British exports caused by Napoleon's 'continental system', his ban on Continental purchases of British goods (incomplete though this was), and by the interruption to American purchases from this country which began in 1807 and culminated in the War of 1812. Though Napoleon's downfall and peace with America removed these obstacles to trade, the change from war to peace in 1815 led to a period of widespread distress and unemployment. There is evidence that these were accompanied by an upsurge of crime.

In 1812 the House of Commons appointed a Select Committee to inquire into the police of London. This was set up primarily as a result of the 'murders in the Ratcliffe Highway' – in December 1811 two families were murdered in a brutal manner, and much public alarm was occasioned[36] – but it seems reasonable to infer also some anxiety about the general crime situation. Be that as it may, there is no doubt about the impact on contemporary minds of the post-war upsurge of crime. One index is the number of Select Committees on the topic of London's police set up after Waterloo: the first was appointed in 1816 and continued to hear evidence and to make reports until 1818, and there were others in 1822 and 1828. Professor Radzinowicz points out that there were nine reports published on this topic in the years 1812 to 1828, as against four in the previous half-century.[37] Contemporaries thought that they were facing a new problem.

The main body of this book examines in detail the criminal scene from 1815 to about 1900, and only the briefest of summaries is necessary here. There was a steady trend to less violence, but it is difficult to be certain of any movement in the level of crime between 1815 and the middle 1850s. In the first half of the nineteenth century generation after generation of youngsters flooded to the growing towns, and in many cases entered the

36. Radzinowicz, op. cit., vol. iii, pp. 315–47.
37. ibid., p. 354.

ranks of the criminals. The prisons were reformed and new methods introduced; the police force was reformed and a new model established. But crime flourished unchecked. The evidence gathered by the Select Committee on Juvenile Offenders of 1847 and 1852–3 tells a story not markedly different from that told to the Select Committee on Police of 1816–18.

At last a change did come. In the latter part of the 1850s contemporary opinion began to see a decline in the number of juvenile offenders, and looking back on that period from later years people saw it as a great watershed. There was a decisive drop in the number of juvenile offenders, a change in the character of juvenile crime and an end of the floating population of young vagrants, or at least a marked reduction in its size. Contemporaries were content to give the credit for this improvement to the reformatory school, but, though the reformatory school helped to inaugurate the change, the real explanation is to be found in the improvement of conditions of life in the country as a whole. England in the second half of the nineteenth century was a richer country than it had been, and it employed some of its wealth in improving the standard of life of the poor people of its towns. It had, moreover, got used to being an urban and an industrialized country. Changes were still proceeding rapidly, but to some extent they were changes in number and not in kind. The pace of change had slowed down, and the children of the towns were to a much greater extent living in the sort of world in which their parents had lived and were prepared to a much greater extent for the sort of life they had to lead.

By the end of the nineteenth century there were voices claiming that crime had begun to rise again. When the evidence is examined it seems probable that crime did not rise in the last forty years of the century, in relation to population. What is certain, however, is that even if it did rise, it did not rise to the level that had existed in the early 1850s and before, nor did the criminal world return to its former size and importance. The criminal youngsters whom Henry Mayhew saw in the early 1850s were virtually the last of the long line. There continued to be small pockets in the towns where such children lived, but Charles Booth and his associates in the 1880s and 90s did not find rookeries of the type that Mayhew saw.

What has happened in the twentieth century? It is difficult to find a clear-cut answer in the works of the authorities on the subject. Professor Radzinowicz refers to an increase of crime starting in the nineteenth century and continuing to the present day. Dr Mannheim says that there was in the inter-war period a 'steady and considerable rise in crimes against property'. For example, the number of indictable offences falling in the statistical category 'offences against property without violence' rose from an annual average of 82,182 in 1920–24 to 219,481 in 1938. He notes signs of 'a crime wave immediately after the War' of 1914–18, a 'steadily rising wave of shop-lifting, railway frauds, etc.' and an 'increase in crime which began in 1930'. In another study he and other writers concluded that 'it seems certain that there was some "real" increase' of juvenile delinquency in the period to 1938. However, Dr Howard Jones appears doubtful about this suggested increase of crime in the inter-war years:

Between 1930 and 1939 there was a very considerable increase, but it is arguable that where this was not due to changes in the methods of police recording . . . it was attributable to the Children and Young Persons Act, 1933, which provided a more humane approach towards the juvenile offender, and so encouraged people to bring children before the courts. . . .There is a remarkable degree of stability in the figures for the over-sixteen group during this period.[38]

Dr Jones sees a different picture during and since the Second World War:

With the outbreak of the Second World War . . . the torrent overflowed its banks. During the war, crime among all age groups rose to a record height, and has remained high ever since. . . . [There

38. L. Radzinowicz, *Ideology and Crime* . . . , 1966, pp. 61, 65, 70; H. Mannheim, *Social Aspects of Crime in England Between the Wars*, 1940, pp. 107, 109, 159, 351; A. M. Carr-Saunders, H. Mannheim and E. C. Rhodes, *Young Offenders* . . . , Cambridge 1942, p. 147; H. Jones, *Crime and the Penal System*, 2nd ed., 1962, pp. 117–18.

has been a] definite swing towards violent crime in the years *since the war*. ... By 1960, the percentage found guilty of crimes of violence in England and Wales had increased from two per cent to six per cent of all findings of guilt for indictable offences. ... It is seen that the actual number of crimes of violence known to the police increased sixfold [comparing the annual average of 1935–9 with 1960], and sex crimes more than fourfold.

Professor J. B. Mays agrees with Dr Jones:

There is more *known* crime nowadays than there was pre-war, and furthermore there seems to have been an increase in the nastier offences involving violence against the person and sexual offences. There has also been a shift from simple larceny towards more breaking and entering. ... Although we can never know in an absolute way what the extent of crime is at any one moment in society, there are good grounds for believing that there has been a substantial increase in this country over the past twenty odd years.

Dr Nigel Walker, after discussing changes in the public's readiness to report crime, says:

It is much more probable that there really has been a marked increase in the rate of these offences [property offences], and while part of the explanation may lie in the psychological and social changes in our population ... we should not overlook the obvious. This is that the rise in property offences has accompanied a rise in the amount of portable property at risk. ... In other words, the affluent society is a society of opportunity, which includes the dishonest as well as the industrious amongst its beneficiaries.

He is less sure than Dr Jones and Professor Mays about the increase in violence:

We cannot, of course, dismiss the whole of the apparent increase ... almost certainly some of it reflects a real trend. But equally certainly the real trend is not nearly as spectacular as the statistics make it seem.[39]

Can we say then that the decline in the amount of crime that occurred in the 1850s has been reversed by later movements and

39. Jones, op. cit., pp. 118, 122; J. B. Mays, *Crime and the Social Structure*, 1963, pp. 30–31, 37; N. Walker, *Crime and Punishment in Britain*, Edinburgh 1965, pp. 28, 20.

that the situation today is approaching that of the first half of the nineteenth century? A plausible case could be made out for an affirmative answer. Anyone who has studied crime in the first half of the nineteenth century will be struck by many resemblances to the present day. Many current controversies were raging then, and many so-called modern views were being put forward. Indeed, for much of the time between 1815 and the mid 1850s the nation was, just as it is today, anxiously talking about an upsurge of crime, especially amongst juveniles, and was wondering what to do about it. Many people believed that the nation was facing a problem the like of which it had never seen before. Just as today, again, there were those who, without denying that a problem existed, felt that talk of an upsurge of crime was exaggerated. Offences which used to be dealt with by parents or schoolmaster now go for trial, we are told; anyone who dealt with a childish offence on the spot as in earlier days would risk a summons for assault. These remarks come from the evidence before a Select Committee of 1828,[40] but it would not be difficult to find modern parallels. Many people in the nineteenth century were sceptical of criminal statistics – and many people are today.[41]

One common view today is that, regardless of quantitative change, the criminal problem is more serious today because of the increase of organized crime. This view too has its parallels in the past. Henry Fielding's comment of 1751 that 'a great Gang of Rogues ... have reduced Theft and Robbery into a regular System' has already been quoted. Jonas Hanway in 1775 wrote that 'in *our days* we feel such grievances the more from being more civilized. In proportion to our superior ingenuity to our forefathers, thieving is reduced to a *system*'. In 1817 the increase in the duration of the London and Middlesex sessions was in part attributed to

robbery being conducted more upon system, since it is no longer an adventitious pursuit, but a regular profession, and [to] many criminals being able to pay (out of funds obtained from plunder) large

40. s.c. on Criminal Commitments, p.p. 1828, vi, pp. 440, 484.
41. e.g. L. T. Wilkins, *Social Deviance* ... , 1964, pp. 142–76.

fees to counsel for the most able and ingenious defences which can be furnished.[42]

The use of firearms is today said to be increasing; the example of Charles Peace (who was hanged for murder in 1879) was said to have led to a fashion amongst thieves for carrying a revolver, 'owing to the unnecessary prominence given to every detail of his career by fevered pressmen in search of copy'. The fashion, said the Rev. J. W. Horsley in 1913, 'has so increased by tolerance that now we think we are obliged to give revolvers to our police'. If the police were armed in 1913 or today, this too would be a feature reminiscent of the nineteenth century, for in 1856 the Metropolitan Police in the outer districts, horse and foot, were said to be armed.[43]

Similarly, many nineteenth-century comments on the causes of crime have parallels in the present day. The people of the nineteenth century could see that poverty, the immediate pressure of want, was not, as it might at first sight have seemed, the only explanation or the most important explanation for crime, and that many stole who were not driven to it by the immediate pressure of necessity. This opinion is of course an age-old one. Aristotle wrote:

There are some crimes which are due to lack of necessities. . . . But want is not the only cause of crimes. Men also commit them simply for the pleasure it gives them, and just to get rid of an unsatisfied desire. . . . The greatest crimes are committed not for the sake of necessities, but for the sake of superfluities.[44]

This truth was rediscovered in the early nineteenth century, when new 'superfluities' were becoming available even though many lacked necessities, and when it must have been rather more difficult to perceive than it is today, now that 'lack of

42. Fielding quoted on p. 26; Hanway, op. cit., p. 5; s.c. on Police, P.P. 1817, vii, pp. 338–9.

43. J. W. Horsley, *How Criminals are Made and Prevented* . . . , 1913, pp. 34–5; *Quarterly Review*, vol. xcix, June 1856, p. 167.

44. Aristotle, *Politics*, translated E. Barker, Oxford 1946, book ii, ch. vii paras. 11–12, pp. 65–6.

necessities' has taken a very different and a much less acute form and is clearly much less satisfactory an explanation. Again, the writer who said that the excitement of dodging the police was as important as the hope of gain could well have been writing in the 1960s instead of in 1852.[45] The writers on crime of the nineteenth century could not envisage a society without unemployment and with all the advantages of a Welfare State; but it is conceivable that some of them, could such a society have been described to them, would have guessed that none the less crime would remain a serious problem.

In much the same way, modern views about the social consequences of life in large cities and its effect on children do not differ markedly from those put forward in the nineteenth century. The 'latch-key child' is a modern name for a phenomenon which existed and was recognized in the earlier period. The influence of family background was important in both periods, and contemporary comment about it is similar in each case. A Liverpool magistrate in 1850 described a family of three brothers each of whom had a lengthening record of crime, following in the footsteps of their father; a London magistrate today tells of a youngster following eight older brothers and sisters into crime.[46] Nineteenth-century remarks about the children of the Irish immigrants are paralleled by similar remarks about similar children today.[47] There would be no difficulty in finding a parallel for Horsley's remark in 1913 that there was a 'curious idea that dishonesty against a corporate body is more venial than if it were against an individual'.[48]

There is a modern note in the nineteenth-century remarks about the way in which lower-class children were brought before the courts for what would have been a prank in a youth of better family, while the crimes of the professional classes

45. *English Review*, vol. xvii, July 1852, p. 243.

46. For the nineteenth-century magistrate see p. 92; the twentieth-century magistrate is the Hon. E. E. S. Montagu C.B.E., Q.C. (personal communication).

47. J. A. Jackson, *The Irish in Britain*, 1963, pp. 66–9, 160.

48. Horsley, op. cit., p. 82,

received little attention.[49] And anyone who reads what is said later about the entertainment offered to the children of the towns, about the way Jack Sheppard and similar heroes bulked large in their lives whilst they did not know more respectable heroes, must hear the echoes of the modern discussions which were in the author's mind as he wrote. A generation after the end of the Second World War, surveys contrasted the children's ignorance of Eisenhower and Montgomery with their detailed knowledge of current variety stars, just as, a generation after the end of the Napoleonic Wars, surveys contrasted ignorance about Wellington with knowledge of Jack Sheppard. Current discussion about television and horror-comics follows the same lines as the earlier discussion of penny theatres and penny books.

Other echoes of modern debates are to be found in the following chapters. The discussion of travelling criminals and their use of turnpikes and railways could be paralleled by modern debate about cars and motorways. The animadversions of nineteenth-century magistrates on the display of goods at shop-doors have been repeated by their modern counterparts in relation to self-service shops and gaudy displays. Edwin Chadwick, who advocated the greater use of banks and cheques to reduce theft, would have heard his arguments being repeated, had he been able to listen to current discussion of bank-raids and the payment of wages by cheque. If the current craze for bingo were to lead to the development in this country of anything like the 'numbers' or 'policy' rackets of present-day America, it would be a reversion to something like the 'insurances on lotteries' of London after Waterloo.[50]

The treatment of prisoners led to much the same sort of discussion in the nineteenth century as it does today. A writer in 1908, looking back on twenty-one years' experience as a police-court missionary, declared:

49. cf. Mays, op. cit., pp. 40–43.
50. T. Sellin, 'Organised Crime: A Business Enterprise', *Annals of American Academy of Political and Social Science*, vol. cccxlvii, May 1963, pp. 12–19; s.c. on Police. P.P. 1816, v, pp. 30–31.

Introduction

I often feel dismayed when I consider some of the present-day tendencies. There is such a feverish and manifest desire among thousands of people to stand between a prisoner and the law, and to relieve him at any cost from the legal consequence of his wrongdoing. Indeed, some folk would move heaven and earth, if it were possible, to keep a heartless young rogue out of prison. I would not lift my finger; to me it seems a most serious matter, for the consequences of criminal actions ought to be as certain as daylight. I would, however, do much to make those consequences, not only certain, but swift, reasonable, and dignified, but not vindictive or revengeful. Punishment should be severe enough to convey an important and a lasting lesson. . . . As a rule, it is not a wise or a good thing to prevent the consequences of crime falling upon the criminal.

All that would today seem remarkable about this statement is its source – it comes from the Secretary of the Howard Association, one of the predecessors of the Howard League for Penal Reform.[51] There were in the nineteenth century advocates of sterner punishments and advocates of softer treatment; and – just as today – each side was able to find in past experience evidence which satisfied its own supporters if nobody else. Just as today, there were plenty of theories but no firm facts.

In one aspect of the use of prison as a punishment we may be going some way to restore the position of the nineteenth century. There was in the nineteenth century a marked trend to shorter sentences. Mr J. E. Hall Williams has shown that this trend was reversed after the Second World War, and suggests that

the chances of getting long sentences for certain crimes are greater now than in 1938. . . . It seems likely that the number of truly long sentences will grow, and that prisons will be expected to accommodate prisoners for terms far in excess of that which the humane practice of the past few generations has sanctioned and decreed as acceptable.[52]

Some of the prisoners of the past seem to have been the same

51. T. Holmes, *Known to the Police*, 1908, pp. 100–101.
52. J. E. Hall Williams, 'The Use the Courts Make of Prison', *The Sociological Review*, Monograph no. 9, June 1965, pp. 66–7.

sort of people as prisoners today. The people who welcomed prison as a place of abode in the nineteenth century were perhaps not very different from the 'drifters' described by modern authors.[53] And the nineteenth-century prison officials who spoke of the unsettling effects on youngsters in homes of race-weeks and (after their invention in 1871) Bank Holidays were anticipating in simpler language the modern comment that 'epidemics of tension states appear at New Year and during the various "Fair" weeks in the summer'.[54] Burt in the 1920s recorded the advice of an experienced youngster to a new hand: 'S'y it's the pitchers: 'e always makes a speech about it and nods at yer for provin' 'is p'int.' Youngsters paid similar attention to the foibles of public officials in the nineteenth century.[55]

Some 'modern' devices to improve criminal and penal procedure were suggested long ago. A public defender and a public prosecutor were both suggested early in the nineteenth century.[56] A 'court of inquiry' to classify prisoners after conviction and on the basis of full reports was advocated in 1833, while the newly created School Boards were in 1876 suggested as suitable tribunals for dealing with juvenile delinquents – an anticipation both of our existing special courts for juveniles and of suggestions that the fate of juvenile delinquents should be decided by bodies concerned with the care of children rather than by courts of any kind.[57]

Yet, despite all these resemblances, it is clear that things are fundamentally different today from the first sixty years of the nineteenth century. It can be shown today that certain streets,

53. Home Office Advisory Council on the Treatment of Offenders, *Report on Preventive Detention*, 1963, pp. 26–7.

54. S.C. on Juvenile Offenders, P.P. 1852–3, xxiii, p. 211 (q. 2105); J. W. Horsley, *Jottings from Jail* . . . , 1877, p. 84; H. S. McWalter, 'A Preliminary Comparative Study of the Treatment of Certain Prison Neuroses', *British Journal of Criminology*, vol. ii, April 1962, no. 4, 382.

55. C. Burt, *The Young Delinquent*, 2nd ed., 1927, p. 143n.; the nineteenth-century quotation is on p. 98.

56. See p. 264.

57. *Fraser's Magazine*, vol. vi, Oct. 1832, p. 300; B. Waugh, *The Gaol Cradle: Who Rocks It?* . . . , 3rd ed., 1876, pp. 87–9.

or even whole areas, of our towns produce an undue proportion of the total number of offenders, but there are no rookeries like the old St Giles'. We have our Teddy-boys and our Mods and Rockers, but even their severest critics could not liken them to the youngsters of the early nineteenth century. Again, though there are frequent complaints of the lax sexual conduct of modern youth, it should be remembered that in 1816 the Ordinary (Chaplain) of Newgate told a Select Committee of the House of Commons that all the boys in that prison – and there were some of nine or ten years old – kept a mistress.[58] We may be right to worry about the crime situation today, but we should not claim that it is worse than it has ever been.

Indeed, if we are to look for a parallel in the field of crime with the England of the first sixty years of the nineteenth century, it is not to the England of the twentieth century that we should look, but to those countries that are today undergoing the experience of industrialization and urbanization. In 1960 the secretariat of a United Nations conference on crime drew attention to the effect on crime of 'cultural instability, the weakening of primary social controls and the exposure to conflicting social standards' such as is found in developing countries; the effects are intensified, it noted, when the rate of social change is rapid, 'the degree of social change is high and when the gap between the breakdown of old social institutions and the creation of new institutions is great'.[59] If the contention of this book is correct, there is a close parallel here with the England of the nineteenth century. The people of nineteenth-century England, like the people of many parts of Africa and Asia today, were not only building physical assets for their descendants. They were, slowly and painfully and at no small price, developing a new way of life. They were learning to live in an urban, industrialized society.

58. See pp. 100–101.
59. Second United Nations Congress on the Prevention of Crime and Treatment of Offenders, London 1960, *Report by Secretariat* (A/Conf.17/20), p. 62, New York 1961.

Part Two

Criminals and the course of crime in the nineteenth century

4. The criminal class

The first point that has to be made in relation to crime in the
nineteenth century is that contemporaries were convinced that
the crux of the question was the existence of a separate criminal
class. In 1854 an article in the *Eclectic Review* said that it was
not a question of dispute that a criminal class existed. 'It is in
very fact a recognized section, and a well-known section, too, in
all towns of great magnitude. . . . It constitutes a new estate, in
utter estrangement from all the rest.'[1] In 1891 the Rev.
W. D. Morrison, a prison chaplain who is regarded today as one
of the most percipient writers on crime of the nineteenth century, expressed the same idea:

There is a population of habitual criminals which forms a class by
itself. Habitual criminals are not to be confounded with the working
or any other class; they are a set of persons who make crime the
object and business of their lives; to commit crime is their trade;
they deliberately scoff at honest ways of earning a living, and must
accordingly be looked upon as a class of a separate and distinct
character from the rest of the community.[2]

It seems possible that this concept developed gradually after
1815. The witnesses before the Select Committee on Police of
1816–18 do not seem to have thought in terms of a criminal
class. A question put to one of them referred to 'that class of
persons who ordinarily commit crimes, meaning the poor and
indigent', a turn of phrase which would not have been used later
in the century (and which would have met with a rebuttal if it
had been used). Another made a clear distinction between the
criminal district of St Giles' and the more respectable (and

1. *Eclectic Review*, new ser., vol. vii, April 1854, p. 387.
2. W. D. Morrison, *Crime and Its Causes*, 1891, pp. 141–2.

poorer) parts of the parish without using the idea of a criminal class. The Keeper of Newgate did indeed make a distinction between the criminal who 'happens among a family, where the family are not criminal themselves' and 'those in the habits of criminality', and here perhaps we can see the idea taking shape.[3]

By 1828, however, the idea seems to be gaining credence. A witness before the Select Committee on Police that reported in that year was asked: 'Are the thieves in general low artizans employed in any trade or business, or are they a class distinct by themselves, who do nothing but thieve?' He replied: 'Generally speaking, I think they are trained up from what I may call juvenile delinquents; they go on step by step, and have no trade at all; certainly a great portion of them have had trades.' A writer the following year commented on this passage: 'They are born [thieves], and it is their inheritance: they form a *caste* of themselves, having their peculiar slang, mode of thinking, habits, and arts of living.'[4] In 1832 an article in *Fraser's Magazine* said:

There is a distinct body of thieves, whose life and business it is to follow up a determined warfare against the constituted authorities, by living in idleness and on plunder. ... So very similar are their ideas and converse, that in a few minutes' conversation with any one of the party, I could always distinguish them, however artfully they might disguise themselves, and attempt to mislead me. They may be known almost by their very gait in the streets from other persons. ... They form a distinct class of men by themselves, very carefully admitting noviciates into their secrets. They form one club.[5]

In 1834 Francis Place assured the Select Committee on Drunkenness that the criminal class was now separate from the orderly part of the community, adding the next year, before the Select Committee on Education, that they no longer mixed in-

3. s.c. on Police, P.P. 1816, v, p. 226; ibid., P.P. 1817, vii, p. 153; ibid., P.P. 1818, viii, p. 185.

4. ibid., P.P. 1828, vi, p. 45; J. Wade, *A Treatise on the Police and Crimes of the Metropolis ... by the Editor of 'The Cabinet Lawyer'*, 1829, p. 159.

5. *Fraser's Magazine*, vol. v, June 1832, pp. 521–2.

discriminately as before.[6] By the middle of the 1830s, too, the distinction between the honest poor and the criminal class was clear enough to the people themselves. W. A. Miles, an investigator who worked for two official inquiries in the 1830s, recounted what a police officer had told him. Speaking of one London tenement (Calmet-buildings, Oxford Street) where 'low Irish' lived four or five families in a room, he said:

In this court, there are two classes, namely, the industrious and the idle, which are distinguished by titles peculiar to this court, and which are often the cause of serious party fights; the parties are the *clock makers*, i.e. the hard-working people, and the *watch makers*, who are the most dissolute persons and young prostitutes.[7]

From this time onwards the idea that criminals formed a separate section of the community was general, and many of the works cited elsewhere in this book took this as axiomatic. The *Oxford English Dictionary* records the use of the phrase 'dangerous class' in 1859, but in fact it was in use ten years earlier. One of those who used it as part of the title of a book was Miss Mary Carpenter, a well-known writer on criminal matters and an advocate of reformatory schools. In 1851 she defined the classes about whom she was writing:[8]

Those who have not yet fallen into actual crime, but who are almost certain from their ignorance, destitution, and the circumstances in which they are growing up, to do so, if a helping hand be not extended to raise them ... form the *perishing classes* ... those who have already received the prison brand, or, if the mark has not been yet visibly set upon them, are notoriously living by plunder – who unblushingly acknowledge that they can gain more for the support of themselves and their parents by stealing than by working ... form the *dangerous classes*.

6. s.c. on Drunkenness, p.p. 1834, viii, pp. 500 (q. 2039), 501 (qq. 2047–8); s.c. on Education, p.p. 1835, vii, p. 851 (q. 939).

7. H. Brandon (ed.), *Poverty, Mendicity and Crime* ... , 1839, p. 140.

8. M. Carpenter, *Reformatory Schools for the Children of the Perishing and Dangerous Classes, and for Juvenile Offenders*, 1851, p. 2; s.c. on Juvenile Offenders, p.p. 1852, vii, pp. 98 (q. 799), 102 (q. 816).

These two classes together seem to have made up what she later called the 'ragged' class:

I have been very much struck with observing the strong line of demarcation which exists between the labouring and the 'ragged' class; a line of demarcation not drawn by actual poverty. ... The line of demarcation consists in the utter want of control existing among the children of the lower class, and in the entire absence of effort among the parents to provide proper education for their children. I believe that juvenile crime is entirely arising from the lower class.

It may well be thought that the distinction being made in all these quotations, and in the others which could be added to their number, is merely the familiar nineteenth-century distinction between the deserving and the undeserving poor. It is, however, clear that this is not the case. Many sympathetic observations were made about juvenile offenders by those who believed in the existence of a criminal class. Two examples will suffice here. The writer in *Fraser's Magazine* already quoted[9] went on:

I wish those who have the management of boys of the description here spoken of, would reflect that, in the majority of cases, there has either been no parent, or those of such habits and temper as would have rendered orphanship a blessing; and that, in all probability, most of them under their care never had a kind or affectionate sentiment imparted to or drawn out of them, by any human being they could look to as a friend; and that they have in a manner been driven to take up arms against society, meeting, from their earliest recollections, with nothing but an enemy in man. Thoughts of this nature ever induced me to adopt a kind mode of treatment; and I have found it to succeed in a wonderful manner, even when others have said that no sense of feeling was left.

A gaol chaplain asked in 1849, in relation to the appearance presented by the prisoners, 'Who would not have evil looks if their lives had been spent in poverty and misery?' An aristocrat, he said, would in similar circumstances look the same.[10]

9. *Fraser's Magazine*, loc. cit., p. 524.
10. W. C. Osborn, *A Lecture on the Prevention of Crime delivered* ... *November 26th, 1849*, Ipswich n.d., p. 6.

Moreover, those who believed in the existence of a criminal class did not think that its members were responsible for all crimes. The writer in *Fraser's Magazine* already quoted spoke the following year of

> working men and labourers, who have not before committed crime ... and yet from the occurrence of particular events, fall into a month's habit of idleness and drunkenness from which they merge in a mental state of confusion into the commission of an accidental offence. Now, in all cases, when these men are treated as common offenders, they are invariably made so from that time henceforward, and probably their posterity also.[11]

The *Edinburgh Review* in 1854 made a clear distinction between men who '*commit crime*' and men who '*become criminals*', and in 1865 it distinguished between 'the isolated offence of a generally well-conducted person' and the offences of 'the vast majority of convicts – those who are members of a sort of criminal race – an order as clearly marked to the eye of the police and the prison-inspector as the gypsies are to us all'. It said that the late Ordinary (Chaplain) of Newgate 'strongly insisted' on the body of prisoners being 'divided, for practical purposes, into two; the one comprehending the habitually corrupt and degraded; and the other, such offenders as have broken the law under some sudden impulse or some single overwhelming temptation'.[12] It was of course difficult for discharged prisoners to find honest jobs, and thus commission of the first offence was very likely to lead to others whatever the character of the prisoner.

To some extent, of course, the belief in a criminal class was self-fulfilling, for it may have led some youngsters to think that there was no other way of life for them. This occurred to the Rev. W. D. Morrison, who wrote in 1896: 'Juveniles in all ranks of life are exceedingly sensitive to public opinion, and, unless

11. *Old Bailey Experience ... by the Author of 'The Schoolmaster's Experiences in Newgate'*, 1833, p. 289. (Much of this book is a reprint of the articles in *Fraser's Magazine*.)

12. *Edinburgh Review*, vol. c, Oct. 1854, p. 598; ibid., vol. cxxii, Oct. 1865, p. 341.

gifted with great inborn force of character, are apt to become what the world in general considers them to be.' In the same year his namesake, Arthur Morrison, used his novelist's imagination to make the same point. His hero Dicky Perrott, having lost (through no fault of his own) the only honest job he ever had the chance of, muses on his situation:

As for himself, he was hopeless: plainly he must have some incomprehensible defect of nature, since he offended, do as he might, and could neither understand nor redeem his fault. . . . Plainly Mr Weech's philosophy was right after all. He was of the Jago, and he must prey on the outer world, as all the Jago did; not stray foolishly off the regular track in chase of visions, and fall headlong. . . . Who was he, Dicky Perrott, that he should break away from the Jago habit, and strain after another nature? What could come of it but defeat and bitterness? As old Beveridge had said, the Jago had got him. Why should he fight against the inevitable, and bruise himself? The ways out of the Jago old Beveridge had told him, years ago. Gaol, the gallows, and the High Mob. There was his chance, his aspiration, his goal: the High Mob. . . . He . . . put away his foolish ambitions, and went forth with a brave heart: to accomplish his destiny, for well or ill – a Jago rat.[13]

Professor Chevalier suggests that part of the population of Paris in the nineteenth century drifted into crime because it was regarded as criminal by the world at large;[14] and this may have been true in England as well.

Another way in which the belief in the existence of the criminal class helped to perpetuate it was by the readiness with which it led everyone to think the worst of those in poor circumstances. As early as 1828 the Select Committee on Criminal Commitments pointed out that offences passed over when committed by sons of the rich led to prosecution when committed by the children of the poor, and the remark later became commonplace. In 1862 Henry Mayhew, after a visit to the House of Correction, Tothill Fields, wrote:

13. W. D. Morrison, *Juvenile Offenders*, 1896, p. 173; A. Morrison, *A Child of the Jago*, Penguin ed., 1946, pp. 116–18.
14. L. Chevalier, *Classes laborieuses et classes dangereuses à Paris pendant la première moitié du 19ème siècle*, Paris 1958, p. 312.

Here we find little creatures of six years of age branded with a felon's badge – boys, not even in their teens, clad in the prison dress, for the heinous offence of throwing stones, or obstructing highways, or unlawfully knocking at doors – crimes which the very magistrates themselves, who committed the youths, must have assuredly perpetrated in their boyhood. ... Suppose you or I, reader, had been consigned to such a place in our school-boy days, for those acts of thoughtlessness which none but fanatics would think of regarding as *crime*. ... On our return from Tothill Fields, we consulted with some of our friends as to the various peccadilloes of their youth, and ... they, one and all, confessed to having committed in their younger days many of the very '*crimes*' for which the boys at Tothill Fields were incarcerated.

A few years earlier, a writer pointed out that the future Lord Eldon had as a schoolboy been caught robbing an orchard. If he had been prosecuted instead of flogged by his father, he asked, how could he have become Lord Chancellor?[15]

The difference of treatment was not entirely a matter of prejudice. Miss Carpenter explained one of the motives: there was very considerable reluctance to prosecute children of respectable background, because of the well-known contaminating effects of prison.[16] It was not only the young members of the respectable classes who received preferential treatment, of course. Adults were similarly treated, and the fixed fines for certain offences made a very different impact on people in poor circumstances than on the well-to-do. The difficulties of obtaining bail also made things harder for the poor:

While the poor man is kept incarcerated at the station-house the whole of the night to be ready at the time he is to make his appearance before the magistrate, the rich one is enabled, by the strength of his purse, to be at large on his parole, until waited on by

15. s.c. on Criminal Commitments, P.P. 1828, vi, p. 430; H. Mayhew and J. Binney, *The Criminal Prisons of London* ..., 1862, pp. 406, 408; A. Thomson, *Punishment and Prevention*, Edinburgh 1857, p. 179n.
16. M. Carpenter, *Juvenile Delinquents – their Condition and Treatment*, London 1853, p. 7.

the officer who had him in charge, whom he leisurely attends to the justice room.[17]

The Metropolitan Police in their early days were rather over-enthusiastic in enforcing the law and dealing with minor offences;[18] and it is legitimate to assume that the poorer classes were the principal sufferers. Moreover, as was pointed out in 1849, one reason why criminals came mainly from the 'un-educated classes' was that those of higher classes were better placed to avoid crime, or at any rate the sort of crime that attracted attention – the Rev. Lord Sidney Godolphin Osborne, a prolific writer of letters to *The Times*, in 1864 complained that the misdeeds of the professional classes were usually ig-nored. The discrimination was not all one way, and Charles Booth noted in 1903 that 'conduct which in Cadogan Square would lead to the police cells, might be passed over in Slaidburn Street'. There is, however, no doubt that the balance was un-favourable to the poorer classes, and we need hardly be sur-prised that these perennial factors operated in the nineteenth century. It is, however, worthy of note that contemporaries were able to perceive their working.[19]

Nineteenth-century opinion was thus not blind to the ways in which circumstances operated against those whom it called the 'criminal class'; but the question now arises whether the concept of a 'criminal class' is a tenable one. The idea is certainly not one which appeals to modern thought, and sociologists of the twentieth century would no doubt have described the situation in very different terms. Yet to some extent it is merely termin-ology that is in question. This may be seen by examining a study of 'Radby' (a name which disguises the identity of a Mid-land mining town) made in 1952-4. One part of the study com-

17. Brandon, op. cit., p. 28.

18. Commissioners' letter dated 9 Aug. 1830, H.O. 61/2, Public Record Office.

19. T. Beggs, *An Inquiry into the Extent and Causes of Juvenile Depravity*, 1849, pp. 53-4; letter dated 23 Aug. 1864 reprinted in A. White (ed.), *The Letters of S.G.O.*, 1890, vol. i, pp. 365-8; C. Booth (ed.), *Life and Labour of the People in London*, 1902-4, final vol., p. 137.

pared two streets, Dyke Street and Gladstone Street, and another part ranged the households in five grades. The following extracts are drawn from the authors' conclusions:

Although both streets are situated in a working class area, two different sets of standards are upheld. ... There is a concentration in the black street [Dyke Street] of cases of adult and juvenile delinquency, and ... there is a similar concentration in the two lower grades. ... In the black street and in the low grades there is ... a disregard of commonly accepted codes of conduct, not enforced by the law of the land. ... Actual delinquency – illegal activity – is more general amongst the lower grade people than the official delinquency figures suggest. This is thought to be true of both adults and juveniles ...

Children brought up in such homes may hardly distinguish between what they have a right to use and what the law says they must not. Even the adults may regard the distinction as less important than do those who live in the 'white' streets. Stealing tends only to be regarded as such if the monetary value of the article is considerable ...

The pleasures of leisure are very dependent on gambling. ... They admire the man who can raise money by means other than his ordinary work. He is patently a smart chap if he can 'make something on the side' at the job itself. Actual theft may come to be regarded as just another legitimate means, parallel to gambling, of getting something without having to pay for it by the grind of the daily job ...

The analysis of factors operating in the black street suggests that there is nothing extraordinary in the occurrence of delinquency in that street. Whereas delinquency occurring in the white street may well be considered as unusual since there are no factors, comparable to those in the black street, operating to encourage delinquency, and many operating in a positive way to prevent its occurrence ...

There is a common sentiment amongst the people of Dyke Street which is remarked upon by other people in the town. They are recognized as a community, differing from other streets in the town, and regarded as a unit. ... Their whole life is tied up with such [delinquent] behaviour in many ways, as has been shown. The man returning to Dyke Street from gaol and the boy from Approved School are not the subjects of ostracism. Our research suggests that they will be welcomed back, or at any rate just received back as if nothing untoward had happened. And they will re-commence life as they left it off, in the moral climate in which they live, which presents a very different code from that by which they were convicted of an offence.[20]

The picture presented by these extracts, and even to some extent the very language used, is not too different from that of the nineteenth century.

One specific criticism of the nineteenth-century concept has been made: the proportion of people in their 'teens and early twenties in the total number of offenders appearing before the courts, it is said, is so high as to suggest that what existed is not so much a criminal class but a criminal generation – that is, that criminal activity was a phase through which many people passed at a certain period of their life and out of which they later grew. There was indeed a predominance of youthful offenders, and this did not escape the notice of nineteenth-century observers. Thus the introduction to the Criminal Statistics for 1842 said:[21]

The comparison of the ages of Offenders, with the population at the same age, shows more strongly the great proportion of Offenders between the age of fifteen and twenty-five years, and how rapidly that proportion declines after the age of thirty, becoming less than the proportion in the general population after forty, and falling suddenly off at each period, on passing that age.

Mayhew, quoting the above passage, adds that

In the year 1848, for instance, those between fifteen and twenty-five years of age who were sent for trial made up exactly forty-nine per cent of the whole commitments; whereas, according to the census returns [for 1841], there are only 19.6 per cent of persons of that age throughout the country.

L. O. Pike in 1876 compared the age-structure of eight agricultural and industrial occupations with that of convicts, and was

20. A. P. Jephcott and M. P. Carter, *The Social Background of Delinquency*, Nottingham 1954 (limited circulation), pp. 275, 283–5, 287, 291–2.
21. Introduction to the Criminal Statistics for 1842, P.P. 1843, xlii, p. 7; Mayhew and Binny, op. cit., p. 453n.

surprised to find that the proportion of convicts over the age of thirty-five was lower than the corresponding figure in all the other cases. It was also lower than that of the total population. (He excluded those below fifteen years of age from all the calculations.)[22]

The dangers of arguing from nineteenth-century criminal statistics have already been shown. Even if the statistics were reliable, however, they would not disprove the existence of a criminal class. A number of factors would increase the proportion of those in the lower age-groups brought before the courts. Older criminals tended to get longer sentences, and thus were not able to appear before the courts as frequently as youngsters with short sentences. Some criminals were transported to Australia or elsewhere – no one knows exactly how many convicts were actually transported, but the figure was something like 160,000. (However, this factor may to some extent have been balanced by the fact that it was harder for those with a criminal record to emigrate in the normal way.) It is probable that older criminals were more skilful than younger ones (just as is the case in most other trades) and hence were caught less often. Most important of all, perhaps, is the fact that the pattern of crime changed as criminals grew older. They took to different forms of crime, and there is no reason why the capture-rate should be the same for different offences. They stole more at a time, and stole less frequently – the Artful Dodger committed several offences every day, but Bill Sikes prepared the 'Chertsey job' for weeks – and the youngsters thus ran more risk of being caught. The older criminals used younger ones for the more dangerous tasks, and thus the younger partner could be caught without the same fate befalling the older one, whilst the reverse was less likely.

The attempt to draw from the statistics conclusions of the sort suggested can perhaps be refuted by a modern comparison. In 1964 the proportion of the population of England and Wales between the ages of fifteen and twenty-four was 14·3 per cent,

22. Pike, *A History of Crime in England* . . . , 1876, vol. ii, pp. 513–16 (cf. pp. 456, 668–70).

and the proportion of those killed in motor vehicle accidents who were between those ages was 25·8 per cent; but the corresponding figures for those aged between twenty-five and forty-four were 26·1 per cent and 18·7 per cent. Clearly, therefore, a higher proportion of those aged fifteen to twenty-four was killed than of those aged twenty-five to forty-four.[23] However, we could not from this contrast deduce anything about the *amount* of use made of the roads by people in those age-groups. We should seek the explanation for the difference in the *ways* in which people of different ages use the roads. In the same way, the differences seen in the criminal statistics may well be due to different patterns of criminal behaviour rather than a different rate of criminality.

On the whole, then, the nineteenth-century concept of a 'criminal class' may be regarded as an acceptable explanation of the phenomena of the time. Even if this is not the case, however, the evidence which has to be used for a survey of criminal conditions in the nineteenth century is couched almost entirely in terms of such a class, and must of necessity be discussed in those terms. Thus, in this book the nineteenth-century expression will be used.

Though they drew this distinction between honest people and the criminals, the people of the nineteenth century of course realized that the criminal class included people of many different types. Henry Mayhew, that great classifier, produced a table of the different types of criminal, which has five major headings, twenty minor headings and over a hundred different categories. The flavour of the table can be shown by an extract. The following is part of the section under the major heading 'Thieves and their Dependants'. Subsection A has disposed of 'Those who Plunder with Violence', ranging them in three groups, and sub-section B of 'Those who "Hocus", or Plunder their Victims when Stupified' (two groups). There follows:

23. The figures have been calculated from General Register Office, *Quarterly Return of Births, Deaths and Marriages,* no. 466, 2nd quarter, 1965, pp. 25, 32–3.

c Those who Plunder by Manual Dexterity, by Stealth, or by Breach of Trust.

1 'Mobsmen', or those who plunder by manual dexterity – as the 'light-fingered gentry'.

  a 'Buzzers', or those who abstract handkerchiefs and other articles from gentlemen's pockets.

    i 'Stook-buzzers', those who steal handkerchiefs.

    ii 'Tail-buzzers', those who dive into coat-pockets for sneezers (snuff-boxes), skins and dummies (purses and pocket-books).

  b 'Wires', or those who pick ladies' pockets.

  c 'Prop-nailers', those who steal pins and brooches.

  d 'Thimble-screwers', those who wrench watches from their guards.

  e 'Shop-lifters', or those who purloin goods while examining articles.

2 'Sneaksmen', or those who plunder by means of stealth.

  a Those who purloin goods, provisions, money, clothes, old metal, &c.

    i 'Drag Sneaks', or those who steal goods or luggage from carts and coaches.

    ii 'Snoozers', or those who sleep at railway hotels, and decamp with some passenger's luggage or property in the morning.

    iii 'Star-glazers', or those who cut the panes out of shop-windows.

    iv 'Till Friskers', or those who empty tills of their contents during the absence of the shopmen.

    v 'Sawney-Hunters', or those who go purloining bacon from cheese-mongers' shop-doors.

    vi 'Noisy-racket Men', or those who steal china and glass from outside of china-shops.

    vii 'Area Sneaks', or those who steal from houses by going down the area steps.

    viii 'Dead Lurkers', or those who steal coats and umbrellas from passages at dusk, or on Sunday afternoons.

    ix 'Snow Gatherers', or those who steal clean clothes off the hedges.

    x 'Skinners', or those women who entice children and sailors to go with them and then strip them of their clothes.

xi 'Bluey-Hunters', or those who purloin lead from the tops of houses.

xii 'Cat and Kitten Hunters', or those who purloin pewter quart and pint pots from the top of area railings.

xiii 'Toshers', or those who purloin copper from the ships along shore.

xiv 'Mudlarks', or those who steal pieces of rope and lumps of coal from among the vessels at the river-side.

Sub-section c continues with 'b Those who steal animals' (in seven categories) and 'c Those who steal dead bodies – as the "Resurrectionists" ' (no sub-division). There then follows '3 Those who plunder by breach of trust', eight types being specified. Sub-section D ranges ' "Shoful Men", or those who Plunder by Means of Counterfeits' under four headings, and sub-section E polishes off the 'Dependents of Thieves' in a mere two categories.[24]

It is clear that Mayhew's zeal and industry as a classifier have carried him too far, but the general picture given by his table is fully confirmed from other sources. Those to whom we refer, hitherto and subsequently, as the 'criminal class' were in fact of almost as many infinite gradations as the nation itself. They had the bond of 'living on the cross', and of having a reckless disregard for their eventual fate, but otherwise they had little in common.

Mayhew emphasized the prestige attached to the 'swell mob', the high-class pickpockets who dressed well and lived in rooms rather in lodging-houses. The swell mobsmen could be mistaken for gentlemen; this was indeed their essential characteristic and their stock-in-trade. The governor of a gaol described them:

The swell-mob, generally speaking, are composed of men who have received education, some respectably connected, all well dressed; in society, except to their immediate associates, they appear and are considered as gentlemen.[25]

Mayhew said of the swell mobsman that he

24. H. Mayhew, *London Labour and the London Poor* . . . , 1861–2, vol. iv, pp. 23–7.

25. R.C. on Constabulary Force, P.P. 1839, xix, p. 222.

'mixes' generally in 'the best of company', frequenting – for the purposes of his business – all the places of public entertainment, and often being a regular attendant at church and the more elegant chapels, especially during charity sermons.[26]

The skilled housebreaker, the cracksman, was rougher and a greater drinker – Bill Sikes, for example, wore

a black velveteen coat, very soiled drab breeches, lace-up half-boots, and grey cotton stockings. . . . He had a brown hat on his head, and a dirty belcher handkerchief round his neck.[27]

To some extent it was not the type but the scale and success of a criminal's operations that determined his prestige. In this connection we may recall Charley Bates's anguish at the injustice which had befallen his friend Jack Dawkins:[28]

'The Artful's booked for a passage out [that is, he was in custody on a charge bound to result in his being transported to Australia]. To think of Jack Dawkins – lummy Jack – the Dodger – the Artful Dodger – going abroad for a common twopenny-halfpenny sneeze-box! I never thought he'd a done it under a gold watch, chain, and seals, at the lowest. Oh, why didn't he rob some rich old gentleman of all his walables, and go out *as* a gentleman, and not like a common prig, without no honour nor glory!'
With this expression of feeling for his unfortunate friend, Master Bates sat himself on the nearest chair with an aspect of chagrin and despondency . . .
'How will he stand in the Newgate Calendar? P'raps not be there at all. Oh, my eye, my eye, wot a blow it is! . . .'
'Never mind, Charley', said Fagin soothingly; 'it'll come out. . . . Think how young he is too! What a distinction, Charley, to be lagged at his time of life!'
'Well, it is a honour that is!' said Charley, a little consoled.

About the time that Dickens was writing *Oliver Twist,* another writer described the ideals of the real-life Charley Bateses:[29]

26. Mayhew, op. cit., vol. iv, p. 32.
27. Dickens, *Oliver Twist,* ch. xii, edited by K. Tillotson, Oxford 1966, pp. 76–7 (all page references are to this edition).
28. ibid., ch. xliii, pp. 295–6.
29. Brandon, op. cit., p. 93.

I have observed that boys in Newgate, who have been sentenced to death (although the boy, as well as the judge and every person present, knew that he would not be hung in pursuance of that sentence,) conduct themselves as boys of a superior class to the transport lads. The boy under sentence of transportation for life is of greater consequence than the boy who is sentenced to seven years, while the lad whose sentence is a short imprisonment is not deemed worthy to associate or converse with them: in short, the daring offender is a member of the prison aristocracy ... and severity of punishment is by them converted into a scale of merit.

Pickpockets and house-breakers, whatever their position in the scale of merit by the test just discussed, looked down on mere shop-lifters, who in their turn were superior to sneak-thieves. The 'pudding snammer', who stole food from those leaving cook-shops, was said to be the lowest class of all thieves, but he in turn looked down on those who were in prison merely for begging – as Mayhew put it, a boy was 'partly forced to steal for his character'. Mayhew summed up the situation: 'The "Cracksman", or housebreaker, would no more think of associating with the "Sneaksman" than a barrister would dream of sitting down to dinner with an attorney.'[30]

Despite these gradations, the criminal class can be divided into two main groups. The division can be seen by considering the group from which nearly all criminals came – what might be described in modern terms as the 'recruitment grade' – the urban juveniles. Some of the boys were out-and-out thieves, active, alert and intelligent; such lads would soon be picked by older thieves for training and would become experts. The boys in Newgate – that is to say, those who were charged with serious offences – were described in the 1830s:

I have found much shrewdness, much talent, and, moreover, much good feeling mixed up with these boys. In fact, shrewdness, bold daring, and close observation is their 'stock-in-trade', and without those requisites they would make but very sorry thieves. There is a library in the boys' ward at Newgate: it contains a great number of evangelical books and lives of a great number of dissenting minis-

30. ibid., p. 92; Mayhew, op. cit., vol. i, p. 411, vol. iv, p. 31.

ters; among the other books, however, there are a few containing history and travels, and it is with these latter books that the boys are delighted; they read them with eagerness, and the more illiterate boys will subscribe portions of food to engage the services of a boy to read to them aloud. The schoolmaster mentioned cases of boys who were so fired with the desire of reading, that, although they did not know their letters when they came to prison, they were enabled to read before they left it.

Thus it is evident, that however lost these children may *now* be, there is 'material' to work upon, if properly managed and directed.[31]

If these boys avoided disease and the law and grew to manhood in England, they would become the adult thieves of standing and ability. Other boys, and probably a greater number, were content to beg when they could, pilfer minor articles as occasion served, but lacked the industry, the intelligence or the drive to undertake the more serious crimes. Those of this group who survived to manhood doubtless were the feckless drifters in and out of prison who figure in contemporary descriptions. The same division obtained amongst the girls as amongst the boys, the less intelligent being prostitutes and beggars while their brighter sisters were primarily thieves who used prostitution merely as a means of taking strangers unawares.

Criminals of both groups and all ages were usually town-based. Contemporaries had no doubt that the criminal class was substantially a phenomenon of the large towns. J. T. Burt wrote in 1863 that the large towns were the nurseries and hiding places of criminal classes, and dense populations gave shelter to the criminals. A witness told the Select Committee on Transportation in 1856 that there were not more than fourteen to sixteen places in the United Kingdom large enough to furnish harbourage for bad characters. The Rev. J. Clay, Chaplain of Preston Gaol, wrote in his 1849 Report:

It is not a manufacturing population, as such, which fosters crime. ... It is not manufacturing Manchester, but multitudinous Manchester, which gives birth to whatever criminality may be imputable to it. It is the *large town* to which both idle profligates and practised

31. Brandon, op. cit., p. 93.

villains resort as a likely field for the indulgence of sensuality or the prosecution of schemes of plunder. It is the *large town* in which disorder and crime are generated.

In his 1850 Report he observed: 'Preston is not yet of sufficient magnitude and importance to maintain a body of *resident* pickpockets.'[32]

These views are paralleled in earlier discussions. Patrick Colquhoun, the pioneer of modern policing and a London police magistrate of many years' standing, had said much the same in 1819, adding a warning that crimes outside the London area were on the increase. The Report of the Royal Commission on a Constabulary Force of 1839 contained many quotations from the statements of magistrates and others emphasizing the urban connections of most criminals. The larger towns had obvious advantages as bases for criminal activity, in the shape of greater opportunity for crime and greater opportunity of escape after its committal.[33]

It was only in the larger towns that distinctively criminal areas were to be found. As the towns grew in the early nineteenth century the separation of the dwellings of the well-to-do from the dwellings of the poor began. As a modern writer has put it, by the 1830s and 40s 'the working people were virtually segregated in their stinking enclaves'.[34] However, it would be wrong to think that the dwellings of the poor were all of a kind. The areas occupied by the lowest classes were called 'rookeries', but there was a distinction between a poor district and the smaller part thereof which was regarded as a criminal area. 'It may be stated in general terms,' wrote the clerical author of many pamphlets on mid-Victorian Liverpool, 'that the area which

32. J. T. Burt, *Irish Facts and Wakefield Figures in Relation to Convict Discipline in Ireland*, 1863, pp. 21–2; s.c. on Transportation, P.P. 1856, xvii, pp. 195–6 (qq. 1793–4); W. L. Clay, *The Prison Chaplain; A Memoir of the Rev. John Clay* . . . , Cambridge 1861, pp. 517–18, 522.

33. s.c. on Criminal Laws, P.P. 1819, viii, p. 66; R.C. on Constabulary Force, P.P. 1839, xix, pp. 19–21 (paras. 19–23), 23–36 (paras. 27–8).

34. E. P. Thompson, *The Making of the English Working Class*, 1963, p. 321.

poverty claims for its own, contains within it the smaller localities which are specially devoted to crime, vice, and immorality'. Of course, not all those who lived in criminal areas were
dishonest. In St Giles's, wrote W. A. Miles, 'the labouring man
is in nightly company with the habitual thief'. In one part of the
parish 'the working men live in rooms facing the street; the bad
idle fellows at the back of the houses; the thieves live up the
courts and alleys'. (We can perhaps see, in this doubtless over-
drawn picture, the combined effect of differential rents and the
thieves' preference for a chance to see who was coming near
their homes.) Sixty years later Charles Booth pointed out that
even the worst streets 'taken together contain some of *every*
class from A to F, or (including the publicans) even G'. Contemporaries were well aware that 'a tenement may get a bad
name through the misconduct of one or two of its inhabitants,
and a street may be regarded as wild although there is only a
minority of rowdy people living in it,' and that 'frequently but
from one small street, or from two or three courts and alleys,
will come nearly all the cases that give the whole parish a bad
name'.[35] 'None the less criminal areas could be identified, and
from them criminals would move out to do their day's or their
night's work; to them they would retire if they were pursued or
when they had made enough for their needs. Their meeting-
places – usually called 'flash-houses' in the earlier part of the
century – were usually in the criminal area, and there too the
receivers were mostly found.

In the country districts, the author of a prize essay wrote in
1853, there was less to steal and less chance of concealing crime
– but there were fewer prosecutions of known crime, for there
were fewer police and there was greater repugnance to prosecute; and a pencil note has been added to one copy that personal chastisement was more frequently inflicted by employers

35. A. Hume, *Condition of Liverpool* . . . , Liverpool 1858, p. 24; Brandon,
op. cit., pp. 88, 98; Booth, op. cit., vol. ii, p. 43; J. Devon, *The Criminal
and the Community*, 1912, p. 84; J. W. Horsley, *How Criminals are made
and Prevented* . . . , 1913, p. 228; R. C. on Housing of Working Classes,
P.P. 1884–5, xxx, pp. 20, 177 (qq. 2236–9), 268 (qq. 5474–6), 275 (q. 5673)

of labour. Country districts had their criminals, of course. They were drawn from the floating population not in regular work – 'living at large, skulking about, and ... always suspected as night marauders, poachers, and that sort of thing', as the Superintendent of the Macclesfield Police put it in the 1830s; but this experienced officer, who had previously served in London and in a country area of Cheshire, emphasized that 'the thieves in a village are not the same as the thieves in a town. They all work occasionally.'[36] The country districts had the Game Laws as well, and many people fell foul of this harsh and restrictive code – and perhaps from the consequent loss of reputation went on to worse things. None the less, the criminal class which forms the subject of this book was essentially town-based.

It was, however, migratory in its habits. Criminals have always found it advantageous to live in one area and work in another, and they would often leave the town in which they lived to steal in the surrounding country districts, or raid towns from unpoliced rural areas. The Royal Commission on a Constabulary Force of 1839 presented much evidence to this effect. The magistrates of the Droitwich Division of Worcestershire said: 'There are reasons to believe that the burglaries, horse-stealing, and cattle-stealing, whenever they occur, are committed by strangers; – that the burglars are supposed to come from Birmingham; the horse-stealers still farther off.' The magistrates of Evesham, Worcester and a number of Warwickshire divisions also spoke of thieves coming from Birmingham. The magistrates of some Middlesex divisions attributed the more serious crimes in their area to London thieves, and similar complaints came from the areas around the other large towns. Some towns complained of raids from the unpoliced rural areas around them. Such evidence must be treated cautiously, for magistrates might well have preferred to think that crimes occurring in their district were largely committed by strangers for whose conduct they could in no way be

36. M. Hill and C. F. Cornwallis, *Two Prize Essays on Juvenile Delinquency*, 1853, pp. 19–20; R.C. on Constabulary Force, P.P. 1839, xix, pp. 120–21 (para 147).

held responsible. There is, however, some evidence that a real distinction between types of crime is being made. For example, the Droitwich magistrates, after making the remarks quoted above, go on: 'The sheep-stealer is generally a labourer resident in the parish where the offence is committed, or of an adjoining parish, and rarely escapes detection.' On the whole, there seems sufficient testimony to make us accept what is after all a very likely story.[37]

There was more than this local, day-by-day movement, however. The thieves of Liverpool and Manchester frequently transferred their operations from one of the towns to the other, as did those of Bristol and Bath. The distances involved were short enough for the criminals, and particularly the youngsters, to transfer their operations from one town to the other without much difficulty. Ellen Reece, a twenty-four-year-old prisoner in Salford Gaol, told the Chaplain that some years previously she had left her Manchester haunts for Liverpool because she had become too well known, returning after a couple of years when nearly all the police and watch had forgotten her. Only her arrest had prevented her doing the same thing again. 'I should have gone this time on Monday to Liverpool, having done the robbery [£34] on the Saturday. I might have stopped there twelve months.'[38] There was a regular correspondence and interchange between the large towns over the whole of the century, and thieves who became known in the provinces would seek safety in London. Indeed, as Ellen Reece's tale suggests, much of the movement was inspired by the fact that the original location had become an unhealthy one for the individual concerned. As a modern police officer has put it, the criminal 'has no need to change his field of activity until he gets caught. . . . The main reason why a criminal travels is to enable him to commit crime in a district where his identity is not known.' He stresses the advantage to the criminal of movement: the acqui-

37. R.C. on Constabulary Force, P.P. 1839, xix, p. 19 (para. 19) for the quotations, and generally pp. 19–21 (paras. 19–23).

38. Chadwick Papers, box 129 (statement of E. Reece), University College, London; cf. Clay, op. cit., pp. 522–7.

sition of means of transport 'widened the scope of his activities and allowed him to operate where he was unknown. . . . The further a criminal travels from his own home ground the better it is for him, and the worse it is for the police and the public.'[39] This motive for travel received a sharp stimulus from the improvements in police forces during the nineteenth century.[40] Of course, fear of detection was not the only reason why criminals travelled. Another motive was to take advantage of openings for crime elsewhere, and perhaps the simple desire for variety played its part. Whatever the reasons, it is clear that movement round the country was a regular feature of criminal life.

A large proportion of the London and other town thieves left their main base of operations for some months of the year, travelling around from town to town, stealing and begging as occasion served, often wearing good clothes on the journey and changing into rags for business purposes. There were even recognized patterns to these movements, and the accounts of them are worthy of discussion.

As far as the young criminals were concerned, London was the best place in which to spend the winter, as it had the best provision of refuges and workhouses. A consequence – and a proof – of its attraction was the winter influx into its Ragged Schools of pupils who deserted them in the spring. The prospects of making a dishonest penny seem to have been better in the provinces, however, for as soon as the weather improved there began a movement to summer pastures (analogous to the geographer's 'transhumance'). In April and May the youngsters would begin to leave London; by then the refuges had closed and they had become known in the workhouses of all the unions in London and even as far out as Richmond, Kingston and Romford (the reference to the Poor Law unions shows that the activities on which the account is based took place after the Poor Law Amendment Act of 1834). By June all those who

39. J. King, 'Mobile Criminals and Organised Crime', *The Police Journal*, vol. xxxviii, no. 1, Jan. 1965, pp. 17–20.
40. See pp. 268 ff.

were leaving London would be gone, some setting out for Cheltenham, Bath or other watering places, others leaving on well-
known circuits. One such passed through Essex, Suffolk and
Lincolnshire on the way to Leeds (a popular place, it was said in
1851, as there relief was given in cash) and thence to North-
umberland or Manchester (also popular, for the same reason).
At one time most youngsters would spend a night in Birmingham workhouse, where they would tear their clothes or
commit some other petty offence against discipline, in order to
be sent to Warwick Gaol; the motive for this was that the
magistrates of Warwickshire granted a shilling to each prisoner
discharged from the Gaol. However, Birmingham's attraction
soon vanished, as the influx was so great that the rules were
changed and the shilling was paid only to those who had not
been there before – and few 'trampers' had not been. Then the
route led back through Northamptonshire and Hertfordshire to
London for the winter. Another route lay through Sussex,
Hampshire (Winchester was another good place to visit) and
Wiltshire. The seaside was a popular place in the later summer,
and many vagrants visited Kent and Sussex for the hopping,
before working their way back to London.

The first-class thieves, the high-class adult pickpockets known
as the 'swell mob', would follow an entirely different pattern as
they moved around the country, even visiting the Continent on
occasion.[41]

They work the Dover packets, and visit the Lakes of Killarney.
They go on the Manchester Exchange, and sleep in the hotels of
New York. They know the way to the Liverpool Docks, and 'wire'
in the streets of Paris. They generally go on the Continent in the
spring, and remain there until the races and fairs are coming off in
England. The London mobs go down to Manchester in December,
there being a large number of commercial men about the town at
that time. . . . Irish thieves come into England in the summer for the
fairs and races. In the latter end of April and the beginning of May,
the London mobs do the May meetings of Exeter Hall and other
places; and then start for Wales and the Midland counties, as the

41. *Cornhill Magazine*, vol. vi, Nov. 1862, p. 650.

fairs are coming on about that time. The pick-pockets are always at work, travelling night or day, or both as it may suit them. The migration of thieves into Wales takes place from March up to May; the time of the fairs.

One prisoner explained the routes based on fairs:[42]

It begins at Wrexham, 7th March; Nottingham, next week Grantham, pleasure fair; Sleaford, pleasure fair; Caiston, P.L. [what 'P.L.' means is not explained]; Lincoln, cattle fair four days, two days pleasure; Horncastle statties ['statties', he explains, 'means fairs held by statute where servants are hired'], Spilsby statties, Tattersall statties, Boston May fair, cattle and pleasure; then to Sleaford, again to the 'big market', Tuxford fair and statties, Newark again. Derby, where some branch off to Birmingham and some to Sheffield.

This is only a brief extract from a long and rambling account, but it suffices to give the flavour of the whole.

Special circumstances would of course alter the normal pattern. Charles Dickens in 1850 said that the police expected a visit from the swell mob on 'all public occasions', and would wait for them at the railway station; on one occasion they were left waiting at Epsom station while the swell mob entered the town by road from the other side.[43] A Royal visit to a provincial town was of course one of these 'public occasions' and London was especially attractive in times of public disturbances such as the Chartist activities. In the exceptionally severe winter of 1860–61 the number of vagrants in the provinces was even lower than usual: 'All the Vagrants had travelled to London to partake in the munificent subscriptions which were placed at the disposal of the police magistrates.'

It might be thought that some of the evidence just cited proves merely the existence of a large number of vagrants; but

42. R.C. on Constabulary Force, P.P. 1839, xix, p. 24 (para. 27); there are other similar accounts in the same paragraph, pp. 23–32.

43. Dickens, *Reprinted Pieces: Three 'Detective' Anecdotes: II, The Artful Touch*, 1850; Reports of Poor Law Inspectors, P.P. 1866, xxxv, pp. 653, 678–702; Mayhew, op. cit., vol. iii, p. 398; R.C. on Constabulary Force, P.P. 1839, xix, p. 39 (para. 32).

there is proof that most vagrants were thieves. Henry Mayhew wrote:

That vagrancy is the nursery of crime, and that the habitual tramps are first the beggars, then the thieves, and, finally, the convicts of the country, the evidence of all parties goes to prove. ... The vagrants form one of the most restless, discontented, vicious, and dangerous elements of society. . . . These constitute ... the main source from which the criminals are continually recruited and augmented.

A Poor Law Inspector in 1866 quoted in his Report estimates of the proportion of vagrants who were professional beggars and thieves ranging from two thirds to ninety-five per cent, ending up with his own comment that 'fully seventy-five per cent' were in this category. There is a wealth of corroborative evidence. The trampers would steal when opportunity presented itself, or would bully and badger women whose husbands were out into giving them food or money. They would indulge in tricks of all kinds to defraud the country-people. One prisoner furnished a description of some of them:

1st. Men who go about the country almost naked begging clothes or food. They get about 3s. a day. They have good clothes at their lodging-house, and travel in them from town to town, if there are not many houses in the way. Before they enter the town, they take them off, as well as their shoes and stockings, put on their Guernsey jackets, send the bundle and the woman forward to the lodging-house, and commence begging at the first house they come to. ... These fellows always sell a gift of clothes.

2nd. Men who are ring-droppers. [The trick here was for one of the gang in company with the dupe to 'find' a ring in circumstances which made it fair to suggest that both had a claim to it. A stranger (who was of course one of the gang) would appear and give an estimate of the ring's value. The dupe would then be persuaded to buy out the other finder by paying him a proportion of the estimated value; needless to say, he parted with more than the value of the article he was left with.] Travelling tinkers make sham gold rings out of old brass buttons ...

3rd. Fellows who go round to different houses, stating their master's stock of rags has been burnt, or that a sudden supply is wanted, and that they are sent forward to collect them. The rags are called for, and one fellow marches off with the bundle, leaving one or more talking with the housewife, who is gravely cavilling about the price, and as gravely informed that the master is coming round, and they leave some private mark on the door-post, which they say is the sign to indicate to him the quantity and the quality taken, and the amount to pay; so they walk off, and 'never tip her anything.' . . .

4th. A set of fellows who go about in decent apparel, leaving small printed handbills at cottages and farm-houses, wherein are set forth the wonderful cures of all sorts of ailments, effected by medicine which they sell. . . . The mixture is only a decoction of any herb or rubbish that may be at hand . . .

11th. Fellows who boil up fat and a little soap over night, run it out in a cloth, and next morning cut it up like cakes of Windsor soap. It's all bad, but they drive a good trade.

12th. Fellows who go from house to house, stating that they live in some neighbouring town, and ask for 'umbrellas to mend'. An active fellow in this line will make a clean sweep of all the umbrellas in a village before dinner.

Gambling games such as thimble-rig, a variant of the three-card trick, seem to have been popular. One police officer told of the arrest of a thimble-rig man by a parish constable on the complaint of a victim. The matter was eventually compromised, the constable being given something for his trouble. The group then sat drinking together, and eventually took to thimble-rig again; the constable lost what he had been given, and all his money besides.[44]

Another favoured and persistent dodge was to pose as a distressed sailor. The Home Office called attention to the practice in a circular to the police officers in 1818, the Royal Commission on a Constabulary Force heard about it from several witnesses, and one of Mayhew's collaborators described it in 1861. The number of 'turnpike sailors' apparently declined towards the end of the century, but there were still some left in 1889.[45] The 1861 description explained that a beggar of this class

44. Chadwick Papers, box 126 (statement of Burgess), University College, London.

45. Circular dated 20 May 1818, H.O. 65/2, Public Record Office; R.C.

has two lays, the 'merchant' lay and the 'R'yal Navy' lay. He adopts either one or the other, according to the exigencies of his wardrobe, his locality, or the person he is addressing. . . . When on the 'merchant lay' his attire consists of a pair of tattered trousers, an old guernsey-shirt, and a torn straw-hat. One of his principal points of 'costume' is his bare feet. . . . In his gait he endeavours to counterfeit the roll of a true seaman, but his hard feet, knock-knees, and imperceptibly acquired turnpike-trot betray him . . .

On the 'R'yal Navy' lay, the turnpike sailor assumes different habiliments, and altogether a smarter trim. He wears coarse blue trousers symmetrically cut about the hips, and baggy over the foot. A 'jumper', or loose shirt of the same material, a tarpaulin hat, with the name of a vessel in letters of faded gold, is struck on the back of his neck, and he has a piece of whipcord, or 'lanyard' round his waist, to which is suspended a jack-knife, which if of but little service in fighting the battles of his country has stood him in good stead in silencing the cackling of any stray poultry that crossed his road, or in frightening into liberality the female tenant of a solitary cottage.

The turnpike sailors would accost people on inland roads with a story that they had been paid off in one port and were tramping to another to get another ship. Occasionally they would run up against someone who knew the captain they claimed to have served under, or the ports they claimed to know, but it must have been a fairly safe ruse on the whole.

Another well-known form of begging was the 'shallow lay' – standing in the streets in cold weather with scanty clothing and trying to excite the compassion of the passers-by. It has often been pointed out that in the nineteenth century three days of wet weather brought ruin to many who made an honest living by selling things in the streets; it is less well known that three days of cold weather brought prosperity to the beggars on the shallow lay. Indeed, one writer records the complaint of a former practitioner that when the weather was very cold people

on Constabulary Force, P.P. 1839, xix, pp. 36–40 (paras. 30–32); Mayhew, op. cit., vol. iv, pp. 415–16; C. T. Clarkson and J. Hall Richardson, *Police!*, 1889, p. 237.

were apt to hamper the shallow-lay artist by giving him food and not money. He would eat as much as he could, hide as much as he could about his person, but in the end was forced to throw it away to avoid the loss of time involved in taking it home or taking it somewhere to sell it.[46]

The 'shallow lay', like many of the others, was exposed from time to time. Someone signing himself 'Australian' wrote to *The Times* in 1862:[47]

On this bitter cold and wet morning . . . my attention was attracted to a little girl, seven or eight years of age, crying bitterly. . . . Her garments were miserably thin, and her poor little feet had scarce any covering, as she dragged herself along on the cold pavement. . . . The poor little thing could only say, 'I'm so cold', and that she had no parents alive. Of course, I gave the child a trifle, and begged the policeman to see what could be done for her; but he could do nothing. . . . I am myself a father, and I am not ashamed to say I was unmanned by the sight.

He was answered a few days later, and was told that he

did precisely the thing he ought not to have done. He gave her 'a trifle'. Did he see what she did with it? His uncommunicative policeman probably did, and smiled grimly as he saw her run round the corner into the adjacent ginshop and give it into the hand of the blear-eyed hag who had hired her for the day, and who, with a greater or lesser blasphemy in proportion to the amount of the contribution, drives her back into the cold to distil more tears of 'unmanned fathers' into gin.

Despite such exposures, the technique no doubt remained a useful source of revenue to adult criminals and to youngsters.

There was nothing unusual in the suggestion that children were employed to beg for others. Beggars would hire children to accompany them, because of the sympathy they attracted. In 1839 a writer gave the rate for the hire of a child as 3d. a day, and spoke of two children of similar age being hired for 4d. or 6d. and represented to be twins; the takings he estimated at 3s. or 4s. a day at the least. He said that a crippled child was worth

46. J. Greenwood, *The Seven Curses of London*, ?1869, pp. 246–8.
47. *The Times*, 22 and 24 March 1862.

6d. a day; a later writer said that as much as 4s. a day had been paid for the hire of a deformed child. Henry Mayhew gave the rates as 9d. a day for one child or 1s. for two, if no food was supplied, or two for 9d. with food and Godfrey's cordial (Godfrey's cordial, a preparation of laudanum, was a well-known quietener of babies). A 'school', say half a dozen, cost 2s. 6d. a day. 2d. extra a child was charged after midnight, and garments were supplied at 2d. a day. 5d. to 7d. a day was the rate quoted in 1869 in a letter to *The Times*. The same paper in 1848 spoke of two girls aged thirteen and eleven sent out by their father to sing in the streets; they carried their two-year-old brother and stuck pins in him in order to make him cry and increase the sympathy of passers-by. The use of children by adult beggars remained a subject of complaint for most of the century.[48]

48. Brandon, op. cit., pp. 89–90, 97; Hill and Cornwallis, op. cit., p. 44; N.A.W., letter to *The Times*, 12 March 1869; *The Times*, 28 Jan, 1848.

5. Juveniles and women

A large proportion of the wandering criminals, and of the criminal class in general, was under the age of twenty or so – as indeed the age-composition of the general population would lead us to expect.[1] There is in the first part of the century much contemporary evidence of the youthfulness of quite experienced criminals. The Hon. Henry Gray Bennet, M.P., Chairman of the Select Committee on Police of 1816–18, told his Committee about four boys in Newgate, none aged more than twelve years, who had between them been in custody over eighty times. In 1816, he said, 514 prisoners under the age of twenty were committed to Newgate, 284 of them under the age of seventeen, and fifty-one under the age of fourteen; one was nine years old. The Superintendent of the Hulks told a similar Committee in 1828 that of the 300 boys in the *Euryalis* hulk (boys, that is, of sixteen years or less who had been sentenced to transportation or had had a sentence of death commuted to transportation), two were eight years old, five were nine years old and 171 in all were under the age of fourteen. People giving an age-range for juvenile criminals took nine or ten years, or sometimes even six or seven years, as their starting-point, though the remark that some were so young that they could 'scarcely crawl' was doubtless not intended to be taken literally. One must of course allow a margin of error to all these estimates of age, but the general picture is clear enough.[2]

The careers of some youngsters can usefully be examined in more detail – though it must be remembered that much of the information comes from the prisoners themselves and is as sus-

1. See p. 96.
2. S.C. on Police, P.P. 1817, vii, pp. 541–3; ibid., P.P. 1828, vi, p. 105; ibid., P.P. 1816, v, p. 229.

pect as statements of age. Pride of place should be given to
Leary, who went

progressively from stealing an apple off a stall, to housebreaking
and highway robbery. He belonged to the Moorfields Catholic
School, and there became acquainted with one Ryan in that school,
by whom he was instructed in the various arts and practices of
delinquency; his first attempts were at tarts, apples, etc., then at
loaves in bakers' baskets; then parcels of halfpence on shop
counters, and money-tills in shops; then to breaking shop windows
and drawing out valuable articles through the aperture; picking
pockets, housebreaking, etc. etc.; and Leary has often gone to
school the next day with several pounds in his pockets as his share
of the produce of the previous day's robberies; he soon became
captain of a gang, generally known since as Leary's gang, with five
boys, and sometimes more, furnished with pistols. ... They would
... divide into parties of two, sometimes only one, and ... go to
farms and other houses, stating their being on their way to see their
families, and begging for some bread and water; by such tales,
united with their youth, they obtained relief, and generally ended by
robbing the house or premises. In one instance Leary was detected
and taken, and committed to Maidstone gaol; but the prosecutor not
appearing against him, he was discharged. In these excursions he
has staid out a week and upwards, when his share has produced him
from fifty to one hundred pounds. He has been concerned in various
robberies in London and its vicinity, and has had property at one
time amounting to £350; but when he had money, he either got
robbed of it by elder thieves who knew he had so much about him,
or he lost it by gambling at flash-houses, or spent it among loose
characters of both sexes.

This career, during which he claimed to have stolen to a total
value of £3,000, took five years. He was imprisoned in every
prison in London, including Newgate two or three times, sentenced to death, respited, sent to a home run by the Philanthropic Institution, escaped from there, resumed his old ways
of living, and in the end he was transported for life. At the end
of his career he was fourteen years old. When Bennet saw him
in Newgate, under sentence of death, 'he was ... good-looking,
sharp, and intelligent, and possessing a manner which seemed to

indicate a character very different from what he really possessed'. Leary was a 'very extraordinary boy', but this comment does not relate to the developing story of crime, which was common enough in its general outlines.[3]

There was indeed general agreement that juvenile thieves passed through a regular progression of crime, and perhaps a better example, because a more typical one, is the case of Thomas M'Nelly (his name is sometimes spelled 'M'Nally' or 'M'Nellay'). His record begins at about the age of thirteen, with an arrest on 15 April 1836 for 'wilfully breaking glass at church'; it is possible that he committed this offence in the hope of spending some time in prison, and the sentence of seven days which he received may not have been an unwelcome one. Eight days after the expiration of the sentence, on 30 April, he was arrested and charged with sleeping in the open air, but was discharged. On 29 May he was sentenced to one month's imprisonment for stealing coal from a barge. A week after the expiry of that sentence, on 6 July, he received three months' imprisonment on 'suspicion of stealing brushes'. He was presumably released about 6 October, but we hear no more of him until 17 November, when he appeared on a charge of stealing two bundles of wood but was discharged. The next entry on his record is a conviction for stealing carrots from a barge on 23 December (fourteen days). He may have had two or three weeks at liberty, but on 31 January 1837 he was sentenced to three months' imprisonment for stealing cheese from a shop. On 29 or 30 April, when he had presumably only just been released, he received another month's imprisonment for 'stealing a pair of drawers'. On 2 August he was accused of stealing a silk handkerchief but was discharged. He may have had over two months' freedom, for the next recorded conviction is on 18 October, when he was sentenced to three months' imprisonment for stealing a pair of trousers. Within a few days of the end of that sentence, on 23 January 1838, he received one month's imprisonment on suspicion of stealing three handkerchiefs. On 23 February he was arrested on suspicion of stealing some

3. S.C. on Police, P.P. 1817, vii, p. 542; cf. ibid., 1816, v, p. 231.

braces but was discharged. On 7 March he received three months' imprisonment and disappears from our view. M'Nelly's record thus comprises thirteen arrests and nine prison sentences totalling fifteen months and three weeks, in a period of two years. His longest period of freedom would seem to have been about $4\frac{1}{2}$ months, with just one court appearance during that time, though it is of course possible that he had convictions in other courts that are not known to us. M'Nelly's story is of interest for two particular reasons. First, it illustrates the trend to increasing seriousness: starting with the trivial offences of breaking glass and sleeping in the open air, he soon graduates to stealing, and at the end has passed from the petty stealing of coal or brushes to thefts of clothing, probably from shops. Secondly, the string of unavailing imprisonments makes understandable the despair which magistrates felt.[4]

Some other case-histories should be given, even at the risk of wearying the reader, in order to make clear that even if the truth of any one tale is doubtful the general pattern must be true. The Honorary Secretary of a Juvenile Delinquency Society told the Select Committee on Police in 1817 of some cases which

convey a general idea of the characters that have come under the notice of the Society.

A.B. aged thirteen years. . . . This boy had been for five years in the commission of crime, and had been imprisoned for three separate offences. Sentence of death has twice been passed on him.

C.D. aged ten years . . . sentenced to seven years imprisonment for picking pockets . . .

E.F. aged eight years. His mother only is living, and she is a very immoral character. He has been brought up to the several police offices upon eighteen separate charges. He has been twice confined in the House of Correction, and three times in Bridewell.

These three cases, it should be said, have been chosen as those which give the longest period of crime and the earliest com-

4. S.C. on Police, P.P. 1837, xii, pp. 355–6 (qq. 444–50); J. Adams, *A Letter to Benjamin Hawes, Esq., M.P. . . .*, 1838, p. 32; Chadwick Papers, box 116 (draft report, p. 9), University College, London.

mencement; the other nine cases include two who began crime at the age of eleven and one who began at fifteen; in the others the age at the time of the first offence is not specifically stated.[5]

The Stipendiary Magistrate of Liverpool in 1850 described the eldest boy in a family of delinquents: 'He was first brought before me on the 9th of June, 1845, charged with stealing ropes. He was then about nine years old. I did not wish to send so young a child to gaol, so, as I usually do, I delivered him to his parents with an admonition to them.' He went through the boy's record of crime, during which he had used four aliases, step by step, ending up: 'Thus, at the age of fourteen, he has been twenty-four times in custody; he has been five times discharged, twice imprisoned for fourteen days, once for one month, once for two months, six times for three months, and tried [at Sessions] and convicted, and sentenced to four months' imprisonment and to be twice whipped.' His nine-year-old brother had been charged with theft eight times in the past year, and an eight-year-old brother had had six arrests in the past year.[6]

Thomas Miller's first known conviction was in August 1845, when he was about eight years old; by the time he was twelve he had been arrested at least ten times, had eight convictions, had served five terms of imprisonment and had been whipped twice. Edward Joyhill (the alternative spelling 'Joghill' is presumably a misprint) started – as far as we know – with two months' imprisonment in 1847 at the age of eight. Two years later he had at least seven other convictions, had received sentences totalling eleven months' imprisonment and had been whipped four times.[7]

It will have been noticed that the descriptions all date from the first half of the century, and the situation changed after the

5. s.c. on Police, P.P. 1817, vii, pp. 438–9.

6. E. Rushton, *A Letter . . . upon Juvenile Crime . . .*, Liverpool 1850, pp. 5–7.

7. J. Adams, *Summary Jurisdiction . . .*, 1849, pp. 21–2; s.c. on Juvenile Offenders, P.P. 1852, vii, pp. 223–4 (q. 1872).

coming of the reformatory schools in the 1850s had at last provided an alternative to the weary alternation of 'one month' – 'three months'. In the last three or four decades of the nineteenth century comments on the progression of crime through which juveniles passed are not couched in such strong terms and have not so hopeless an air. Things did not change all at once, and the Rev. J. W. Horsley, the Chaplain of Clerkenwell Gaol, protested in his 1878 report that children of six and seven years had been remanded to that prison – but when in 1913 he recorded the episode he added an exclamation mark which shows how the situation had changed.[8]

John Binny, one of Henry Mayhew's collaborators, provides a description of the juvenile thieves:

Some have no jacket, cap, or shoes, and wander about London with their ragged trowsers hung by one brace; some have an old tattered coat, much too large for them, without shoes and stockings, and with one leg of the trowsers rolled up to the knee; others have on an old greasy grey or black cap, with an old jacket rent at the elbows, and strips of the lining hanging down behind; others have on an old dirty pinafore; while some have petticoats. They are generally in a squalid and unwashed condition, with their hair clustered in wild disorder like a mop, or hanging down in dishevelled locks – in some cases cropped close to the head. . . . They are generally very acute and ready-witted, and have a knowing twinkle in their eye which exhibits the precocity of their minds.

Their prison clothing and footwear were better than their own. W. A. Miles in the 1830s recorded the following story:

A poor ragged sweep, about sixteen years of age, without shoes or stockings, and his red legs cracked with the cold, was brought into prison for some trifling offence. The warm bath into which he was put much delighted him, but nothing could exceed his astonishment on being told to put on shoes and stockings. 'And am I to *wear* them? and this? and this too?' he said, as each article of dress was

8. B. Waugh, *The Gaol Cradle: Who Rocks It ?* . . . , 3rd ed., 1876, chs. ii–iv; J. W. Horsley, *How Criminals are Made and Prevented* . . . , 1913, p. 22, and *'I Remember'* – *Memories of a 'Sky Pilot' in the Prison and the Slum*, 1911, pp. 86–7.

given to him. [The rest of the story is not strictly relevant here, but it should not be suppressed.] His joy was complete when they took him to his cell; he turned down the bed-clothes with great delight, and, half-doubting his good fortune, hesitatingly asked if he was really to sleep in the bed! On the following morning, the governor, who had observed the lad's surprise, asked him what he thought of his situation? 'Think of it, master! why I'm damn'd if ever I do another stroke of work!' The boy kept his word, and was ultimately transported.

It must often have been a bitter wrench when the thick, sound prison clothing had to be laid aside in favour of the thin and ragged garments that would not do much to keep out the weather – though rags and filth were to some extent tools of the trade, and much of Binny's description would no doubt have applied well enough to many youngsters not in the criminal class.[9]

By the end of the century a difference had come over the criminal youngsters, as no doubt it had the others as well. Thomas Holmes, a police court missionary and Secretary of the Howard Association, wrote in 1908:

While offences remain much the same, and the ways in which offences are committed have not altered greatly, the bearing and appearance of the offenders have completely changed. Rags are not as plentiful as they were, and child offenders are very much better dressed; for civilization cannot endure rags, and shoeless feet are an abomination. . . . The change in speech, too, is strongly noticeable; the old blood-curdling oaths and curses spiced with blasphemy are quite out of fashion. Emphasis can only be given to speech today by interlarding it with filthy words and obscene allusions.[10]

Sympathetic comments on the conditions in which the youngsters were brought up are not hard to find. The Select Committee on Police of 1816–18 was told:

It is very easy to blame these poor children, and to ascribe their

9. H. Mayhew, *London Labour and the London Poor* . . . , 1861–2, vol iv, pp. 277–8; H. Brandon (ed.), *Poverty, Mendicity and Crime* . . . , 1839, p. 87.
10. T. Holmes, *Known to the Police*, 1908, pp. 22–3.

misconduct to an innate propensity to vice; but I much question whether any human being, circumstanced as many of them are, can reasonably be expected to act otherwise; numbers are brought up to thieve as a trade ⁝⁝⁝ others are orphans, or completely abandoned by their parents; they subsist by begging or pilfering, and at night they often sleep under the sheds in the streets and in the market places, when in prison no one visits them, nor do they seem to possess one friend in the world; they are occasionally treated with severity, sometimes sentenced to be flogged, a practice than which nothing tends more to harden and degrade. Much may be done with those boys by kindness; there is scarcely one who will not be powerfully affected by it, but they are so accustomed to be considered as destitute of all moral feeling, that when they receive assurances of kindness, they can hardly believe them to be sincere.

'I do not suppose they have ever heard a dozen kind words spoken to them at their homes,' said the Chaplain of Preston Gaol in 1852; they 'require humanizing rather than deterring from crime.' He had written earlier that most juveniles 'never had been spoken to in a kind tone till they came into our Gaol'. His Bath colleague a few years earlier described the future criminals as 'neglected, untaught, unfed, unhoused, uncared for in their childhood', and the *Eclectic Review* in 1854 spoke of the 'negative conditions under which the child of the adult criminal, in such places as London or Liverpool, is brought up. Parental love and tenderness he scarcely knows.' Very often the children's first experience of counsel and sympathy was in gaol, which was really their only home.[11]

For many this latter remark had an added truth because they slept out in the streets. Those who could not enter the workhouse, who escaped prison, who had not a penny for a bed in a lodging house, slept in groups in the arches of bridges, in markets, under the porches of houses, under the arches of Blackwall railway (a 'human zoo'), or under the trees of Hyde

11. s.c. on Police, P.P. 1817, vii, pp. 431–2; s.c. on Juvenile Offenders, P.P. 1852, vii, p. 198 (q. 1622); W. L. Clay, *The Prison Chaplain; A Memoir of the Rev. John Clay* ..., Cambridge 1861, p. 451; W. C. Osborn, *A Lecture on the Prevention of Crime delivered ... November 26th, 1849*, Ipswich, n.d., p. 6 (cf. p. 16); *Eclectic Review*, new ser., vol. vii, April 1854, p. 388.

Park, wrote Moreau-Christophe in 1851. 'Hundreds of these miserable little creatures may be found sleeping, night after night, in Covent Garden, in the pens of Smithfield, in the barrels in Whitechapel, and in the markets and squares of the Metropolis,' the Common Sergeant of London wrote in 1840. A Manchester clergyman in 1856 spoke of

young adepts in crime spending the hours of darkness in the strangest of places, locating themselves under a waggon, or a market standing, in old conveyances, and (in a case falling under my own observation) in an omnibus, or in any out of the way and unwatched hiding place into which they are able to squeeze their supple limbs. They issue forth from their secret haunts as the morning breaks.

The pavement outside a sugar bakery in Leman Street, Whitechapel, was a favourite spot in the 1850s – twenty children at a time could sleep on the warm flags. There was a similar favoured spot at the corner of Canning Place, Liverpool, about the same time, but in wet weather its warmth was abandoned for the dryness of 'a yard near the Sailors' Home'. In 1865 Archer wrote that the children had 'better be in prison, aye, had better even be in the worst workhouse [the order of preference is noteworthy] than thrown as they are upon the streets'. Dr Barnardo estimated in 1876 that about 30,000 neglected children under sixteen years old slept out on the streets of London. Perhaps the last word on this topic may be left with the party of Ojibway Indians who visited London in the 1840s and who are reported to have said, in reply to attempts at conversation, that they were

willing to talk with you, if it can do any good to the hundreds and thousands of poor and hungry people that we see in your streets every day. . . . We see hundreds of little children with their naked feet in the snow, and we pity them, for we know they are hungry. . . . You talk about sending blackcoats [missionaries] among the Indians; now we have no such poor children among us. . . . Now we think it would be better for your teachers all to stay at home, and go to work right here in your own streets.

The Ojibways were of course right in suggesting that missionaries could have found plenty to do at home, for the criminals were in many cases virtually heathens. In this, of course, and in much else of what has just been recorded, there was often little difference between criminal and many non-criminal children; but it is of interest that these things were said of criminal children by those who were concerned with the problem of juvenile crime.[12]

However, not all juvenile delinquents were in the circumstances just described. In some cases the motive was 'less the acquisition of property or money, than a sort of wilful defiance of authority – a conceited disdain of domestic restraint', 'that love of enterprize and daring so common among boys of all classes'. The excitement of dodging the police was as important as the hope of gain. As one writer put it, 'There is, moreover, a kind of lottery adventure in each day's life; and as these excitements are attainable at so easy a rate, is it strange that these children are fascinated with and abandon themselves to crime?'[13]

Dickens shows us the Artful Dodger in the dock demanding his 'priwileges' and showing that he is not to be put upon. He threatens the magistrates with an action for damages, and

with a show of being very particular with a view to proceedings to be had thereafter, desired the jailer to communicate 'the names of them two files as was on the bench. . . . Ah! (to the Bench) it's no use your looking frightened; I won't show you no mercy, not a ha'porth of it. *You'll* pay for this, my fine fellers. I wouldn't be you for

12. L. M. Moreau-Christophe, *Du problème de la misère et de sa solution chez les peuples anciens et modernes*, Paris 1851, vol. iii, pp. 148–9; J. Mirehouse, *Crime and its Causes* . . . , London 1840, pp. 18–19; J. F. Bryan, *A Lecture on Ragged Schools delivered March 11th, 1856, in . . . Ardwick*, 2nd ed., Manchester 1857, p. 5; *Liverpool Life, its Pleasures, Practices and Pastimes*, Liverpool 1857, 2nd ser., pp. 38–40; T. Archer, *The Pauper, the Thief, and the Convict* . . . , London 1865, p. 97; K. Heasman, *Evangelicals in Action* . . . , London 1962, p. 69; J. C. Symons, *Tactics for the Times* . . . , London 1849, p. 66.

13. Sir George Stephen's comments on the draft report (opposite p. 23) of the R.C. on Constabulary Force, H.O. 73/4, Part 1, P.R.O.; M. Carpenter, *Juvenile Delinquents – Their Condition and Treatment*, 1853, p. 27; Brandon, op. cit., p. 92.

something! I wouldn't go free, now, if you was to fall down on your knees and ask me.'

This is an accurate picture. Young criminals at sessions and assizes were often 'wholly absorbed in maintaining their characters as bold and ardent sinners' in front of their associates who attended the trial, while their ego was inflated by the attention the police and prison officers were bound to give them. One observer commented:

> I have seen young children, not in their 'teens', placed behind large iron bars, strong enough to restrain an elephant. And what is the effect? It is this: the mind of the boy becomes impressed with an idea that he must be a very clever lad to require such barricadoes, and that society has a great dread of his talents. ... The pomp and panoply of justice only gives to these lads a feeling of self-importance: they never had any feeling of shame or disgrace.

Newspaper publicity was a matter of glory to those mentioned.[14]

A talent for deceiving prison officials was highly regarded by the youngsters. The governor of one gaol thought the principal cause of crime was smoking. 'His old customers never fail. ... "It is all through smoking, sir; I never knowed what bad 'abits was afore I took to 'bacca'." ' Another governor thought the blame belonged to cheap literature – ' "It was them there penny numbers what I used to take in, sir." ' The same governor also had a firm belief in appealing to a boy's love for his mother – 'they all most dutifully wept, in some cases bellowed as loudly as the stern restriction of the silent system would permit, as soon as the delicate subject was broached'.[15]

Petty crimes were regarded by the youngsters as only 'taking', not stealing, and a theft was, in their eyes, of merit by any other law than that of the land. Imprisonment in the event of failure was regarded as the purchase price of the right to steal, and accepted as a soldier accepted the risk of capture or death.

14. Dickens, *Oliver Twist*, ch. xliii, pp. 299–300; s.c. on Juvenile Offenders, P.P. 1852, vii, p. 336 (q. 3596); Brandon, op. cit., p. 93.

15. J. Greenwood, *The Seven Curses of London*, ?1869, pp. 178–9.

Indeed, the youngsters, like adult criminals, viewed their career as a gamble, expecting to draw a prize though others drew the blanks, accepting capture as ill-luck but looking forward to the next opportunity for better fortune. W. A. Miles in his report of 1835 said:[16] 'A thief speculates upon chance, "chance" is his favourite word, and however remote a chance may be, he trusts to his ingenuity and "good luck" to reduce it to a certainty. "Chance" is the Alpha and Omega of a thief's existence.' One corollary of this belief in chance was that the thieves were very superstitious. The same report described what were called 'Newgate tokens':

They are circular thin pieces of metal, of various sizes. The initials or names of a loving pair are punched upon them, together with a heart, or some symbol of affection; sometimes with a motto, as 'True for ever', 'Love for life', &c. &c. &c. These tokens are manufactured in Newgate, and I am informed that the parties attach the greatest value to them, wearing them constantly about their persons, attaching to them in many cases a superstitious value, and deeming them as amulets to preserve them from danger and detection.

Despite their good-luck charms and their hopes of good fortune, however, the youngsters took a fatalistic view of their prospects, and until its abolition transportation was the eventual fate that they expected.

The impact on the popular imagination made by Jack Sheppard, Dick Turpin and other heroes of crime was such that they had become almost legendary by the nineteenth century, and they played an important part in the lives of the juvenile criminals. Contemporaries found that their names and adventures were familiar to many youngsters who did not know the name of the Queen of England and were ignorant about more conventional heroes. In 1876 Greenwood wrote:[17]

At the present writing there are thousands of young gentlemen varying in years from ten to eighteen, and born and bred in and about the most enlightened city in the world, who in the secrecy of

16. Brandon, op. cit., pp. 47, 45–6.
17. J. Greenwood, *The Wilds of London*, 1876, p. 246.

their hearts hold it to be true that Jack Sheppard, house-breaker, prison-breaker, thief, and murderer, was the most splendid fellow the sun ever shone upon, and who find their *beau ideal* of a hero, not in Lord Nelson or the Duke of Wellington, but in 'Blueskin', Claude Duval, or some similar ruffian.

Tales of Jack Sheppard and the others were told by one youngster to another in gaol or lodging-house, and also formed the principal part of the repertoire of the low theatres and singing-rooms in which boys and girls spent much of their time. Such places do not seem to have blossomed in full vigour until the 1820s, but thereafter they were much patronized. Boys and girls would make a visit to the theatre their first business on release from gaol, and would go hungry in order to spend 6d. on admission to a theatre, such was their desire for entertainment.

Stories of Jack Sheppard and the others were disseminated by the printed word as well. The sale of tales of this sort in penny parts was said to have been proceeding in the large towns since 1844; a hundred such series were circulating in London in 1850, we are told, and they were taken round the provinces by hawkers. They could be read by those who could not manage the books contemporaries would have liked them to read, and the familiarity of the names and words was part of their appeal.

Contemporaries were of course conscious of the part that Jack Sheppard played in the life of the youngsters, and were worried about it. The plays, songs and stories were thought to be harmful, and crimes were often said to have been inspired by the desire to emulate Jack Sheppard. Critics also mentioned the bad company and the drinking which were features of the theatres and singing-rooms, and some attached importance to the mere temptation to acquire money. It was said that the first crime was often the use of the Monday school money for admission to a theatre, or some petty pilfering for the same purpose.

Whether or not the plays they saw and the books they read had anything to do with it, the boys and girls of the criminal class were promiscuous from an early age. Gibbon Wakefield, on the basis of his experiences as a prisoner in Newgate, said that most of the boys there over twelve years old, and some younger ones, had mistresses who visited them as their sisters, and the Select Committee on Police of 1816–18 heard similar testimony. The Prison Inspectors for the Home District in 1836 confirmed the story; they said that some of these girls were only twelve or thirteen years old, and that some prostitutes visited more than one prisoner in the guise of wife or sister. The Select Committee on Juvenile Offenders of 1852 was told that many of the young criminals lived with prostitutes, and that they had been known to have venereal disease at the age of twelve.[18]

The Select Committee of 1816–18 had obviously received allegations about brothels catering principally for 'children', for it frequently asked witnesses about such places. Some witnesses denied that such places existed, but others described and identified in a convincing manner brothels where the prostitutes were mainly under fourteen years and some as young as eleven or twelve, and where the customers were also mainly youngsters.[19] Another witness named a girl then aged sixteen who had been working as a prostitute in her father's brothel for the past five or six years. Representatives of the Magdalen Hospital and the London Female Penitentiary gave the lowest ages at which girls had been admitted as twelve years and eleven years respectively, though these were exceptional cases and the usual age was fourteen or fifteen years. A London judge in 1852 told a Select Committee about girls fourteen or fifteen years old who could not remember their first intercourse.[20]

This composite description of the juvenile delinquents invites comparison with the honest children of the poor. Some contemporaries felt that the criminal youngsters had a pleasant enough life. Miss Mary Carpenter was by no means unsym-

18. E. G. Wakefield, *Facts Relating to the Punishment of Death in the Metropolis*, 2nd ed., 1832, p. 18; s.c. on Police, P.P. 1816, v, p. 232; ibid., P.P. 1817, vii, p. 542; Report of Prison Inspectors, P.P. 1836, xxxv, p. 8; s.c. on Juvenile Offenders, P.P. 1852, vii, pp. 21–2 (qq. 154, 160–62).

19. s.c. on Police, P.P. 1816, v, p. 170; ibid. P.P. 1817, vii, pp. 166, 430, 534.

20. ibid., pp. 351, 504, 507; s.c. on Juvenile Offenders, P.P. 1852, vii, p. 217 (q. 1823).

pathetic towards them, and we may therefore believe her when she declared:[21]

Their present mode of life is so lucrative and so pleasant, that they will not exchange it for another apparently presenting far greater advantages. Their filth and rags are no annoyances to them, for they are the implements of their trade; the cold and hunger which they continually endure are most amply compensated by an occasional luxurious meal. The close and noisome dens in which they are stowed at night presents nothing revolting to their feelings, and they prefer them to a clean abode where they must resign their occupation and some portion of their liberty.

The Royal Commission on a Constabulary Force – that is to say, Edwin Chadwick, who knew what he was talking about when it came to the living conditions of the poor – said that 'in point of sensual gratification, the condition of the habitual depredator is, during his career, much higher than that of the honest labourer, living on wages which afford a share of the comforts of life'.[22]

On the other hand, there were those who were impressed with the miseries of a criminal life. 'The thief always was and always will be the hardest worked and most miserable of all labourers,' wrote Greenwood in 1876.[23] A decade earlier the *Cornhill Magazine* had said that 'the professional thieves have a miserable time of it' and spoke of the 'ills of a life which, from its nature, must be very much made up of hardship and misery'.[24] Dickens, in the 1841 preface to *Oliver Twist*, declared that his intention had been to paint the criminals[25]

in all their deformity, in all their wretchedness, in all the squalid poverty of their lives; to show them as they really are, for ever skulking uneasily through the dirtiest paths of life. . . . The cold wet shelterless midnight streets of London; the foul and frowsy dens, where vice is closely packed and lacks the room to turn; the haunts

21. M. Carpenter, *Reformatory Schools for the Children of the Perishing and Dangerous Classes, and for Juvenile Offenders*, 1851, p. 72.

22. R.C. on Constabulary Force, P.P. 1839, xix, p. 17 (para. 14).

23. J. Greenwood, *The Wilds of London*, 1876, p. 254.

24. *Cornhill Magazine*, vol. vi, Nov. 1862, pp. 652–3.

25. Dickens, *Oliver Twist*, pp. lxii–iii.

of hunger and disease; the shabby rags that scarcely hold together; where are the attractions of these things?

No doubt both points of view were partly true. We must of course remember that there were many honest children who lived lives of great hardship. Miss Pinchbeck, for example, said that in the agricultural labour-gangs of the Castle Acre district of Norfolk children seven years old or even younger sometimes had to walk seven or eight miles each way to and from their work, and were at work from 8.30 a.m. to 5.30 p.m. A girl of eleven walked ten miles in a day and worked perhaps seven hours, all on one piece of bread. The Hammonds described the conditions of the pauper apprentices:

Their regular working hours, Saturdays included, were from 5 a.m. till 8 p.m., and, with the exception of half an hour at 7 a.m. for breakfast, and half an hour at 12 for dinner, they were working continuously the whole time. They were, however, allowed to eat something while working in the afternoon. ... The bedding was simple and unclean; a blanket to lie on and another blanket, with a horse cover, to throw over them.[26]

These are extreme cases; but some of the children of the criminal class were in no better state, walking as far if not working as hard, often eating as little, and having no family to return to and no bed but the pavement. Yet many criminal children could and did do better than that. If they were often cold and often wet, and always uncared for and unloved, at any rate they had a varied life, adventure and freedom (apart from occasional periods during which they were fed and kept warm without worry). They had the compensation of times of plenty when they could eat and drink their fill and enjoy the luxury of squandering their temporary riches in cheerful company. If one had to be an Oliver Twist, then – failing the unlikely chance of a Mr Brownlow – in material terms one might be well advised to enter into the care of a Fagin.

Women were well represented in the criminal class, and acted

26. I. Pinchbeck, *Women Workers and the Industrial Revolution, 1750–1850*, 1930, pp. 87, 98; J. L. and B. Hammond, *The Town Labourer*, Guild Books edition, 1949, vol. i, p. 148.

as accomplices in a number of ways. They were used as 'look-outs'. They would carry a housebreaker's tools to and from the scene of operations so that if he were stopped and searched by a too-curious policeman the incriminating equipment would not be found on him; for the same reason they would often be entrusted with the stolen property. Prostitutes would sometimes start a riot in a public house to draw the police away from the scene of an intended burglary, and were often in league with pickpockets.

The women of the criminal class did not of course restrict their activities to aiding the men; many of them were thieves themselves. The girls would beg or steal like the boys, with of course the additional resort of prostitution when occasion served; as they grew older, prostitution doubtless became more important. The girl vagrants would very often pair off with a boy for a time, separating when one or the other was sent to gaol or took a fancy to move off independently. Though there were proportionately far fewer women criminals than men, they were said to be worse than most of the men – Cesar Lombroso, a leading criminologist of the nineteenth century, later reached the same conclusion.[27]

The law helped women in one respect. A married woman was in certain circumstances not answerable for offences committed in the presence of her husband, on the supposition that she acted under his direction – it was this supposition that convinced Mr Bumble that the law was 'a ass – a idiot'. One professional coiner, a widow, traded on this blindness of the law. She is said to have inveigled a young man into marriage with it in mind, and what she anticipated came to pass. They were taken together in the act of coining money; he was hanged, and she spent the night before the execution 'in riot and debauchery'.[28]

27. Brandon, op. cit., p. 139; M. Carpenter, *Juvenile Delinquents*, op. cit., p. 85, and *Our Convicts*, 1864, vol. ii, pp. 207–11; C. Lombroso and W. Ferraro, *The Female Offender*, English trans., 1895, p. 150.

28. W. O. Russell, *A Treatise on Crimes and Misdemeanours*, 4th ed., 1865, vol. i, pp. 33–9; s.c. on Juvenile Offenders, P.P. 1852, vii, p. 73 (q. 569).

Descriptions of the prostitute-thieves and their associates abound in the first sixty years of the century. Patrick Colquhoun told the Select Committee on Police in 1816 that

the major part of them derive a considerable proportion of their subsistence by the robbery of those who come into contact with them, of their watches and money; a vast proportion of them are associated with thieves, who actually live with them, and who follow them in the streets, not only to tutor them in the way they are to commit robberies, by pulling out watches, money, etc. etc. but also are near at hand, ready to attend them when they commit those robberies, in order to receive the booty and run off.

A parish constable said that in one of the brothels in St Giles's

there was a gentleman robbed about a week or a fortnight since of all his clothes and his watch; they left him stark naked, and the girl was stopped with his clothes, and brought down to the watch-house.

The owner of this brothel and two others near by, a man named Danser, was 'clerk to the Bedford Chapel, in Charlotte-street'! The 1828 Committee was told that 'when the girls got a man into Wentworth-street, they did not get him for the purposes of prostitution, but they are in league with the notorious thieves, and then they rob him'.[29]

In 1837 Ellen Reece, a twenty-four-year-old prisoner in Salford Gaol who had been sentenced to fourteen years' transportation, told the Chaplain that from about fourteen years of age

I have lived entirely by prostitution and plunder. Seven times as much by robbery as the hire of prostitution. None of the girls think so much of prostitution but as it furnishes opportunities of robbing men. ... Most girls will rob by violence and especially drunken men. ... [They] will not go to a house if they can help it; to some back Street. Gentlemen notice the features so much better when you go to a house.

When possible they would take a client's purse or wallet and

29. s.c. on Police, P.P. 1816, v, p. 50; ibid., P.P. 1817, vii, p. 361; ibid., P.P. 1828, vi, p. 93.

make their escape before completing the transaction which had
been negotiated. Ellen Reece's companion, Jane Doyle, described how they would pick their would-be client's pocket
while his breeches were down and run off while his disarray
hampered pursuit. Another dodge was for an accomplice to
raise a false cry of 'Watch!' after a cough had signalled that the
money had been taken; prostitute and man would then run off –
in opposite directions.[30]

Sometimes of course the girls were seized and taken to the
police office, and it was then important to hide the stolen money
before they were searched – though the women at the police
office did not search very well. Ellen Reece continued her
story:

The places for hiding money are pockets in the underside of the
Stays towards the lower part. . . . Also wrapping it in a piece of rag
or paper and putting it in the hair. Also pockets inside the Stocking
below the Garter. Also putting it where decency forbids to name –
has known thirty Sovereigns hidden there at one time and secured.
Also swallowing it – has known eleven swallowed. It has been swallowed once or twice by Girls on Deansgate beat whilst in the Lock
ups. Relieve themselves on the Floor. If they don't get it for two or
three days they get opening Medicine. Never heard of any one being
injured by disposing of it either way. Has herself hid money in that
way (not swallowing) perhaps thirty times. Was only three times
searched there, and only once it was found. That was by the bad
house woman and the Watchman, who made her jump off the Bed
Stocks twice. Putting it in the Shoes another way. If a Girl heard the
Constables were after her, she would swallow her money for fear –
it is done regular by two or three every night almost.

Ellen had been a shop-lifter, her targets being linens of
various kinds or jewellery. She claimed that she and another girl
had devised for themselves 'a large square fustian pocket
fastened round the waist and hanging nearly to the knees' as a

30. Chadwick Papers, box 129, University College, London. Readers of
Majbritt Morrison's account of her life as a prostitute-thief in London after
the Second World War – *Jungle West 11*, 1964 – will notice certain resemblances.

means of carrying off their booty. She was 'miserable both ways, but going on the Streets was most profitable'. Shop-lifting was not as 'safe as street-walking. Generally young hands that got to this who are not old enough to go on the Streets.'

Mayhew's collaborators found similar activities in London in 1861. A member of the Metropolitan Police explained the art of 'picking-up':[31]

The woman looks out for a 'mug', that is a drunken fellow, or a stupid, foolish sort of fellow. She then stops him in the street, talks to him, and pays particular attention to his jewellery, watch, and every thing of that sort, of which she attempts to rob him. If he offers any resistance, or makes a noise, one of her bullies comes up, and either knocks him down by a blow under the ear, or exclaims: 'What are you talking to my wife for?' and that is how the thing is done, sir.

They added the comforting assurance:

If a well-dressed man went into an immoral house in Spitalfields, Whitechapel, or Shadwell, he would assuredly be robbed, but not maltreated to any greater extent than was absolutely requisite to obtain his money, and other valuables.

This close association between prostitution and crime was, said one writer, 'peculiar to this country, and is often the cause of just surprise to foreigners, who find nothing approximating thereto at home'.[32] Later writers do not throw as much emphasis on the association between the two as do those in the earlier part of the century. For example, Pike wrote in 1876 that

Prostitution . . . may afford opportunities for robbery, especially to the lowest class of prostitutes, who are probably associated by indissoluble bonds with the habitual criminals of the male sex.[33]

It is possible, therefore, that crime and prostitution were no longer so closely linked as in the first sixty years of the century.

31. Mayhew, op. cit., vol. iv, pp. 237–8, 253.
32. S. P. Day, *Juvenile Crime, its Causes, Character, and Cure*, 1858, p. 318.
33. L. O. Pike, *A History of Crime in England . . .*, 1876, vol. ii, p. 527.

6. The institutions of the criminal class

The existence of the criminal class was important because of its role in providing support for its members. The large towns during much of the nineteenth century failed to provide the support which former country-dwellers had known in the smaller communities from which they came. Entry into the criminal class was a means of finding support; it was entry into an association, informal but none the less real, members of which could be found almost everywhere. In gaol or lodging-house or on the road, criminals could find companions in like situation, could exchange experiences and discover common acquaintanceships. To many of them the world had been an empty and friendless place; many of them had never been able to find anyone to listen to them or sympathize with them, or speak to them save to command or criticize. Now all this was changed. They were welcomed – especially if they had money, but if they had not they would often be given advice how to get some. They were received on equal terms with others of their group, and were regarded as independent persons. Their tales were listened to, and the more crimes they could relate, the better would their reception be. Membership of the criminal class met a real need – 'I shall be all right when I find somebody to pal in with', an orphan released from gaol told Greenwood in 1876.[1] Everything combined to make both recruits and old hands glad to be criminals, to strengthen their feeling of belonging and to reinforce the patterns of behaviour which were their membership-card to this desirable association.

Contemporaries saw what was happening. W. A. Miles recorded in the 1830s that[2]

1. J. Greenwood, *The Wilds of London*, 1876, p. 244.
2. H. Brandon (ed.), *Poverty, Mendicity and Crime ...*, 1839, p. 92.

Young thieves have often confessed to me, that ... having acquired confidence by a few successful adventures, they have gradually progressed in crime, allured by others, and in their turn alluring. They find companions to cheer them and instruct them, girls to share their booty and applaud them, and every facility to sell their daily booty.

Things were no better at mid-century:[3]

If a youth takes to thieving and is alone in his course, he soon finds company and a home in the thieves' quarter, where his lagging courage will be stimulated and the ignorance of his inexperience be corrected by the craft of old and practised rogues.

L. O. Pike in 1876 analysed the situation in terms which need not be challenged:[4]

The criminal has ... ideas of right and wrong, but he differs from his fellow-countrymen in the signification which he attaches to the words. He is rarely or never without associates whose ideas of right and wrong are the same as his; he has, therefore, a public opinion which not only supports him in his own views, but would cease to support him if he substituted for them the views of the non-criminal classes. Thus one of the motives which might deter a man who habitually lived within the law has precisely the opposite effect upon a man whose life is a war against society.

Of course there were limits to the reliance which could be placed on these bonds of friendship.[5] 'There is a sort of honour amongst us until we fall asleep or get drunk and then they will "barber" one another, "skewer them of all they have",' said one prisoner. Criminals would sometimes betray one another as the result of a quarrel. The following was given as an example of what often occurred:

Two women living with thieves are taking their 'drop of ruin' together, a quarrel arises as to the superiority of their fancy men in their line of life; one swears her man is the best burglar, and the other as stanchly [sic] upholds the superiority of hers; a species of

3. *Cornhill Magazine*, vol. ii, Sept. 1860, p. 331.
4. L. O. Pike, *A History of Crime in England* ..., 1876, vol. ii, p. 508.
5. R.C. on Constabulary Force, P.P. 1839, xix, pp. 25 (para. 27), 221; cf. S.C. on Police, P.P. 1816, v, p. 142.

jealousy arises, and each, to substantiate their case, tells the feats performed by their men, but in too loud a tone of voice; the conversation is overheard, and the necessary information is given to cause the apprehension of the offenders: or, in other instances, one of the females, fired with envy, perhaps in a state of intoxication, and thinking that by so doing she will deprive her acquaintance of that which she values so much, her fancy man, and thus gain a victory, gives the information herself to the police; and thus criminals are now and then brought to justice.

Sometimes the betrayal was a means of evading pursuit and satisfying the police, and the old thieves who trained youngsters in the fashion of Fagin would occasionally sacrifice one of their followers for this reason. Despite these limitations, however, criminals could on the whole look to one another for help.

The swell mob would send money and such necessaries as the regulations permitted to members in prison, and would wait for them on release, and a thief's mistress would raise what funds she could for him. When someone was released from gaol, a collection or a raffle would be organized for him – partly for celebration, partly to put him on his feet again. Greenwood in 1876 quoted a ticket he had obtained:[6]

A raffle will take place at the Ram and Teazle, for a silk handkerchief, for the benefit of Plummy Jukes, who was trotted in on the 2nd of this month, and needs your kind assistance. Many can help one when one can't help himself. Tickets, one shilling.

The object of the raffle was to provide funds with which to brief counsel for this pickpocket, who had two previous convictions and thus expected a severe sentence. The raffle raised £2 13s. 0d., and it was made up to the necessary £3 by a whip-round. The provision of counsel was indeed a matter to which the prisoners usually attached great importance; the briefing of counsel even at the police offices (i.e. the magistrates' courts) was common in London by the middle 1820s. The accused's mistress would regard the provision of counsel as her duty. Gang-leaders would provide them for valuable boy-pickpockets; and if necessary, crimes would be committed to get the

6. Greenwood, op. cit., pp. 250–53.

sum required. Criminals often used attorneys of low reputation who would attempt to bully the police out of their evidence and to persuade prosecutors to drop the case; the London ones were worse than those of the provinces in this respect. They would tell the prisoners what evidence to give, would suborn the prosecutor or procure false witnesses. This much rests on the testimony of respectable witnesses; Ellen Reece, a prostitute-thief, adds that if a prostitute had no money for her defence there were, in Manchester at any rate, some attorneys who would provide their professional services in exchange for hers.[7]

It was sometimes a formal gang which provided these facilities and which organized criminal operations. Often enough, of course, the references to 'gangs' which are frequent in the literature are to casual partnerships of a few youngsters without any element of permanence or subordination. However, there were some gangs which can properly be so called. This was mainly the case with boys, who would often receive orders from a 'captain' who might be an older boy or an adult thief. This could well arise from the natural tendency of boys to form gangs, but it could also be a consequence of one of the more active and intelligent youngsters gathering round him a group of less bright ones who were glad to put their brawn at the service of his brains and who, even as criminals, liked to have someone to tell them what to do.

There was in addition one case where the gang was part of the technique of operation and a feature of adult criminal life: pickpockets of higher classes very often worked in gangs. The actual thief, who was often a boy, needed help if his activities were not to be severely curtailed by the risk of apprehension. He needed assistants to jostle the victim or to mask his own movements, and above all to receive the booty the moment it had been taken, so that if the alarm was given nothing would be found on those near enough to the victim to be accused of the theft – property was often in the hands of a prostitute down

7. Chadwick Papers, box 129 (statement of Ellen Reece). For the respectable witnesses see ibid., boxes 126 (statement of J. Bishop, p. 69) and 131 (statement of A. J. List).

the road within seconds of being stolen. The methods of the swell mob were described:

> Two go before their man, the others close up behind; their victim is hemmed in, a push takes place, he is jostled and hustled about, the thieves cry out to those behind not to press so, the press is increased; the victim being surrounded, his pockets are presently turned inside out. No time is lost; if he does not readily raise his hands, but keeps them in his pockets, or at his side, to guard his property, his hat gets a tip behind, perhaps it is knocked over his eyes. To right his hat he raises his arms, nor does he get them down again till eased of everything in his possession. His fob and vest-pockets are emptied by the thief standing beside him ... the trousers-pockets and coat-pockets are emptied by those behind.[8]

The victim is unlikely to discover his loss quickly enough to pin suspicion on the right persons – and even if he does accuse one of the gang, failure to recover the property will often enough mean that after a search the accused has to be released with an apology.

These gangs of pickpockets were sometimes said to have areas allocated to them; 'I have been informed that the town is divided into different walks for gangs of pickpockets,' said the Recorder of the City of London in 1816. Another witness about the same time spoke of youngsters dividing themselves into parties to work certain districts, one party by day and another party by night, the whole group meeting at stated times to divide the proceeds; a boy had claimed that one group had one day divided £400.[9] Both adult and juvenile gangs had their own special meeting-places, which also acted as houses of resort for criminals not organized into gangs.

These houses of resort, indeed, played an important part in the supporting organization of the criminal class. In the earlier part of the century they were often called 'flash-houses', a term covering low public houses and lodging-houses, and coffee-shops and cook-shops which were the resort of thieves and prostitutes. Though the opening of coffee-houses in the 1850s

8. r.c. on Constabulary Force, p.p. 1839, xix, p. 221.
9. s.c. on Police, p.p. 1816, v, p. 224; ibid., p.p. 1817, vii, p. 429.

represented a movement of reform, such places had earlier had a less savoury reputation, and an increase in their number during the Napoleonic Wars had harmful effects. They became alternatives to public houses, particularly attractive to the criminal class because the magistrates had no powers of regulation or supervision. A number of them seem to have become the meeting-places of criminals. Later on – from about the time of the Report of the Royal Commission on a Constabulary Force in 1839, in fact – lodging-houses and beer-houses were the principal places condemned as centres of crime.

The flash-houses were headquarters of gangs and places of general resort for the exchange of gossip and the arrangement of business. They were houses of call for wandering criminals, where all could be sure of welcome and companionship, information about local conditions, and assistance if they had just come from prison. Flash-house keepers who still retained a shred of good character were said often to help young customers who were appearing before the magistrates by giving false testimony to their previous blameless record. In all these ways the flash-houses performed the function of facilitating the criminals' movement round the country.

The thieves' houses of resort had their uses from the police point of view; it was convenient to know where the thieves could be found if wanted. This of course had been a familiar idea ever since Sir Samuel Romilly spoke in 1812 of police officers going 'into places open for the reception and entertainment of thieves and other abandoned characters, as openly as a merchant would go to the Exchange, or a gentleman to that part of his manor where he expected any particular kind of game'.[10] The condemnatory tone in which this practice was discussed was due largely to the effect of the Parliamentary Reward payable on conviction for certain offences, an undesirable feature of the law at the beginning of the century. One important aspect of the matter was that police officers and police magistrates were said to be insufficiently active in seeking

10. S. Romilly, *The Speeches of Sir Samuel Romilly in the House of Commons*, 1820, vol. i, p. 370.

to put down the flash-houses. This complaint was met partly by a denial of the fact and partly – and more convincingly – by an attempt at justification. Thieves, it was said, were bound to meet somewhere and might just as well meet openly as secretly. Patrick Colquhoun put this view to the Select Committee on Police in 1816:[11]

It has been frequently stated that the existence of such houses is necessary for the purpose of enabling the Police officers to know where to find criminal persons accused or suspected of having committed specific felonies; and it must be acknowledged that it frequently happens that the landlords or occupiers of those houses do give useful information to the officers.

[Question] Then in fact there are houses which are overlooked by the Police, for the purpose of gaining information? – I cannot exactly say they are overlooked; I speak of houses where there is no particular disorder, except that they are frequented by reputed thieves; if such houses merely on this account are put down, others will rise up immediately, and there would be no useful practical result . . .

Do you not think that the existence of houses of resort for thieves, from the combination which they occasion of one with another, encourage [sic] the habits of the people who frequent them? – I certainly do think so; the conclusion is obvious . . .

Do you think the system of permitting public-houses, which are the resort of thieves, for the sake of gaining information, is really necessary to obtaining such information? – Upon the general principle that every thing that can contribute to the detection and apprehension of thieves, may be useful in bringing criminal offenders to justice; if one house of this description is put down, another will immediately rise up.

Are you of opinion the detections would be as frequent and as speedy, if the licences of those houses to which they resort, were taken away? – I should doubt it.

Robert Raynsford, another police magistrate, backed him up:

Certainly it is a great evil to society that such houses should be

11. s.c. on Police, P.P. 1816, v, pp. 48–9, 57–8, 147, 178–80, 262–3; ibid., P.P. 1817, vii, p. 17.

permitted, yet at the same time as a Police Magistrate I am bound to tell the Committee that many of the most notorious thieves would escape if it were not for those particular places of rendezvous, which afford us the means of getting those offenders into our power . . .

If it came to our knowledge that there was any particular house that was a notorious receptacle for thieves, we should . . . certainly try to put a stop to the licence; the consequence of that would be, they would be driven from that house and would go to another; and as there will always be thieves, the place of resort for those thieves will naturally be the public-houses; and it certainly is the principal means of our knowing where notorious offenders are to be taken. . . . In my opinion we should very rarely get hold of notorious offenders if every place of this sort was done away.

John Lavender, a police officer, was equally emphatic: 'They are certainly a necessary evil; if those houses were done away we should have the thieves resort to private houses and holes of their own, and we should never find them.' John Vickery, a police officer of great experience, was less decided:

They often furnish the means of detecting great offenders . . . they materially help in the detection of offenders, and if the officers did not go round where these men frequent, we should never know how to proceed after those parties that are connected together in gangs, and bring them to conviction: I think, however, it would be much better if these houses were done away with altogether . . .

It is impossible to prevent these men having their meetings: and suppose they were to meet at each man's private lodging at different times, we should have no sort of admission to the private lodging, where they might mature their crimes better than at a public house.

Philip Holdsworth, who had after eighteen years' service just vacated the office of Upper Marshal of the City of London (the permanent head of its police under the Lord Mayor), told the Committee that no such houses were allowed in the City – 'Not one; whenever there is, it is stopped immediately. . . . We do not allow them a place of rest if we can help it.' However, his evidence allows one to believe that the City officers only took the view they did because they could make use of the flash-houses in the parts of London outside their jurisdiction: 'The officers sometimes go out of the City, they know where to look for them, and see them together. . . . The officers go out of the City, and are always well treated.'

The Select Committee had no hesitation in deciding against the flash-houses:

> Your Committee feel that though the criminal may be there apprehended; crimes also there are planned; and that in these schools and academies for vice, adapted to both sexes and to all ages, where one thief is seized a hundred are trained. . . . Thus is a chain of connection kept up, known to and tolerated by the police officers, by which, in the opinion of Your Committee, under the disguise and pretence of furthering the detection of crime and the apprehension of criminals, the guilty may be allowed to escape, the penalties of the law eluded, the officers of justice exposed to dangerous temptations, and their character brought into great disrepute.

But of course it was easier to condemn the flash-houses than to close them and to prevent their reopening, as no doubt the Select Committee realized. There do indeed seem to have been attempts from time to time to take a stricter attitude, especially after the formation of the Metropolitan Police and the other new police forces. However, Dickens in 1851 described a tour round the lodging-houses with a police officer who was clearly as much at home there as any Bow Street Runner could have been.[12] Moreover, though in 1856 the *Quarterly Review* declared 'all known flash-houses have long been discontinued', the *Cornhill Magazine* in 1862 showed that things had not changed much:

> Two detectives, perhaps, come in quietly, look round the rooms, and then pass out, without anything being said. Should a man whom they want be present in the rooms, they will give him a tap on the shoulder, and say, 'You are wanted; come with me.' . . . Should there be an individual in the room, a stranger to the detectives, they

12. Dickens, *Reprinted Pieces: On Duty with Inspector Field*, 1851; *Quarterly Review*, vol. xcix, June 1856, p. 193; *Cornhill Magazine*, vol. vi, Nov. 1862, pp. 645–6; letter from N.A.W. and leading article, *The Times*, 10 March 1869.

will bid him stand up, and then, 'take off your hat, sir': this, that they may know him another day.

In 1869 a letter to *The Times* declared: 'There are recognized haunts and thieves' houses in London, which are as well known to the police as the Bank, and which are in fact visited by the police every night.' The writer accompanied two police officers to a house frequented by the swell mob.

The landlord and landlady ... both are known to be convicted thieves, both are known to be lucrative receivers and expert disposers of stolen goods. ... Some eight or nine well-dressed men are sitting over their cigars and beer. These were the *élite* of the swell mob. ... Our entry, I am sorry to say, seemed to throw a general damp upon the company. There was an utter silence, and then, at intervals of a few seconds, one after another went out to get a cigar or a glass of 'old and bitter', all of which they must have found it particularly difficult to find, as none of them came back.

A leading article, commenting on this letter, said:

The police ... can take us at a minute's notice to the places where they [the criminals] are drinking, resting, gambling, or scheming. Powerless as they are in other respects, they can enter the very houses and rooms in which these gangs are assembled, can point out the members of the company one by one, and tell off their 'previous convictions' on their fingers. ... The understanding which prevails all through is perfect. The police know the thieves and the receivers as well as they know each other, and the thieves and receivers know the police. ... They all knew ... that though the police might make a visit of inspection, count them, mark them, see what they were about, and show them off to any inquiring friend, they could not lay a finger on them to stop their doings.

The suggestion in the 1869 letter that the detectives' visit was an unwelcome one and not treated as a matter of course is a new feature, but otherwise there is little that is different from what had been said soon after Waterloo.

The network of supporting institutions not only provided the criminals with meeting-places; it also had the important function of facilitating the disposal of stolen goods. In every age observers of the criminal scene have been conscious of the importance of the receiver, and the nineteenth century was no exception. 'If there were no receivers there would be no thieves' was a familiar saying. Throughout the century stolen property could easily be disposed of – even handfuls of hay, it was said, could be sold to donkeymen, and brickdust had its buyers.

The name of Fagin comes immediately to mind when this subject is raised, and there is no doubt that many receivers operated in the way Dickens described. Indeed, it is sometimes suggested that the character of Fagin was based on the real-life Isaac Solomons, of Spitalfields and Rosemary Lane, London – 'the great Ikey Solomons', as he was often called – who was arrested for receiving in 1827.[13] A playbill for the Royal Surrey Theatre in 1838, advertising a stage version of *Oliver Twist,* emphasized the accuracy of its general picture by pointing out that the officers who pursued Solomons 'discovered cellars and trap-doors, and all sorts of places of concealment, which they found full of stolen goods'. When Mrs Solomons was arrested a few months later, two coach-loads of property were said to have been removed from the house on the first visit, and two subsequent visits were made. The goods were placed in a room above one of the police offices to be viewed by tradesmen who might be able to identify things stolen from them – the office was during the whole morning 'a complete Bazaar'. Ikey Solomons was eventually transported to Van Diemen's Land, but he had made enough of a mark for Arthur Morrison, writing in 1896, to speak of receivers using 'the simple system first called into being seventy years back and more by the prince of fences, Ikey Solomons. A breastpin brought a fixed sum, good or bad, and a roll of cloth brought the fixed price of a roll of cloth, regardless of quality.' There is no evidence that Solomons really was the originator of this system, or that he even used it, but the comment is testimony

13. Royal Surrey Theatre Playbill for 19 Nov. 1838; *Morning Post,* 1 Sept. 1827; A. Morrison, *A Child of the Jago,* Penguin ed., 1946, p. 136. For further details about this fascinating villain and a discussion of the suggestion that he formed the basis for the character Fagin, see my forthcoming *The Life and Times of Ikey Solomons.*

to the impact he made on the memory of some Londoners.

The novel just quoted, Morrison's *A Child of the Jago*, contains another fictional fence. Aaron Weech, a sanctimonious, sabbath-observing coffee-shop proprietor, gives some cake and coffee to eight-year-old Dicky Perrott, the hero of the tale, and then sends him out to steal to pay for it. Here is the technique in operation:[14]

'If you *find* somethink . . . you come to me an' I'll give ye somethink for it, if it's any good. It ain't no business of anybody's *where* you find it, o' course. . . . Bring it 'ere quiet, when there ain't no p'liceman in the street . . . An' then I'll give you somethink for it – money p'raps, or p'raps cake. . . . There's no end o' things to be found all over the place, an' a sharp boy like you can find 'em every day. If you don't find 'em, someone else will. . . . That's twopence you owe me, an' you better bring somethink an' pay it off quick.'

Weech takes care to regulate the account so that Dicky is always in debt to him and thus cannot transfer his custom elsewhere.

Dicky came moodily back from his dinner at Mr Weech's, plunged in mystified computation: starting with a debt of twopence, he had paid Mr Weech an excellent clock – a luxurious article in Dicky's eyes – had eaten a bloater, and had emerged from the transaction owing threepence halfpenny. . . . As Mr Weech put it, the adjustment of accounts would seem to be quite correct; but the broad fact that all had ended in increasing his debt by three halfpence, remained and perplexed him.

When Dicky starts an honest job found for him by a local clergyman, Weech soon gets to hear of it and blackens his character to his employer so that he gets the sack, and is thus thrust back into his old ways.

Aaron Weech seems to have been as accurately drawn a character as Fagin. In Manchester about the middle of the century there was a receiver known as One-armed Dick; two prisoners told the prison chaplain about him: 'We used to play cards at Dick D.'s, and when we lost, he would send to the jerry-shop next door to his house, and get drink on credit, and then

14. ibid., pp. 41–3, 49, 112–13.

set us thieving to pay him again,' said one, and the other added:
'He keeps a good many lads to go about stealing lead.'[15]

The keepers of flash-houses were often receivers. They would
perhaps take a handkerchief in payment for a 4d. dinner, while
a watch worth £20 was enough for a week's keep. Mayhew said
that the lodging-house keepers of the middle of the century
would assist the pickpockets who stayed in their houses by
pledging their booty at a pawnbroker's, the regular payment for
this service being 'twopence and the duplicate'; the duplicate,
the title to the goods, could be sold in its turn or, if it subsequently seemed safe to do so, the property could be redeemed
and sold. Mayhew described also a group of speculators who
bought stolen goods from their fellow-lodgers:

These may be dock-labourers or Billingsgate porters having a few
shillings in their pockets. With these they purchase the booty of the
juvenile thieves. 'I have known,' says my informant, 'these speculators wait in the kitchen . . . till a little fellow would come in with
such a thing as a cap, or a piece of bacon, or a piece of mutton.
They would purchase it, and then either retail it amongst the other
lodgers in the kitchen, or take it to some 'fence', where they would
receive a profit on it.'[16]

Pawnbrokers were often receivers, or in some cases were
merely very slow to guess that a ragged youngster was unlikely
to be the owner of the goods he was offering as a pledge (they
would take property even from children of six or seven years).
A police officer in 1817 put the point very delicately: 'I have
reason to believe, that occasionally there may be pawnbrokers
whom we have reason to suspect as not of the purest minds,' he
said, adding that there would be less crime if they 'were more
careful how they took pledges in'.[17] Other witnesses, then and
later, were less mealy-mouthed, and there is no doubt that
young and inexperienced thieves often, and those of some
standing sometimes, disposed of stolen property by pawning it.
In one case a pawnbroker insisted on giving a shilling for an

15. H. S. Joseph, *Memoirs of Convicted Prisoners* . . . , 1853, pp. 62–3.

16. *Morning Chronicle*, 6 Nov. 1849; Mayhew, *London Labour and the London Poor* . . . , 1861–2, vol. i, pp. 255–6, vol. iii, p. 315.

17. s.c. on Police, P.P. 1817, vii, pp. 369–70.

article for which a boy had asked only sixpence – the smaller sum would have been evidence of 'guilty knowledge'.

'Leaving shops' (whence unlicensed pawnbrokers operated), chandlers' shops, 'green-stalls', marine-stores, metal-dealers' stores – all these places were said often to be the bases of receivers, and many private houses were used for the same purpose, of course. Jewish old-clothes-men and others who wandered round the streets early in the morning were also frequently suspected, and pedlars acted as travelling fences. Such receivers were of course for the smaller fry. The more experienced thieves disposed of their takings to the better-class receivers, who kept themselves aloof from the other criminals and specialized in valuable goods and in bank-notes. Then as now, the arrangement to buy the goods was often made before they were stolen.

Some receivers had specially constructed premises. The Select Committee on Police was told in 1817 that the houses often had two or three inner doors to delay the officers' entry. It heard about a house in Field Lane which had a species of night-safe, a hinged trap through which booty could be pushed in a moment, 'so that if you see a person with a bundle, if you pursue him ever so, he will throw it in there, and that will swing back'. (Aaron Weech had a convenient yard into which goods could be thrown if pursuit was too close.) W. A. Miles in the 1830s heard of a fence's house in Petticoat Lane:

Near the window is a small hatch door, tap at it, it opens, nobody is seen, put the property in, the door closes; generally a bit of paper with the price marked on it is handed out, if agreeable to the parties it is given back, when the door opens and the money put out; if the paper is not pushed back, the door opens and the property is returned ... so there is no bargaining, no person is ever seen, and all is done with impunity.[18]

In 1817 it was said bank-notes sometimes turned up in the hands of tradesmen who 'have not actually refused' to give any account of how they came by them,

18. ibid., pp. 355–6; Brandon, op. cit., p. 148.

but the purpose has been served by pretending not to be able to give information, and saying, they never take the names of the persons from whom they received the notes ⋯. speaking of higher notes, as a hundred pounds, there have been instances where a party has [said] that the note was taken on a certain day, and no particular account was taken of it; and it has also occurred with notes of ten pounds and twenty pounds.

Mayhew gave the price of a £5 note on the illicit market as £3 10s. 0d. Metal objects, precious or base, could lose their identity in a moment if they were thrown into a melting pot, and tales were occasionally told of places where a furnace was always kept hot so that this could be done. Watches were 'christened' – i.e. given new makers' names and numbers; alternatively the movement might be put into a different case. Edwin Chadwick in 1829 told the story that in earlier days a sort of second market had operated in Billingsgate for the sale of stolen fish; the stealers not unnaturally had been able to undersell the legitimate dealers, and the market had had a turnover of £8,000–£10,000 a year. It had, however, been broken up 'by an active officer' by the date of the article.[19]

Stolen property was frequently moved around the country. There were more receivers in Liverpool than in Manchester and they paid a better price, so it would often pay to buy stolen goods in Manchester and resell them in Liverpool; a great deal of the property stolen in Manchester passed through the hands of the Liverpool receivers. Romford thieves would dispose of much of their booty in Brentwood and vice versa; if the goods were sufficiently valuable someone from London would come down to buy them. In this trade as in others, London dominated the area around it, and at the upper end of the trade it dominated the whole country. Really valuable articles stolen anywhere in the country would go to London, and if identifiable would often be sent abroad, just as similar goods from abroad came to London. Bank-notes of high value often went abroad,

19. s.c. on Police, P.P. 1817, vii, pp. 493–4; Mayhew, op. cit., vol. iii, p. 317; E. Chadwick, 'Preventive Police', *London Review*, vol. i, Feb. 1829, p. 287.

and valuable horses were passed over to the Continent. Many stolen watches were sent to the United States.

Though so much was known about the workings of the thieves' market, it was difficult to suppress it. As the Recorder of Birmingham put it, 'it would be of no avail, if a hundred persons, each of unspotted character, were to testify to their belief that a given individual carried on the trade of receiving stolen goods ... until some specified criminal act could be brought home to him'. Thus parish officers could say to the Select Committee on Police in 1817 that they 'had no doubt' that certain people were receivers, that they were 'quite convinced' of it, that it was their 'firm belief' – and yet only be able to talk of bringing them to justice 'in the course of time'. As Miles wrote,

juries are so delicate with regard to convicting a receiver of stolen property; there is great difficulty in obtaining a verdict, because a host of neighbours, out of kindness, come forward to give testimonials as to character, &c.; the man escapes, unless he happens to be a Jew, then he is fully suspected and convicted as a matter of course.[20]

In 1828 a police magistrate of eleven years' experience suggested that there was a need for

a very extensive power in the police magistracy of searching premises. For example, when property is stolen, and the owner is not able to swear to the usual affidavit, that he suspects the stolen property, or some part of it, to be concealed in such a particular place, I would give authority to the magistrate to issue his warrant to search any houses or premises regarding which any credible person would swear, that he has known, or has reason to believe that it is a house for reception of stolen property. The Committee will readily imagine that the natural feelings of a professional man would not in the first instance have led him to jump to such a conclusion ... but I was satisfied, on mature reflection, that the liberties of such persons should give way to the public advantage.[21]

20. M. D. Hill, *Suggestions for the Repression of Crime* ..., 1857, p. 67 s.c. on Police, P.P. 1817, vii, pp. 167–8; Brandon, op. cit., p. 59.
21. s.c. on Police, P.P. 1828, vi, p. 178.

Moreover, in the earlier part of the century receiving stolen goods was in some circumstances only a misdemeanour carrying relatively light penalties. The various changes during the century in the law relating to receivers give support to the view that at the time of Waterloo the powers given to police and magistrates were inadequate.

Despite increased powers and an increased number of police to use them, there is little suggestion at any time that the disposal of stolen goods presented any real difficulty. It is true that Ellen Reece in the 1830s said that after several years of shoplifting she faced a problem when the fence with whom she did business was transported.

After he was gone could not find anyone else to take 'em and thought it dangerous to go to pawnbrokers, so gave over Shoplifting and took entirely to the Streets and robbing Mens pockets. . . . She did not become a regular Prostitute till Shoplifting failed.[22]

It is, however, rather difficult to accept that after some seven years – by her own account – living by 'plunder' in Manchester and Liverpool she knew no other outlet for stolen property; perhaps she wanted to give a reason for going on the streets. Despite her claim, it may be said that in broad terms the picture was the same in all places and throughout the century, and though receivers may not have been quite so numerous or so blatant in their conduct at the end of it we need have little doubt that those who stole could readily find a means of disposing of their booty.

Both flash-houses and receivers were associated with another important aspect of the criminal world, the training of youngsters. No doubt these words at once conjure up a picture of Fagin exercising the Artful Dodger and Charley Bates in the art of picking pockets, and there is much contemporary testimony that the picture is an accurate one. John Binny, one of Mayhew's collaborators – who, it is true, must be assumed to have read *Oliver Twist* – described the way in which the youngsters

are learned to be expert. . . . A coat is suspended on the wall with a

22. Chadwick Papers, box 129.

bell attached to it, and the boy attempts to take the handkerchief from the pocket without the bell ringing. Until he is able to do this with proficiency he is not considered well trained. Another way in which they are trained is this: The trainer – if a man – walks up and down the room with a handkerchief in the tail of his coat, and the ragged boys amuse themselves abstracting it until they learn to do it in an adroit manner. We could point our finger to three of these execrable wretches, who are well known to train schools of juvenile thieves – one of them, a young man at Whitechapel; another, a young woman at Clerkenwell; and a third, a middle-aged man residing about Lambeth Walk. . . . We have also heard of some being taught to pick pockets by means of an effigy; but this is not so well authenticated.[23]

It must be admitted that throughout the century there were those who denied the existence of formal training establishments, or thought them a thing of the past. Thus the Royal Commission on a Constabulary Force of 1839 was told:

It is a common opinion that schools for the tuition of the younger thieves exist at these [flash-] houses, but no regular system of such instruction is now carried on. Some years ago it was customary for old thieves to select young ones and form them into a mob to act under their direction, and then a system of teaching was practised; but since the establishment of the new police the same facilities do not present themselves, and no regular system is now in practice.[24]

It may have been true that the Metropolitan Police had begun to have an effect, but subsequent writers make it quite clear that these categorical statements are too optimistic. Adult trainers continued to run formal training establishments in London and elsewhere for many years. In 1858, for instance, S. P. Day wrote:

There are several establishments throughout the metropolis – and very comfortable places they are too – kept by the proprietors of juvenile thieves. Herein the novice is initiated into his future art, and practised daily in sleight-of-hand exercises. . . . Herein, too, he is well fed and well clad, and instructed how to behave in mixed company, so as to disarm suspicion. . . . From these thieves'

23. Mayhew, op. cit., vol. iv, p. 304.
24. R.C. on Constabulary Force, P.P. 1839, xix, p. 214.

domiciles, or training seminaries, occasionally sally forth gangs of young depredators, accompanied by their masters.

And in 1862 the *Cornhill Magazine* observed 'for a superior education the professional trainer, or coaching by a first-class thief in full practice, is necessary'.[25] However, in the 1850s and 1860s the police seem to have been able to interfere more with these activities and to reduce the numbers involved.

Even if the more formal training was handicapped by police activity, there is ample evidence that throughout the century informal training by relatives, friends and casual acquaintances continued. The sort of thing that happened is well described in the story Binny obtained in 1861 from a former pickpocket. It should be said that the narrator had become a patterer, i.e. (in Mayhew's own words) one of those 'who beg on the "blob", that is, by word of mouth', and he had thus no doubt acquired the gift of telling a convincing tale; his story is, however, plausible. He said that he ran away from home at the age of nine (this was in 1840) and managed to get to London; after some weeks, totally destitute,[26]

I was taken by several poor ragged boys to sleep in the dark arches of the Adelphi. I often saw the boys follow the male passengers when the halfpenny boats came to the Adelphi stairs. . . . I could not at first make out the meaning of this, but I soon found they generally had one or two handkerchiefs when the passengers left. . . . Joe said to me, that when the next boat came in, if any man came out likely to carry a good handkerchief, he would let me have a chance at it. . . . I saw an elderly gentleman step ashore. . . . Before Joe said anything to me, he had 'fanned' the gentleman's pocket, i.e., had felt the pocket and knew there was a handkerchief.

He whispered to me, 'Now, Dick, have a try,' and I went to the old gentleman's side, trembling all the time, and Joe standing close to me in the dark, and went with him up the steep hill of the Adelphi. . . . Joe still following us, encouraging me all the time. . . . I took out a green 'kingsman' . . .

After that I gained confidence, and in the course of a few weeks I was considered the cleverest of the little band . . .

25. S. P. Day, *Juvenile Crime, its Causes, Character, and Cure*, 1858, pp. 44–5; *Cornhill Magazine*, vol. vi, Nov. 1862, p. 644.

26. Mayhew, op. cit., vol. iv, pp. 318–20.

[In January 1841] several men came to us. I did not know, although I afterwards heard, they were brought by 'Larry' [the fence who took the boys' goods] to watch me, as he had been speaking of my cleverness. ... It seemed that they were not satisfied altogether with me, for they did not tell me what they wanted ...

The narrator then spent some weeks in prison. He came out in March 1841. Two of the men who had seen him at work were waiting for him with a cab, and invited him to join their gang. 'I was willing to go anywhere to better myself,' and the men took him to their home in Flower and Dean Street, Whitechapel. 'I found out shortly afterwards that these men had lately had a boy, but he was transported.' The replacement was after a few days taken out to work: he was to pick ladies' pockets with the help of the others.

As this was my first essay in having anything to do in stealing from a woman, I believe they were nervous themselves, but they had well tutored me during the two or three days I had been out of prison. They had stood against me in the room while Emily walked to and fro, and I had practised on her pocket.

Within three hours they had taken five purses. 'I recollect how they praised me afterwards that night for my cleverness.'

The details of this patterer's story may have been improved by his skill in his second profession, but that the sort of thing that he described was all too common is clear enough. 'Nearly every adult criminal – usually when in prison, always when out of it – is busy in training younger sinners' – this remark of 1869 seems fair comment for the whole of the century.[27]

This education was sometimes given in a spirit of philanthropy, with motives as disinterested as those which led to the extension of more widely approved forms of education in the same period – Joe the Adelphi boy is a case in point. (It is pleasant to be able to record that Joe 'was afterwards transported, and is now in a comfortable position in Australia'.) Much of the informal training imparted in conversation brought no monetary benefit to the teacher; this was particularly true of the training picked up in gaol. But older criminals

27. *St Paul's Magazine*, vol. iii, Feb. 1869, p. 602.

frequently trained youngsters because they could make use of their services. Fagin not only trained the Artful Dodger and Charley Bates, he provided board and lodging and directed their activities as well – and doubtless took most of the profit. Many emulated him. The clerk of the peace for Surrey said in 1828:

> I can mention a remarkable circumstance that occurred within my own knowledge; I was passing along the road in the neighbourhood of the King's Bench Prison, and upon a vacant spot of ground I observed a collection of boys and a man in the midst of them, with a basket in his hand, doling out provisions. I observed also a peace-officer in altercation with him; and, upon my inquiring the cause, the officer said, Here is an old thief, who keeps all these boys in pay, and comes out regularly in the middle of the day, and brings them their food, and receives the produce of their plunder; and yet he had no power, he said, to apprehend the one or the other.

A writer in 1856 said that 'some years since' he had seen a bill for board and lodging – two guineas a week – made out by a man known as 'Mo' Clarke, of South London, who had a crowd of youngsters with whom he would go to the races looking like a widower out with his children. 'Their appearance disarmed suspicion, and enabled them to empty the pockets of those around them at their leisure.' In 1865 it was said that

> The methods in which thieves are kept and trained differ little from that which obtained when our great novelist wrote for us an account of the doings of Mr Fagin, Charley Bates and the Artful Dodger. But it so happens that Mr Fagin now sometimes keeps a common lodging-house, and that – to appear respectable – he provides his pupils with pencils, oranges, memorandum-books, or some small wares for sale. He is still held in such awe by his satellites, that they would go to prison, to save him from the clutches of the law; and he passes amongst them by the endearing appellation of 'Father'.[28]

Dickens did, however, exaggerate the ease with which youngsters could obtain a place in one of these schools. The criminal section of the juvenile labour market was as over-supplied as

28. s.c. on Police, P.P. 1828, vi, p. 152; *Quarterly Review*, vol. xcix, June 1856, pp. 185–6; T. Archer, *The Pauper, the Thief, and the Convict* ..., 1865, p. 8.

the rest of it, and in the buyer's market that resulted some aptitude for crime had to be shown. A green hand like Oliver Twist was unlikely to have been recruited directly into a top-class organization like Fagin's. Dickens indeed appears to have realized this, for Sikes asks Fagin:

'Wot makes you take so much pains about one chalk-faced kid, when you know there are fifty boys snoozing about Common Garden [this, of course, is Covent Garden market] every night, as you might pick and choose from?'

'Because they're of no use to me, my dear,' replied the Jew with some confusion, 'not worth the taking. Their looks convict 'em when they get into trouble; and I lose 'em all. With this boy, properly managed, my dears, I could do what I couldn't with twenty of them.'[29]

The answer is a lame one, and it is of course not true: Fagin's confusion is due to the fact that he is concealing Monks's interest in the boy. But this interest was not aroused at the time Oliver was admitted into Fagin's band; and it is unlikely that this dangerous step would so lightheartedly have been taken. Noah Claypole, too, would probably have had to serve a longer apprenticeship. A writer in 1833 stressed that it was wrong to think that receivers sought to entice strangers into crime. 'The risk here is too great, and the parties too wary.' In his articles in *Fraser's Magazine* he had explained that the criminal class were very careful in admitting noviciates into their secrets. 'They form one club, to whom all the *fences* are known ... who will never purchase of a new hand without a proper introduction, for fear of "*a plant*" (being betrayed). An initiate is, in consequence, constrained to trust his spoils to some old offender, until he can himself become better acquainted, and gain confidence with the buyer.'[30] The patterer's tale just quoted shows the care taken in selecting someone for the higher training of the criminal world.

29. Dickens, *Oliver Twist*, ch. xix, p. 126.
30. *Old Bailey Experience ... by the Author of 'The Schoolmaster's Experiences in Newgate'*, 1833, p. 41; *Fraser's Magazine*, vol. v, June 1832, p. 522.

When the selection was made the youngsters were well looked after. Gibbon Wakefield in 1832 said that adult thieves often spent as much as £10 in a few days in providing food, drink, theatres and women for a likely lad. This was of course because a well-trained youngster was a most valuable asset. We have already seen that adult pickpockets very often used a boy for the actual theft. The patterer quoted earlier went on to say that a boy like him was always given 'his proper share equal with the others, because he is their sole support. If they should lose him they would be unable to do anything until they got another'. The bargain was not all one way: on one occasion the alarm was given 'but I was got away by two of my comrades. The other threw himself in the way, and kept them back.'

The Select Committee on Police in 1828 heard of another way in which gangs tried to save boys from arrest: 'They were dressed as well as any nobleman's sons, in neat great coats and trowsers, and dressed as fashionably as any boys I ever saw.' If the boys are caught, the adult members of the gang 'go up, and say directly, "This is a gentleman's son; it is impossible he could do such a thing as that." '[31]

Despite such devices the boys were of course from time to time convicted, and imprisonment or disagreement was bound sooner or later to break up a partnership. But both the boys and the adults benefited from the existence of the gang, and such groupings seem to have been numerous until the virtual elimination of the boy-pickpockets in the 1850s and 1860s.

Other adult criminals used youngsters. A Manchester writer in 1840 said: 'It is well known that young children are often employed by more experienced thieves, to bring them information as to where and how property is situated; and they are also employed by house-breakers, to enter through windows and small apertures, and at the proper time to open the doors for the admission of their older accomplices.' It will be remembered that Bill Sikes bemoaned the shortage of boys for this

31. E. G. Wakefield, *Facts Relating to the Punishment of Death in the Metropolis*, 2nd ed., 1832, pp. 16–28; Mayhew, loc. cit.; s.c. on Police, P.P. 1828, vi, p. 91.

purpose; the 'Juvenile Delinquent Society' had taken one useful lad and apprenticed him to some honest calling – 'and so they go on;' grumbled Sikes, 'and, if they'd got money enough (which it's a Providence they haven't) we shouldn't have half-a-dozen boys left in the whole trade, in a year or two.'[32] It is doubtful whether this unhappy state of affairs came to pass, but in fact references to the use of boys in this way have not been met with in the second half of the century.

Forgers and coiners needed youngsters to act as go-betweens.

The bill or cheque is generally given to some porter or boy, of whom there are too many loitering about the streets, who, for a shilling or sixpence, would take the cheque to the bankers, where, if it is discovered at the counter, to be a forgery, the man is on the look out at the door or the neighbourhood to ascertain that fact, and immediately he finds his messenger does not return within the time by which he supposes he could get the money, he is gone, and before you can get out of the house he is out of the way.

A twelve-year-old used to utter false money in a similar fashion was asked what his employer (his father) gave him for the work: 'His answer was, "Plenty of victuals, and a penny a-day if I did well, and a good hiding if I did not." '[33] Witnesses before the Select Committee on Gaols in 1835 spoke of coiners and others visiting the Westminster Bridewell to assure youngsters that their jobs would still be waiting for them on release.[34]

In some of these cases youngsters were, so to speak, necessary from a technical point of view, while in others it was a matter of convenience to use them for the actual criminal act. This might be done in order to facilitate the escape of the adult thief, or in the hope that, if the worst came to the worst, the youngsters would get off lightly because of their age, and the adults because they had not committed the actual criminal act themselves.

32. W. B. Neale, *Juvenile Delinquency in Manchester* ..., Manchester 1840, p. 14; Dickens, *Oliver Twist*, ch. xix, p. 124.
33. s.c. on Police, p.p. 1828, vi, p. 133; M. Carpenter, *Juvenile Delinquents – their Condition and Treatment*, 1853, p. 25.
34. s.c. on Gaols, p.p. 1835, xi, pp. 87–8, 94.

This latter point was especially important in the days when principals but not accessories were liable to capital punishment. And sometimes adults, especially parents, and older children used young ones to do the stealing just as they used them to do any task that needed doing. Children were sent out to get a certain sum, by stealing, begging, sweeping a crossing, holding horses or anything else, on pain of a beating if they returned without it. The story was often told.[35] In 1817 a witness told the Select Committee on Police that children 'are driven into the streets every morning, and dare not return but with plunder'. Another included in a list of juvenile delinquents the case of a twelve-year-old boy whose mother 'subsists by his depredations. She turns him into the street every morning, and chastises him severely when he returns in the evening without some article of value.' In 1828 others took up the tale:

There were last night, and it will be the same tonight, perhaps from ten to fifteen or eighteen boys sleeping under the green stalls in Covent Garden, who dare not go home without money, sent out by their parents, to beg ostensibly, but to steal if they can get it; and I have reason to believe ... that it is the same in Fleet market, and other markets, little urchins that I have taken out at night, with no home to go to, or if they have, they dare not go home under sixpence ...

It is no uncommon thing ... to see infants of five, six or seven years old, with a few matches in their hands, at ten, eleven or twelve o'clock at night; and on being questioned why they do not go home, they answer that their mothers will beat them if they go without money, or at least that they shall get no supper.

These quotations come from the earlier part of the century, but in 1865 a writer referred to 'the horde of lawless young Arabs who infest the streets and beg or steal, under the direction of those cadgers who own them either by right of parentage or the demand for a miserable lodging and a mouthful of food'. In 1883 another writer said that 'children who can scarcely walk are ... mercilessly beaten if they come back from

35. s.c. on Police, P.P. 1817, vii, pp. 431, 439; ibid., P.P. 1828, vi, pp. 39, 152–3; Archer, op. cit., pp. 163–4; W. C. Preston, *The Bitter Cry of Outcast London*, 1883, p. 8.

their daily expeditions without money or money's worth'. Indeed, by the middle of the century it had become so common for children to be sent out in this way, and it had become so widely known that it happened, that 'even where it does not exist, it is a ready tale with young vagrants, who, when soliciting relief, seek to excite sympathy for their case by declaring that they dare not venture home unprovided'.[36]

Not all the children concerned were expected by their parents to steal, perhaps. Certainly the most honest and well-meaning of nineteenth-century parents might beat a child who returned from crossing-sweeping without an adequate sum of money, in the same spirit as that in which Northern parents beat their children to drive them to the factory on time: if the child was not beaten it would not eat. But the long-run effects are likely to have been the same, in any event. Any children sent out in this way were likely to follow the train of reasoning of the young-ster who said to the Ordinary of Newgate: 'If I did not get any thing I had no dinner or supper; and a handkerchief always fetches sixpence in Field Lane.'[37] Children sent out to forage in this way were likely to end by committing crime, whatever the intentions of their parents – and their intentions were not always strictly honourable.

There is some ground for thinking that the use of children by older thieves in all these ways declined from about the 1850s. The Chief Constable of Newcastle-upon-Tyne, writing in 1856 and referring not merely to his own town but to the north of England generally, said:

I know that many of the parents, who heretofore were in the habit of sending their children into the streets for the purposes of stealing, begging, and plunder, have quite discontinued that prac-tice, and several of the children so used and brought up as thieves and mendicants, are now at some of the free schools of the town, others are at work, and thereby obtain an honest livelihood; and, so far as I can ascertain, they seem to be thoroughly altered, and appear likely to become good and honest members of society.[38]

36. Neale, op. cit., p. 13.
37. s.c. on Police, p.p. 1818, viii, p. 184.
38. Quoted in M. D. Hill, op. cit., p. 358.

7. Changes over time, and differences between places

It is of course necessary to be very cautious before making pronouncements about changes in the nature or level of crime over any period of time, let alone one so remote as the nineteenth century. However, there are two propositions on this topic that can be put forward with some assurance.

The first of these is that there was a continuing trend to less violence in crime over the century. Such a trend probably existed in the eighteenth century; the evidence for its existence in the nineteenth century is even stronger. Throughout the century contemporaries accepted that criminals were becoming less violent, each generation seeing an improvement over the previous one.

The evidence before the Select Committee on Police of 1816–18 sets the tone. 'Daring, desperate things seem to be worn out, except daring forgeries,' said one police officer, and the question put to John Nares, a police magistrate of over twenty years' experience, and his reply will serve as a summary of the rest of the evidence: 'The Committee have had in evidence, and indeed the observation of every one must have given him the information without that evidence, that atrocious crimes have of late years considerably diminished? – I have no doubt of that.'

Blackwood's Magazine did indeed in 1818 write that 'one strong feature of the times is the prevalence of atrocious crime. This is the common remark of every day.' However, the Select Committee's reports leave no doubt that many people in the post-Waterloo period took the more optimistic view.[1]

1. S.C. on Police, P.P. 1816, v, pp. 261, 255; *Blackwood's Magazine*, vol. iii, May 1818, p. 176.

Street robberies in London increased dramatically in the early 1820s, and one writer in 1829 spoke of gangs being ready to 'hustle, rob, or knock down' anyone carrying valuables; but he also said that 'there have been few instances lately of forcing houses in the old-fashioned way, at the front, and taking possession by *coup de main*'. Francis Place in 1831 was sure that crimes had decreased 'in atrocity'; Edwin Chadwick too had no doubt about the matter. In 1829 he wrote: 'It is acknowledged on every side, that crimes attended with acts of violence have diminished,' and in 1839 the Report of the Royal Commission on a Constabulary Force, drafted by him, said that 'Crimes of violence committed for the sake of obtaining property have diminished. . . . In the towns, burglaries and depredations in the streets are now rarely accompanied by violence.' In 1832 a writer in *Fraser's Magazine* attempted an explanation:

The character and feelings of the public thief, as of all other classes of society, have undergone a visible and marked change within the last thirty years. . . . Formerly, the heroes of their party were fellows conspicuous and famed for open and daring acts of plunder, in whom the whole body had a pride, and whom they all felt ambitious to imitate; failing only to do so for lack of the same quantum of courage. The more desperate and numerous the instances of robbery, the more were the parties lauded and admired. . . . All this kind of heroism has subsided; their leaders now are men rendered famous for scheming, subtlety, and astuteness. Formerly, the passport to enrolment under their banners was a name for boldness and monstrous acts of outrage; now a certificate must be brought of the man never having committed an indiscreet act in his calling.[2]

Opinion remained the same at mid century. Thus, despite outbreaks of violent crime over the whole country between 1850 and 1853, Frederic Hill, a former Inspector of Prisons,

2. J. Wade, *A Treatise on the Police and Crimes of the Metropolis . . . by the Editor of the 'Cabinet Lawyer'*, 1829, pp. 195, 192; 'Rough Notes made for Mr. Hume', 19 June 1831, Place Papers, Add. MSS. 27, 827, f. 191, British Museum; E. Chadwick, 'Preventive Police', *London Review*, vol. i, Feb. 1829, p. 262; R.C. on Constabulary Force, P.P. 1839, xix, p. 48 (para. 45); *Fraser's Magazine*, vol. vi, Nov. 1832, pp. 464–5.

could write in the latter year that crimes were 'taking a milder and milder form'. Violent crimes continued to attract public attention on various occasions during the 1850s and 1860s, particularly of course during the famous garrotting attacks in London in 1862 (see page 163). They caused much public alarm – perhaps more acute because of the relative safety of recent years – but belief that there had been an improvement over earlier years persisted. In 1862 the *Cornhill Magazine* wrote that the criminals' 'character in respect of violence and cruelty has been much ameliorated during the last fifteen or twenty years. They do not like resorting to violence if it can possibly be avoided. ... The modern thief depends upon his skill.'[3]

In the closing years of the nineteenth century the story was unchanged. Looking back over his long life a few days before his death in 1890, Edwin Chadwick summed up his views on this point in a letter to the Editor of the *Daily Chronicle* prepared for his signature but never signed:

When the Police were first instituted [presumably the reference is to the establishment of the Metropolitan Police in 1829], men who were mechanics in good position were asked why they did not have a watch to mark the time. 'Yes' was the reply 'and get my head broken by thieves.' They could hold in safety no personal property of any sort, and life would have been insecure. So with their families. They had no silver spoons, nor any other article of that kind. The possession of such property at that time endangered their lives.

It must be admitted that in 1891 the Rev. W. D. Morrison wrote that 'offences against property with violence display a tendency to increase', but he was talking about the number of cases recorded in a particular statistical category rather than the quality of the acts themselves. Charles Booth in the 1890s found that violence was regarded by criminals and police alike as a breach of the 'rules of the game, which provide the rough outlines of a code of what is regarded as fair or unfair'. Thomas Holmes, surveying in 1908 his twenty-one years' experience as a

3. F. Hill, *Crime, its Amount, Causes and Remedies*, 1853, p. 3; *Cornhill Magazine*, vol. vi, Nov. 1862, pp. 646–7.

police-court missionary, was satisfied that there were fewer crimes of violence.[4]

Thus over the whole of the century there is evidence, much of it from sources entitled to our respect, that the use of violence in crime had decreased; and the conclusion that this is true seems irresistible.

A qualitative change in criminality can thus be established; what can we say about quantitative change? Here it is much more difficult to make definite statements. The difficulties of ascertaining changes in the level of crime are well known, and the people of the nineteenth century were not likely to have had any clearer idea of what was going on than we have of what is going on today. The evidence of what they thought was happening is, moreover, hard to interpret. What exactly do we understand when someone says that 'the tranquillity . . . of the whole town is miraculous . . . very different from what I remember, even within a few years,' but adds 'we have a vast number of pickpockets occasionally, and frauds in abundance'? How far is he being contradicted by a witness who affirms that 'the petty offences' and 'the juvenile depredators' have increased? Does either of them mean the same thing as the witness who thought that there had been an increase but only in 'simple larcenys, burglaries and so on, nothing very enormous' or the witness who agrees that crime is on the increase 'in numbers certainly, but not in depravity by any means; we have . . . less serious offences'?[5] Despite these difficulties, however, it is worth surveying the evidence, and for this purpose it is convenient to divide the century into two parts, the division occurring in the middle 1850s.

The phrases quoted in the previous paragraph show that it is easy to produce testimony to an increase in non-violent crime in

4. Unsigned letter dated 2 July 1890. Chadwick Papers, box 120 (that this is the fair copy for signature is an inference from its appearance); W. D. Morrison, *Crime and its Causes*, 1891, p. 169; C. Booth (ed.), *Life and Labour of the People in London*, 1902–4, 3rd ser., vol. ii, pp. 111–12; T. Holmes, *Known to the Police*, 1908, p. 11.

5. s.c. on Police, P.P. 1817, vii, p. 402; ibid., P.P. 1816, v, pp. 56, 185, 222.

the first of these two periods. Other evidence can be quoted. The Under-Sheriff of London and Middlesex said in 1817:

As to the length of the Old Bailey sessions, it is within the memory of most persons who are now engaged in its business, that if a session continued from the Wednesday in one week to the Monday in the next (or five days) it was an extraordinary circumstance, whereas it has now become a common occurrence for a session to last a fortnight and three weeks. . . . I am persuaded that the actual increase of crime will alone explain the increased length of sessions and assizes.

The Rev. W. L. Clay, writing in 1861, had no doubt that in the early part of the century 'the real increase of crime had been very serious, the apparent increase terrible', and though the comment quoted was made in relation to the ten years from 1825 to 1834, it represents his view of the whole period from about 1810. Several witnesses before parliamentary committees of inquiry and others whose opinions are on record put forward similar views. On the other hand, the contrary view is well supported, and if the bulk of the evidence is for an increase, there are one or two powerful names in the opposing camp. Alderman Matthew Wood, M.P., who was a leading figure in the affairs of the City of London but who on this occasion can be regarded as a disinterested witness, as he was talking about London outside the City, said in 1828 that there were fewer offences but that more were being detected because of improved policing – 'that is a fact I have no doubt about'. Francis Place was of the same opinion.[6]

Moreover, some observers of the criminal scene in the postwar years were not prepared to accept that any change had really taken place. In 1816 a witness had said that juvenile delinquencies had not increased 'so much as is generally supposed; I apprehend that they are more known from being more inves-

6. ibid, P.P. 1817, vii, pp. 338–9; W. L. Clay, *The Prison Chaplain; A Memoir of the Rev. John Clay* . . . , Cambridge 1861, p. 163, and cf. pp. 67–8, 113, 179–80, and his *Our Convict Systems*, Cambridge 1862, p. 12; S.C. on Police P.P. 1828, vi, p. 84; Place Papers, Add. MSS. 27,825, f.233, 27,826, ff.185, 194, 27,827, f.191, British Museum.

tigated'. He 'hoped, and was inclined to think' that there had been an increase in police activity rather than a 'real augmentation in the number of crimes'. In 1828 the Superintendent of the Hulks said that 'The increase of crime has not been much beyond the increased population of the country; I do not state that it has not increased, but not to that extent that seems to be the prevailing opinion.' 'Do not you think,' he was asked, 'that on the whole the general notion as to the great increase of crime is exaggerated, and not quite founded in fact?' and he replied: 'Certainly.' The Select Committee on Police before which he was speaking was the one which reversed the tenor of previous reports and recommended a change in the police of the metropolis, and thus gave Sir Robert Peel the opportunity to create the Metropolitan Police. However, even they did not go further than to say that they had obtained 'no information which justifies them in reporting further, than that' the increase in commitments and convictions in the metropolis must be considered to emanate

from a combination of causes. ... A portion only of the accession to Criminal Commitments, is to be deemed indicative of a proportionate increase of Crime; and even of that portion, much may be accounted for in the more ready detection and trial of culprits, also in less disinclination to prosecute, in consequence of improved facilities afforded at the courts to prosecutors and witnesses, and of the increased allowance of costs.

Edwin Chadwick observed in 1829 that for the previous six to eight years there had been a general belief that crime in the metropolis had been steadily increasing since before 1815 but that there was no evidence for this belief; all that had happened was that crime was more prosecuted and more exposed to view.[7]

This game of matching quotation to quotation could go on for a long time; until the early 1850s the argument between the

7. s.c. on Police, P.P.1816, v, pp. 169–70; ibid., P.P. 1828, vi, pp. 110, 8–9; E. Chadwick, 'Preventive Police', *London Review*, vol. i, Feb. 1829, pp. 259–62.

three points of view continued. Enough has been said, however, to show the difficulty of reaching any conclusion. It seems probable that the level of crime after about 1810 was higher than that of the previous two decades. Professor Radzinowicz has recorded the view that crime in the early nineteenth century was on the increase,[8] but despite this powerful authority it is difficult to reach any firm conclusion about changes in the amount of crime in the period from Waterloo to the middle 1850s.

When we turn to the second part of the century, from the middle 1850s to its end, we reach the second point about which a reasonable degree of certainty is attainable. There was a marked drop in juvenile crime and in the number of juvenile criminals in the 1850s and 1860s. In the 1850s some writers were still speaking of an increase of juvenile crime, but already opinion was beginning to change. The Rev. John Clay, the Chaplain of Preston Gaol, in his report for 1855–6 wrote:

Any doubts which may have been entertained as to the successful issue of reformatory schools, when the great movement in their favour took place a few years ago, ought now to be set at rest, for it has been sufficiently proved that wherever they have been earnestly and judiciously worked, there criminality has received a check.

In 1859, T. B. L. Baker, a Gloucestershire magistrate and a prominent writer on criminal matters, claimed that a reduction in juvenile crime had commenced, and he later gave details of what he thought had happened. He regarded 1856 as the year in which the decisive change took place, that being the year in which it became the general practice to commit all qualified offenders to reformatory school on a second conviction, almost regardless of the actual offence. He thought that the progress was maintained despite a minor increase of crime in 1860–63. It must be admitted that he was relying, in part at any rate, on the criminal statistics, as indeed other people may have been; but some of the names on the list of those who shared his opinions

8. L. Radzinowicz, *History of the English Criminal Law*, 1948–56, vol. i, pp. 588–9, and *Ideology and Crime . . .* , 1966, pp. 60–61.

are impressive. The Rev. John Clay has already been quoted; the others include the Rev. S. Turner, the Inspector of Reformatory Schools, in his 1859–60 Report, the Rev. W. L. Clay in 1861 and Miss Carpenter in 1861 and 1864. These are powerful authorities.[9]

The case for saying that there was a marked reduction of crime in the 1850s does not rest merely on the testimony of those active at the time. Looking back over the perspective of a decade or two, people could see that the change was not merely quantitative but qualitative as well. The hardened juvenile thief, the hordes of criminal youngsters, had disappeared from English towns. There were few children left as bad as those of twenty years before, wrote C. B. Adderley in 1874. 'It is almost impossible in these days,' wrote the *Gloucestershire Chronicle* in 1886, 'to realize the extent to which juvenile crime prevailed forty years ago.' The Royal Commission on the Reformatories and Industrial Schools of 1884 accepted that the gangs of young criminals had been broken up, and an end put to the training of boys as professional thieves.[10]

There were dissenting voices, of course. W. Hoyle, an ardent advocate of temperance, used the criminal statistics to show that an increase of crime had taken place.[11] Rather more weight should perhaps be given to the Rev. W. D. Morrison, who in 1892 argued that crime had increased during the previous thirty years, i.e. from a period just after the reformatory schools had begun to have an effect. In his view 'whatever the prisons have lost', the reformatory schools and the industrial

9. Clay, *The Prison Chaplain* ... , pp. 379, 463; T. B. L. Baker, *War With Crime* ... , 1889, pp. 44, 73–4, 226, 228–9; Report of Inspector of Reformatory Schools, P.P. 1860, xxxv, pp. 779–80; M. Carpenter, *What Shall We Do with our Pauper Children?*, 1861, p. 6, and *Our Convicts*, 1864, vol. ii, pp. 342–4.

10. C. B. Adderley, *A Few Thoughts on National Education and Punishments*, 1874, p. 47; R.C. on Reformatories and Industrial Schools, P.P. 1884, xlv, p. 10 (para. 3); *Gloucestershire Chronicle*, 11 Dec. 1886.

11. W. Hoyle, *Crime in England and Wales in the 19th Century* ... , 1876, and *Crime and Pauperism – a Letter to ... W. E. Gladstone*, Manchester 1881, passim.

schools have 'more than gained'. His argument was in part based on the number of juveniles in these three types of establishment taken together but, as Captain Anson, the Chief Constable of Staffordshire, pointed out, the increase was mainly in the number of those in industrial schools, not all of whom were offenders. Moreover, Morrison himself had the previous year said that 'crime in England is not making more rapid strides than the growth of the population'; this is at any rate an acceptance that there was no increase in crime relative to the population.[12]

It thus seems certain that a marked decline in the level of juvenile crime took place in the 1850s and 1860s, and that at the end of the century the general level of crime was lower than it had been during most of its course. The Rev. J. W. Horsley felt that the last twenty years of the century had seen a real decrease in crime and a steady improvement in conduct in general.[13] Sidney and Beatrice Webb wrote that 'It is clear that the proved criminality of the eighteenth century was enormously in excess, both absolutely and relatively, of that which prevails at the opening of the twentieth century.'[14] It may fairly be claimed that it is only in the decades indicated that there is any sign of this 'enormous' decrease taking place. R. F. Quinton just before the First World War wrote of the steady decrease of crime, and especially of serious crime, in the past thirty years. He too spoke of an 'enormous' decline, this time of the number of professional criminals; he was quite sure there was an 'actual decrease in crime'.[15] Mr B. D. White, in his survey of the history of Liverpool, notices a fall in crime

12. W. D. Morrison, 'The Increase of Crime', *Nineteenth Century*, vol. xxxi, June 1892, pp. 950–57, and *Crime and its Causes*, 1891, p. 18; G. A. Anson, *The Fluctuations of Crime*, Stafford 1895, p. 5.

13. J. W. Horsley, *Prisons and Prisoners*, 1898, pp. 19–20, and *How Criminals are Made and Prevented* . . . , 1913, pp. 27, 227, 271–2, 289–96.

14. Webb Local Government Collection, vol. xxxi, London School of Economics.

15. R. F. Quinton, *Crime and Criminals, 1876–1910*, 1910, pp. 7, 11, 74, 218–19, 246–7, and *The Modern Prison Curriculum* . . . , 1912, p. ix.

from 1875 to the end of the nineteenth century (and an increase in the first fourteen years of the twentieth).[16]

There is a further piece of evidence that a marked change had come over the criminal scene by the end of the nineteenth century. Charles Booth's survey of London in the 1890s affords an opportunity to compare conditions then with those earlier in the century; and one can only conclude that things had vastly improved. Booth gives details of specimen streets to illustrate his methods of classification, and the worst of these, St Hubert Street, is described as

An awful place; the worst street in the district. The families are mostly of the lowest class. . . . The children are rarely brought up to any kind of work, but loaf about, and no doubt form the nucleus for future generations of thieves and other bad characters. ... A number of the rooms are occupied by prostitutes of the most pronounced order.

Yet, of the fifty-eight heads of households in the street who are put into Booth's grading, only twelve fall into Class A – 'the lowest class of occasional labourers, loafers and semi-criminals'. The occupants of the street are listed tenement by tenement and family by family. In one case a member of the family is in prison, and in another the husband is just out of prison; two families have boys at industrial school (not, be it noted, reformatory school, where those convicted of the more serious offences were sent). All the people in Class A have some occupation listed, even if it is nearly always 'casual labourer' or 'hawker'. It is true that Booth warns us that 'Class A must not be confounded with the criminal classes', but he goes on to say that the lowest grade of criminals 'mix freely with Class A, and are not to be distinguished from it'. If, as we must assume, St Hubert Street is a fair specimen of the worst types of street found by Booth and his investigators, the criminal scene had vastly improved.[17]

16. B. D. White, *A History of the Corporation of Liverpool, 1835–1914*, Liverpool 1951, pp. 110–11, 191.
17. Booth, op. cit., 1st ser., vol. i, pp. 7–13, 33, 175.

Criminals and crime in the nineteenth century

Earlier in the century descriptions of the criminal districts of London laid emphasis on the existence of the separate thieves' quarter. Henry Mayhew suggested that the rookeries, the lowest areas of the town, grew up around the sanctuaries and the older hospitals of London, and it would be interesting to examine this theory and to see how far the criminal areas of the century corresponded to those of earlier periods or to those of the present day.[18] Though so ambitious a project has not been undertaken, the following pages trace some changes in the criminal districts of London in the nineteenth century and paint a picture of criminal life there during the period.

At the beginning of the nineteenth century St Giles's was firmly established in people's minds as the criminal area of London *par excellence*; indeed, it was used as a yardstick against which to measure other areas, in London or in the provinces. The core of the area was defined in 1816 by a beadle of the parish:[19]

> One part of the High Street, back of Great Russell Street, and what we call the back settlement, down the right-hand side of George Street [otherwise Dyott Street], including Buckeridge Street, Church Street, Church Lane, Bainbridge Street, Carrier Street, and Lawrence Street.

(Though there was no clear line of separation between this district and the shady area of courts and alleys to the south, the latter can more conveniently be dealt with separately.) W. A. Miles, collecting information for another official inquiry in the 1830s, noted that:[20]

> The nucleus of crime in St Giles's consists of about six streets, riddled with courts, alleys, passages, and dark entries, all leading to

18. H. Mayhew and J. Binny, *The Criminal Prisons of London* . . . , 1862, pp. 354–8. For a discussion along these lines of the criminal districts of Paris in the nineteenth century, see L. Chevalier, *Classes laborieuses et classes dangereuses à Paris pendant la première moitié du 19ème siècle*, Paris 1958, esp. pp. 99–100, 370–71.

19. s.c. on Police, P.P. 1817, vii, pp. 149–53.

20. H. Brandon (ed.), *Poverty, Mendicity and Crime* . . . , 1839, pp. 87–8, 141.

rooms and smaller tenements, crowded with a population existing in all the filth attendant upon improvidence, crime and profligacy, as if the inhabitants by common consent deem themselves only 'tenants at will', till the gallows or the hulks should require them. ... There is, moreover, an open communication at the backs of all the houses, so that directly a panic is created, men, women, and boys may be seen scrambling in all directions through the back yards and over the party walls, to effect an escape ...

The lowest grade of thieves and dissolute people live in the immediate neighbourhood of the station-house (George-street, late Dyott-street). ... The clerk of this division [of the Metropolitan Police] thinks every publican, except two, in St Giles's are fences.

Confirmation of this picture is provided by the recollections of a police officer, an inspector of lodging-houses, published by Mayhew's collaborator in 1861. Writing of the period twenty years earlier, the inspector defined the area much as had been done in 1816, declaring that the many cross-streets

with an almost endless intricacy of courts and yards crossing each other, rendered the place like a rabbit-warren . . . Both sides of Buckeridge Street, abounded in courts, particularly the north side, and these, with the connected backyards and low walls in the rear of the street, afforded an easy escape to any thief when pursued by officers of justice ... In Bainbridge Street ... were found some of the most intricate and dangerous places in this low locality. The most notorious of these was Jones Court, inhabited by coiners, utterers of base coin, and thieves ... The houses in Jones Court were connected by roof, yard, and cellar with those in Bainbridge and Buckeridge Streets ... [Off Buckeridge Street was a building known as Rats' Castle] a large dirty building occupied by thieves and prostitutes, and boys who lived by plunder ... Maynard Street and Carrier Street were occupied by costermongers and a few thieves and cadgers. George Street ... consisted of lodging-houses for tramps, thieves, and beggars, together with a few brothels.[21]

St Giles's speciality was, as it had long been, the false beggar. Miles recorded that when he visited the parish one autumn in the 1830s most of the beggars were away in the country. The

21. H. Mayhew, *London Labour and the London Poor ...* , 1861–2, vol. iv, pp. 229–300.

local inspector of police 'considers St Giles's to be empty this time of the year (September), at present the only residents are labouring men, a few hawkers, and thieves'. While the beggars were on their rounds, living by charity, pilfering and passing false money, they stayed at lodging-houses – where 'they did not see a face they had not observed at St Giles's'. They would, however, all be at home by Christmas.[22] Mayhew's informant too waxed eloquent on the beggars of St Giles's:[23]

The kitchens of some houses in Buckeridge Street afforded a specimen of life in London rarely seen elsewhere. ... There in the evenings suppers were discussed by the cadgers an alderman might almost have envied – rich steaks and onions, mutton and pork chops, fried potatoes, sausages. ... In the morning they often sat down to a breakfast of tea, coffee, eggs ... and other good things which would be considered luxuries by working people, when each discussed his plans for the day's rambles, and arranged as to the exchange of garments, bandages, etc., considered necessary to prevent recognition in those areas recently worked. ... There are among them sailors, whose largest voyage has been to Tothill Fields prison, or to Gravesend on a pleasure trip. Cripples with their arms in slings, or feet, swathed in blood-stained rags, swollen to double the size, who may be seen dancing when in their lodging at their evening revels.

The cutting of New Oxford Street had a material effect on the St Giles's criminal area. First impressions, indeed, were that the old St Giles's was no more. In the first edition of his book in 1850, Thomas Beames spoke in the past tense of what he called, with a variety of typographical emphasis, 'THE Rookery' of 'but four years since', though he noted that Church Lane received some of the people displaced from the streets to the north and used it as a standard of comparison with the worst part of Paris. He soon changed his mind; in 1851 the preface to the Second Edition of Gore's *On the Dwellings of the Poor* quoted a long note from Beames, later to appear in the Second Edition of his own book. In this George Street and Church

22. Brandon, op. cit., pp. 97, 100, 117–18.
23. Mayhew, op. cit., pp. 300–301. cf. s.c. on Mendicity, P.P. 1814–15, iii, pp. 243, 267, 278, 281–4, 289, 295, 315.

Lane are described as 'the remains of the famous Rookery – the still standing plague-spots of that Colony', and the description of the criminals and their houses uses the present tense.[24] Binny in 1861 quoted a police definition of the then remaining rookery – 'Church Lane, with its courts, a small part of Carrier Street, and a smaller portion of one side of Church Street'. It was perhaps too near New Oxford Street to remain untouched, and by 1889 Church Lane had disappeared and Booth marked the whole area on his map with the pink or red that denoted the residences of the 'fairly comfortable' or the middle classes.[25]

The area to the south of High Street St Giles and Broad Street also had a bad reputation. Seven Dials and the streets around it, Drury Lane and the turnings off it on either side (especially Short's Garden and Parker Street), Covent Garden to the south – these places were for much of the nineteenth century regarded as the haunts of thieves and prostitutes. As someone put it in 1816, because it was so near the theatres 'the girls lodge round there: Drury Lane, and the parts adjoining, are quite full of them; it is quite handy for them to go on with their purposes'.[26] The clearances to the north crowded people into the streets around Seven Dials and the upper part of Drury Lane, and it became a principal district for the low lodging-houses.[27]

By 1880 Ritchie found that Drury Lane had a certain shabby respectability, but the side-streets and courts were as bad as ever. Charles Booth declared in 1891 that 'the dark side [of Central London] lies about Drury Lane. From Seven Dials going east the tone gets lower and lower till we reach that black patch consisting of Macklin Street, Shelton Street and Parker Street.' The district was still noted for low lodging-houses – 'for

24. T. Beames, *The Rookeries of London, Past, Present and Prospective*, 1st edition, 1850, pp. xii, 30–39, 46–63, 129, 2nd edition, 1852, pp. 29–38; M. Gore, *On the Dwellings of the Poor* . . . , 2nd edition, 1851, pp. vii-xiii.

25. Mayhew, op. cit., vol. iv, pp. 281, 301; Booth, op. cit., map of 1889.

26. s.c. on Police, P.P. 1816, v, pp. 149–50.

27. T. Archer, *The Pauper, the Thief, and the Convict* . . . , 1865, pp. 65–6; G. Goodwin, *London Shadows* . . . , 1854, pp. 29, 42.

these places no better title can be found than thieves' or prostitutes' kitchens'. However, G. A. Duckworth, making further investigations for Booth in 1898, was told that the inhabitants of the lodging-houses in Parker Street and Goldsmith Street were a class above the 'Whitechapel dosser', because they all worked for a living when they could. Here again the demolition contractor did his work, and Booth's 1889 map has more black spots – denoting the residences of 'the lowest class – vicious, semi-criminal' – than that published in 1902; yet despite the improvements there were a number of bad spots around Drury Lane to the end of our period.[28]

Perhaps the most persistent of London's criminal areas was the district on the City's north-eastern boundary, the Spitalfields-Whitechapel area. This district shared with others the advantage of being just outside the City, and thus before 1829 thieves had easy access to the City's riches but could equally easily evade the attentions of its more vigorous police. After the establishment of the Metropolitan Police in 1829 the area provided the opposite advantage of easy escape into the City, whose police was not reformed until 1838–9. Even after these inequalities of policing had disappeared, however, there were advantages in being on the border between two jurisdictions. It was indeed the district outside the City limits, on the arc from Bishopsgate round to Aldgate and beyond, which figured most prominently in lists of criminal areas. The most famous street, and perhaps the key to the persistence of its reputation, was Petticoat Lane, with its unrivalled facilities for the disposal of stolen goods. 'If the King's crown were to come within half-a-mile of Petticoat-lane,' boasted a thief in 1835, 'money would be found in an hour for its purchase.'[29] Petticoat Lane was a place where petty criminals carried on much of their business – certainly selling their loot, and perhaps steal-

28. J. E. Ritchie, *Days and Nights in London*, 1890, p. 120; Booth, op. cit., 1st ser., vol. i, p. 184, vol. ii, pp. 46–82, 3rd ser., vol. ii, map between pp. 208–9; London School of Economics, Booth Collection, Police Notebooks (this valuable but neglected source is hereafter cited as Booth Collection), B. 354, pp. 97–103, 131, 135–7, 145.

29. Brandon, op. cit., p. 101.

ing some of it from the crowds in the street-market. Brick Lane and Church Lane were main thoroughfares where petty criminals could steal and could fence their takings. However, the main residences of the poorer classes, criminal and non-criminal, were in the mass of streets and alleys between Petticoat Lane and Brick Lane. The principal street was Wentworth Street, which enjoyed a bad reputation even above the area in which it was situated. In the 1830s the area figured frequently in W. A. Miles's notes, one notable feature being that six consecutive houses in Wentworth Street, Nos. 102–107, were said to be brothels – 'these houses have an outlet at top to facilitate escape; so have many others in this division'. In 1851 Mayhew bracketed Wentworth Street with St Giles's as 'the worst places, both as regards filth and immorality', and though St Giles's soon dropped out of the lists Whitechapel did not. Essex Street, Church Street, Fashion Street, Flower and Dean Street, Thrawl Street, Lower Keate (or Kate) Street and George Yard – these streets, and their courts and alleys, were the worst part of the area.[30]

A marked reduction in the size of the criminal area was brought about in the 1850s, when Commercial Street was cut. Mayhew's collaborator Binny defined as criminal the area enclosed between Commercial Street and Brick Lane, Church Street and Wentworth Street: it contained '800 thieves, vagabonds, beggars, and prostitutes, a large proportion of whom may be traced to the old criminal inhabitants of the now extinct Essex Street and old Rose Lane'. In the early 1860s George Yard 'and its outlying network of unsavoury streets, courts and alleys' was regarded as one of the most dangerous districts in London, but by the beginning of the 1880s it was 'greatly improved'. By that time Flower and Dean Street, though it too had now 'probably less of a criminal element in its population' than hitherto, was the worst street of the area – 'one naturally assumes that no good can come out of Flower and Dean Street'. Indeed, at the end of the century a police officer could use as the

30. ibid., p. 102; Mayhew, op. cit., vol. i, pp. 246, 248–9, 252–7, 317 (cf. cover of part no. 21, dated 3rd May 1851).

standard of a bad street 'Flower and Dean Street in the old days'.[31]

On Booth's map of the area published in 1889 a smaller area is coloured black, though two other notorious centres had developed, Dorset Street and Great Pearl Street. When G. A. Duckworth, one of Booth's secretaries, visited the area in 1898, change was in progress, partly because of the work of the demolition contractor and partly because of the coming of the Jews.[32] C. Russell, writing in 1900 a not entirely favourable account of the Jewish immigration to East London, said that 'there are certain districts of Whitechapel, which – before they were over-run by the foreigners – were haunted by roughs and criminals of the worst description. ... These are now exceptionally quiet and orderly.' His co-author H. S. Lewis added that 'whole streets, formerly Gentile, have within the last three years become almost completely foreign'. He listed some streets, which had been black on Booth's map, as being 'now Jewish and respectable'; they include Thrawl Street and Flower and Dean Street, though he noted that 'a few bad houses' remained there. The streets of Whitechapel regarded as Gentile by Russell and Lewis were marked as black areas by Booth. This is true also of Dorset Street to the north, 'the worst street in respect of poverty, misery and vice in the whole of London', Duckworth was told, especially noted for the prostitutes, bullies and thieves who thronged its lodging-houses. Indeed, Booth wrote that it would probably be 'the Jews alone' who would turn the prostitutes out of Great Pearl Street.[33] By 1906 Olive Malvery could declare that 'Today, the Brick Lane end of Went-

31. ibid., vol. iv, pp. 304, 311–16; J. Hollingshead, *Ragged London in 1861*, pp. 40–52; Ritchie, op. cit., pp. 133–45; G. H. Pike, *Pity for the Perishing* ..., 1887, pp. 91–7; Booth Collection, B. 353, p. 213.

32. The writer should declare an interest: his grandparents were amongst the immigrants in question – 'clean windows' was Duckworth's only comment on the court where one pair of them lived.

33. Booth, op. cit., 3rd ser., vol. ii, p. 7, map between pp. 110–11; Booth Collection, B.351, pp. 53–5, 103–9, 112, 117, 123–31, 135–7, B.355, p. 185; C. Russell and H. S. Lewis, *The Jew in London* ..., 1900, pp. 13–14, 176 and n., 196, and map.

worth Street, Whitechapel, is one of the most un-English spots in the British Isles'; some lodging-houses in Brick Lane, Flower and Dean Street and Dorset Street were practically the only houses in the neighbourhood occupied by English people – and they were an 'oasis of vagabondage'.[34]

In 1816 Field Lane, Smithfield, was the most notorious of a cluster of bad streets, which included Saffron Hill, Shoe Lane, and courts and alleys as well. There were receivers in Field Lane, and many young thieves lived around there. In the 1830s the area received advertisement from being made the scene of Fagin's activities, and its notoriety increased in the 1840s. During the demolitions for Farringdon Road, two houses in West Street were found to contain 'dark closets, trap-doors, sliding panels, and means of escape'; said to have been built two hundred years before for criminal purposes, the houses were put on exhibition and attracted large crowds. This did not mean that the area ceased to be used by the criminals: the building work was suspended because of a legal dispute, and the cleared land became a rendezvous of the ragged and homeless, while the untouched houses retained their former population. Thomas Beames regarded Saffron Hill – the bounds being Ely Place, Mutton Hill, Holborn Hill and the boundary of Clerkenwell parish – as having a good claim to second place (behind St Giles's) among London's criminal areas. It continued to attract attention, so much so indeed that Hollingshead in 1861 wrote 'We have heard enough of Saffron Hill'; he felt that the area was no longer one of the worst parts of London. Others agreed with him: the completion of Farringdon Road and other clearances had driven the criminals away. Some of the lower class went westward and northward to the courts around Grays Inn Road and Baldwin's Gardens, but most went east to Clerkenwell.[35]

34. O. C. Malvery, *The Soul Market* . . . , 1906, pp. 217, 278.
35. s.c. on Police, p.p. 1816, v, pp. 41, 263; ibid., p.p. 1817, vii, pp. 349–51, 355, 429; J. Garwood, *The Million-Peopled City* . . . , 1853, pp. 45–8, 54; Beames, op. cit., 2nd edition, pp. 64–6, 75–8, 129, 349–50; Hollingshead, op. cit., pp. 13–14; G. Godwin, *London Shadows* . . . , 1854, pp. 10, 15, 48, and *Town Swamps* . . . , 1859, pp. 2, 9–10.

The Whitecross Street part of St Luke's, Clerkenwell – that street, Golden Lane, Bunhill Row and Grub Street – was 'the known resort of thieves and prostitutes', the Select Committee on Police was told in 1817. 'If the magistrates were to refuse licences to all those houses against which they have had complaints, they would suppress at least one half of those in Whitecross Street, Golden Lane, and the alleys leading out of them.' This was another district that had the advantage of lying at the border between two jurisdictions. Its importance in criminal London was enhanced by an access of population from St Giles's and from the Field Lane area, and it succeeded to the latter's role of housing fences – by the beginning of the 1860s there were said to be forty 'leaving shops' (petty pawnbrokers and fences) in the two streets.[36]

From the 1860s the rising value of land drove the criminal area northward across Old Street. On Booth's 1889 map the part of Clerkenwell with the most extensive black areas was that around Old Street and Goswell Road, but the shift to less valuable districts continued, at any rate as far as the poorer members of the criminal class were concerned. G. A. Duckworth was told in 1898 that the Old Street-Clerkenwell area was still a great receivers' centre – 'the melting-pot of London', where practically all stolen silver and jewellery was fenced – and it still had black spots where pickpockets and housebreakers resided, but, the police told him, only the skilled criminals remained and the rough working class had moved out. The rough working class and the lesser criminals who were indistinguishable from them had gone to Hoxton.[37]

Hoxton had had a bad reputation at the beginning of the century, when it had been said:[38]

The village of Haggerstone [part of Hoxton] is inhabited chiefly by brick-makers of the very lowest class of society, and perhaps

36. s.c. on Police, P.P. 1817, vii, pp. 159, 225–7; Mayhew, op. cit., vol. iv, p. 237; Hollingshead, op. cit., p. 18; Pike, op. cit., pp. 66–7.

37. Booth Collection, B.353, pp. 5–9, 33–39, 45–53, 63, 135, 157–9, 165–7, 177, 221–5, B.354, pp. 11–13.

38. s.c. on Mendicity, P.P. 1814–15, iii, p. 308.

some of them of the very worst characters; so much so, that no man or woman towards dark will walk across that way towards Hackney, though it might be somewhat nearer; and so bad, that if a thief was pursued and ran to Haggerstone, no constable or runner would go beyond a certain line: it has been called The City of Refuge.

Moreover, the Rev. A. O. M. Jay's district of the Old Nichol – which appears in fiction as the Old Jago, scene of Dicky Perrott's exploits – was not far away.[39] But the area did not figure prominently in lists of criminal districts for most of the century, and Hoxton did not receive special mention in this context in Booth's 1891 volume. However, in 1902 Booth started his account of it 'Hoxton is the leading criminal quarter of London, and indeed of all England', and it had by then become the standard of comparison used by police officers, much as St Giles's had been used earlier. Professor Higgins crushed the troublesome stranger by identifying his accent as that of Hoxton, and perhaps this had more impact for the audiences who first heard it than it has today.[40]

Another notorious criminal area was the district south and west of Westminster Abbey. According to Miles in the 1830s, it housed adult cracksmen, but it was principally the resort of prostitute-thieves and the male thieves who lived with them. So notorious was one court for young thieves that 'the police would not allow a bundle to be carried into or out of the court without searching them, and that all stolen goods were consequently "fenced", or disposed of before the boys came home'. The fences were however only in a small way of business, and more valuable goods had to be taken eastwards to areas around the City of London. About the same time, a police report noted that some of the low prostitutes who walked the streets of Lambeth lived around Tothill Fields.[41]

39. For the connection between the Old Nichol and the Old Jago, see P. L. Keating's edition of A. Morrison, *A Child of the Jago*, 1969, pp. 23–33.
40. Booth, op. cit., 1st ser., vol. ii, appendix pp. 17–18, 3rd ser., vol. ii, p. 111, map between pp. 168–9; G. B. Shaw, *Pygmalion*, 1912, Act I.
41. Brandon, op. cit., pp. 45, 113, 134–5; Public Record Office, H.O. 73/3.

Charles Dickens in 1850 called attention to the area known as Devil's Acre – the area around Pye Street. Though the final line of Victoria Street was chosen to cut through the worst part of Westminster, there was no great improvement. Hollingshead described the resultant overcrowding, declaring that there were 70 black streets, with the worst kinds of courts, either side of it. Orchard Street was like Field Lane 'in the old days', and Pye Street was the 'openly acknowledged high street of thieves and prostitutes'. The area had many common lodging houses. Beames spoke of the inhabitants using violence or obstruction to defeat forays by the police.[42]

Improvements began in the late 1870s, and by 1889 Booth's map had only a few black spots around Great Peter Street, though the 1891 text described the people as having a vicious look. Booth's secretary who visited the area in the later survey found much evidence of prostitution and plenty of people of low class, but the criminal area had been further reduced by major clearances, which were in progress at the time south of Victoria Street and east of Rochester Row. Chadwick Street was still notorious for thieves and prostitutes, as were parts of Great Peter Street and Marsham Street. There is however rather less black on the 1902 map than the earlier one, and though the text of 1902 declared that 'At present the disreputable classes are still very much in evidence in Westminster. ... There is nothing much lower to be found anywhere in London than the life led in some of the Westminster courts and streets,' yet clearly the area was not as bad as it had once been.[43]

Another part of London with a long-standing reputation as the home of criminals was Southwark. The Rev. G. Weight, writing in 1841, declared that the public house where Jonathan Wild had kept his horses was still to be seen in Red Cross Street,

42. *Household Words*, vol. i, 1850, p. 297; Hollingshead, op. cit., pp. 9, 102–12; Beames, op. cit., 2nd edition, pp. 115, 125–31, 133, 202–3.

43. Booth, op. cit., 1st ser., vol. i, p. 243, 3rd ser., vol. iii, p. 79, map between pp. 92–3; Booth Collection, B.360, pp. 193, 203, 207–9, 223–5, 235, 247–9.

one of the main thoroughfares of the Mint, the worst part of the Borough. The Mint had developed its character as a refuge for criminals from the days when it conferred an immunity from process for debt, but long after those days it was notorious as the resort of criminals. Kent Street (the later Tabard Street) was almost as bad – 'in Kent Street there are houses which it is notorious are filled every night with desperate thieves,' a Select Committee was told in 1828.[44]

Things changed little. In 1861 Hollingshead wrote that 'No speculator has ever been bold enough to grapple with the back streets – the human warrens – on the south side of the metropolis; to start from Bermondsey, on the borders of Deptford, and wriggle through the existing miles of dirt, vice, and crime as far as the Lambeth Marshes.' This mass of poverty was dotted with 'dark areas of crime, and covered everywhere with the vilest sores of prostitution'. Scores of streets were 'filled with nothing but thieves, brown, unwholesome tramps' lodging-houses, and smokey receptacles for stolen goods'. One of Mayhew's collaborators wrote in similar terms of his visits to the Mint and Kent Street, and to the only slightly less criminal areas around Union Street and Friar Street.[45]

In 1891 Charles Booth wrote of 'nests of courts and alleys' around St George's church, 'still harbouring an appalling amount of destitution not unmixed with crime', even though the Marshalsea Road had been cut through the Mint. The Mint still contained 'a very large amount of poverty and lawlessness, particularly in the many common lodging-houses'. The Kent Street area, however, was commented on in slightly more favourable terms: 'One of the poorest spots in London. Main part just struggling with poverty; much apathy, drunkenness, and prostitution ... a poor ignorant lot of people in very casual work ... a fringe of the semi-criminal class.' However, the 1889

44. G. Weight, 'Statistics of the Parish of St George the Martyr Southwark', *Journal of the Statistical Society*,, vol. iii, Apr. 1841, pp. 50–71; s.c. on Police, P.P. 1828, vi, p. 154.
45. Hollingshead, op. cit., pp. 9, 165–79; Mayhew, op. cit., vol. iv, pp. 278–80, 281, 330–33.

Central London Rookeries

N

Scale
0   ¼   ½ MILE

City Boundaries

New Roads   NEW OXFORD ST

FARRINGDON RD.

SAFFRON HILL

FIELD LA.

CHART

CHARLOTTE ST

ST

NEW OXFORD ST.

MUSEUM ST

GT. RUSSELL

DYOTT ST

HIGH HOLBORN   HOLBORN

SHOE LANE

FLEET MARKET

OXFORD ST

HIGH ST BROAD ST

DRURY LANE

FLEET STREET

WYCH ST

HOLYWELL ST

THE STRAND

RIVER THAMES

This map is based on *Pigot's New Plan of London* of *c.* 1840,
with new roads added from Bacon's *New Plan of London* of 1876

OLD STREET
GOLDEN LANE
WHITECROSS ST
BUNHILL ROW
CHISWELL ST
GRUB ST

COMMERCIAL ST
BRICK LANE
CHURCH ST
FLOWER & DEAN ST
FASHION ST
BISHOPSGATE
OSBORN ST
MONTAGUE ST
HIGH ST
WENTWORTH ST.
HOUNDSDITCH
PETTICOAT LA.
WHITECHAPEL
CHURCH LA.

City of London

ALDGATE
COMMERCIAL RD.

ROSEMARY LANE

map showed black in both areas. The 1902 volume declared that Booth, revisiting the district after ten years, 'brought away the same black picture, the same depression of soul'. His secretary's notes provide support. The whole area between Union Street, Borough High Street, Borough Road and Blackfriars Road was still bad – and nothing could be worse than the narrower portion north and east of Marshalsea Road and Southwark Bridge Road, or the area between Long Lane and Tabard Street. The Superintendent of the M Division told the inquirer that the low population of his district, which included Southwark and much else besides, at least did not include the beggars called into existence north of the river by the possibility of casual charity in the street; most people in South London, he felt, would take work if opportunity offered. Crime was however associated with the activities of low prostitutes, just as it was across the river. Here as elsewhere demolition had removed many of the worst places, but once more the inhabitants had merely crowded in on others as near as they could to their old haunts. The 1902 map shows more black than the earlier one, and Charles Booth's despondency was clearly justified.[46]

There were of course other well-known criminal haunts in London.[47] A prescient observer forecast in 1828 that the Lisson Grove area of Marylebone would soon become a new St Giles's, and he was proved right. A policeman told W. A. Miles in the 1830s that

Lisson Grove is the haunt of thieves. . . . The worst and of all sorts, were about Lisson Grove; but they spread themselves over London by day, in order to work (i.e. thieve). The neighbourhood is swarming with youth of both sexes, from eight to twenty years of age – all thieves. He thinks they fence the property in the Grove.

In 1852 the area was said to have become 'of late' one of the worst parts of London, sharing with others the incursion of

46. Booth, op. cit., 1st ser., vol. i, pp. 279–80, vol. ii, app. pp. 34–5, 49, 3rd ser., vol. iv, p. 8, map between pp. 170–71; Booth Collection, B.367, pp. 119–23, B.363, pp. 109–11, 148–52, 171–9, B.364, pp. 21, 33.
47. Wych Street and Holywell Street were the centres of the trade in pornographic literature.

thieves from other rookeries as they were reduced in size. However, Booth recorded that there had been in Lisson Grove 'a "great toning-up", caused by removals, resulting in less poverty and less crime'.[48] But the removals did not of course alter the fact that criminals, like those of other callings, tended to live in specialized localities, and the criminal areas persisted long after the end of the period with which this book is concerned.

London's criminal problem was inevitably larger in scale than that of other places, but it was different in kind as well. The London thief was recognized to be in a class of his own; he was more skilled than others, but above all more hardened and irreclaimable. London abounded in pickpockets and in prostitutes. There were 'more pickpockets in and about London than in all Europe beside', wrote someone in 1805;[49] they naturally haunted the busier and better streets and the theatres and other places attracting well-to-do people – coaching inns at one period, railway stations later on. In this field also Holdsworth claimed superiority for the City police, saying that his force kept down the number of pickpockets in the City. He told how a notorious pickpocket was arrested:

Soames just came through Temple-bar to take a peep in the City, and just beyond the Temple-gate he picked a pocket, and was retiring with the pocket-book he had taken, when he was seized; one of our patrole saw him do it, and immediately took him by the collar, and found the gentleman whose pocket he saw picked; the case was as plain and clear as possible.

Soames showed a few years later that he had learned his lesson. He had had the good fortune to be brought back from transportation and released because his conviction had been based on the evidence of Vaughan, a police officer who was convicted in 1816 of perjury, and was thus able to take up his career once again. In 1821 he was leader of a gang of pickpockets which worked the Strand between Somerset House and Temple Bar

48. s.c. on Police, P.P. 1828, vi., p. 133; Brandon, op, cit., p. 138; s.c. on Juvenile Offenders, P.P. 1852–3, xxiii, p. 219 (qq. 2211–13); Booth, op. cit., 3rd ser., vol. i, p. 197.

49. G. Barrington, *New London Spy for 1805*, 4th ed., 1805, p. 61.

but was careful not to go into the City.[50] In 1837, too, young-sters were said to prowl around Whitechapel until 8 p.m. when the City day police went off duty and it was safe for them to go along Aldgate and up to the Mansion House.[51] There were of course some pickpockets at work in the City, particularly be-tween Temple Bar and Cheapside and in and near the Bank of England, especially on the days on which it paid out dividends in cash.

Picking pockets seems to have flourished in London over much of the century, but the detailed description given by Mayhew's collaborators in 1861 was probably written whilst a change was in progress, for there was about that time a re-duction in the number of the skilled boy-pickpockets. T. B. L. Baker said that in 1859 there were in London 456 boys under sixteen years of age with four or more convictions, but that by 1863 there were not ten.[52] Whether or not this precise claim was justified, there are grounds for accepting that a dra-matic change did come in this field.

London was noted for the number of its prostitutes as well. The Select Committee on Police of 1816–18 was left in no doubt on the matter. The Chief Metropolitan Magistrate accepted that there were 'crowds of women, some in a state of intoxi-cation, infesting the streets and annoying the passengers during the best part of the night. . . . Amongst the great capitals of the Continent, Paris in particular, no such evil as exists in the streets of London is to be found.'[53] Patrick Colquhoun did not demur when it was suggested that 'It is a well-known fact, that in no other Capital in the world is there the same outrageous be-haviour on the part of prostitutes infesting the streets, which there is in this City.' William Fielding, like his father Henry a

50. s.c. on Police, P.P. 1816, v, p. 263; L. B. Allen, *Brief Considerations on the Present State of the Police of the Metropolis*, 1821, pp. 9–11. I have assumed that the two references are to the same person.

51. s.c. on Police, P.P. 1837, xii, p. 488 (q. 1654).

52. Mayhew, op. cit., vol. iv, pp. 303–10; Baker, op. cit., p. 229 (cf. pp. 23, 74).

53. s.c. on Police, P.P. 1816, v, pp. 23, 50; ibid., P.P. 1817, vii, pp. 405, 524; Place Papers, Add. MSS. 27,826, f.195, British Museum.

police magistrate, said: 'About this town, within our present district of Westminster, or half way down the Strand towards Temple-bar, there would every night be found above five hundred or one thousand of that description of wretches: how they can gain any profit by their prostitution one can hardly conceive.' (William Fielding's evidence provides an excuse for quoting Francis Place's comment on him: 'as profligate an old fellow as perhaps any of his day'.) The prostitutes were becoming bolder, thought another witness: 'It is now become the practice of girls of the town (those of an alluring description) to parade the most frequented of the city streets at noonday.'

Supporting evidence can be found elsewhere. In 1816 Defauconpret said that there were many more prostitutes in London than in Paris, and that the danger of theft was much greater.[54] In 1826 another Continental visitor commented on 'the unhappy women with whom London swarms. ... In no country on earth is this afflicting and humiliating spectacle so openly exhibited as in the religious and decorous England.'[55] In 1826, too, it was said that in Cheapside and the Poultry and at the Bank of England the prostitutes were to be found 'almost in stands, like the hackney coaches'[56] – and this by an alderman and former Lord Mayor who was defending the policing system of the City!

Things may have been changing by mid century. A German visitor in 1835 felt that the number of prostitutes in London was no greater than in Paris. Frederic Hill wrote in 1853 that 'effrontery' by London prostitutes was 'becoming a fact of the past'. J. E. Ritchie wrote in 1857 of prostitutes stopping almost every man in the Strand, mildly in the early evening, with rudeness and freedom later on when they had drunk more, and he kept the remark in the present tense in the revised edition of his

54. A. J. B. Defauconpret, *Quinze jours à Londres, à la fin de 1815,* Paris 1816, p. 98.

55. *A Regency Visitor: the English Tour of Prince Peuckler-Muskau described in his letters, 1826–8,* 1957, pp. 83–4.

56. Cutting from an unnamed paper, Place Papers, Add. MSS. 27,828, f.128, British Museum.

book in 1869; but he changed some sentences of the surrounding description into the past tense, and the chapter-title became 'The Strand as it was'. It is, however, true that Hippolyte Taine wrote in the 1860s of seeing twenty harlots every hundred steps in the Haymarket and the Strand. In 1908 Thomas Holmes wrote of a great increase over the last twenty years in the number of prostitutes in London (and other large towns), but none of the later descriptions are couched in terms approaching those of the post-Waterloo period.[57]

At the beginning of the century, before the establishment of the Metropolitan Police, London had also a bad reputation because of the frequency of street robberies – the snatching of property from people in the street. An increase in the frequency of such offences towards the end of 1820 led to a reorganization of the Bow Street patrols, and this brought about an immediate improvement, according to those connected with the courts at any rate. In 1829, however, a writer could say:

> Street robberies have multiplied in the metropolis to a dangerous extent, and are perpetrated in the most daring manner. Gentlemen have frequently their watches plucked out of the fob, or their pocket-book or purse snatched or cut away, in the most crowded thoroughfares. . . . Robberies in the street are more frequent in the day-time, and in the most busy thoroughfares.

Others about the same time made similar comments. The line between this sort of crime and picking pockets was of course a narrow one, but it seems that the Metropolitan Police was able to check the snatching of valuables if not the more careful picking of pockets, for a London judge said in 1833 that 'Street robberies are becoming comparatively very rare; there are very few cases now occur of street robberies, which I attribute entirely to the vigilant conduct of the police.' Little is heard of

57. F. von Raumer, *England in 1835* . . . , English trans. 1836, vol. ii, p. 24; F. Hill, op. cit., p. 79; J. E. Ritchie, *The Night Side of London*, 1st ed., 1857, p. 37, revised and enlarged ed., 1869, pp. 187–9; H. Taine, *Notes on England*, English trans. 1872, pp. 36, 44–6, T. Holmes, *Known to the Police*, 1908, p. 17.

street robberies after 1829 until the very different outbreaks in the 1850s and 1860s.[58]

The most famous of these outbreaks was of course the wave of garrotting in London in the autumn of 1862. This was not the first; there had been a similar one in Manchester in 1850 and another in London in the 1850s, but neither of them received the publicity of the 1862 epidemic. The effect of the latter was described in the *Cornhill Magazine* in 1863: 'Once more the streets of London are unsafe by day or night. . . . The public dread has almost become a panic.' The writer went on to describe the method used by the garrotters:

> The first stall lifts his hat from his head in token that all is clear beyond; the second stall makes no sign to the contrary; and then the third ruffian, coming swiftly up, flings his right arm round the victim, striking him smartly on the forehead. Instinctively he throws his head back, and in that movement loses every chance of escape. His throat is fully offered to his assailant, who instantly embraces it with his left arm, the bone just above the wrist being pressed against the 'apple' of the throat. At the same moment the garotter, dropping his right hand, seizes the other's left wrist; and thus supplied with a powerful lever, draws him back upon his breast and there holds him. The 'nasty man's' part is done.

A few thieves introduced the technique, and by skill (maintained by regular practice) and careful study of the victim before the attack they avoided inflicting permanent injury. Other less careful thieves copied them. 'More brutal and inexpert thieves press the fingers of both hands into the victim's throat; others use a short stick, which is passed across the throat from behind, and hauled back at both ends – a plan seldom adopted, though.' Greenwood in 1888 interviewed a retired garrotter who added a further detail: 'If a man shows fight and struggles, a hit in the pit of the stomach quiets him. If he takes it easy, nothing more happens to him, than a extra squeeze of his throat before he's left, just to keep him still long enough for us to get off.'

58. s.c. on Police, P.P. 1828, vi, pp. 35, 256, 269; Wade, op. cit., pp. 194–5; s.c. on Police, P.P. 1834, xvi, p. 299 (q. 3922).

Criminals and crime in the nineteenth century

The streets of London were dangerous places, day and night, for some months, and many people carried arms. Flogging was introduced as a penalty, and was said by some to have stopped garrotting, but other contemporary observers attributed the cessation of the offence to the conviction of the criminals concerned and to warnings given by the police to convicts on ticket-of-leave. One later outbreak appears to have been, like the garrotting, mainly a London affair; a well-publicized robbery in June 1867 led to a fashion for such crimes which seems to have persisted at least until October 1868.[59]

Many of the young thieves described earlier were of course Londoners or spent part of their time in the capital; the Select Committees of Police of 1816–18 and 1828 whose reports have been quoted so frequently were concerned with the metropolis and not the country as a whole. Petty theft abounded both in the central areas and in the suburbs. Youngsters would snatch goods from kitchen-areas, stalls, shops or vehicles, would pilfer whenever the opportunity presented itself. We can believe the witness who in 1828 said: 'Every shopkeeper in the Strand, and in Bond-street is well acquainted with these juvenile offenders.'[60]

Though London was the main centre of the criminal class, it was by no means the only one. Some of the larger provincial towns were recognized to be criminal centres in their own right, receiving criminals from London and other towns from time to time, making their own contributions to the criminal problems of other places. It is possible to make a distinction between the major towns. In one group fell London, Liverpool, Bristol and perhaps Bath (which had a claim to be regarded as a 'major town' when crime was under consideration). In these towns the

59. Report of Chief Constable, *Criminal and Miscellaneous Returns, Manchester Police, 1850*, Manchester 1851; *Cornhill Magazine*, vol. vii, Jan. 1863, pp. 79–81; J. Greenwood, *The Policeman's Lantern; Strange Stories of London Life*, 1888, p. 52; L. O. Pike, *A History of Crime in England* . . . , 1876, vol. ii, p. 575; R. and F. Davenport-Hill, *The Recorder of Birmingham: a Memoir of Matthew Davenport Hill* . . . , 1878, pp. 192, 195–202; Baker, op. cit., p. 20; Departmental Committee on Corporal Punishment, P.P. 1937–8, ix, pp. 549–50 (para. 56(a)).
60. S.C. on Police, P.P. 1828, vi, p. 35.

ypical juvenile criminal looked to crime alone for his livelihood (though many mixed begging and petty pilfering as occasion served). In the other group were Manchester,
Birmingham and Leeds. In these towns, in addition to a number
of criminals similar to those of the type just defined, there were
also juveniles who had honest jobs, or who would take one if
possible, but who regularly engaged in crime as a species of
bye-employment.[61] London's crime has already been described in some detail and this will serve as an example of the
towns of the first type. Manchester is a convenient example of
the second type of town.

Captain Willis, the Chief Constable of Manchester, told a
correspondent of the *Morning Chronicle* in 1849 that 'there is
. . a considerable floating criminal population in Manchester, a
considerable fixed criminal population, and a smaller number
of persons who are known both to work and steal.'[62] The
difference from the towns of the first type lies in the existence of
this group of criminals who both worked and stole. (It would
obviously be absurd to claim that there was nobody in this
category in London; the point is that the towns of the second
type had an identifiable group of such people.) The town's
youngsters were therefore not the hardened, skilled thieves of
London or Liverpool. As Faucher put it, there were not so
many professional thieves there as in the 'capitals of commerce
and aristocracy', but the working population committed minor
but repeated crimes.[63] Much juvenile crime was committed as
a side-line by those who, when possible, took honest jobs.
Though of course cotton and other materials were stolen from
the mills or other places of work if opportunity served, the
trades of Manchester did not lend themselves to theft from
one's place of work, and in consequence these boys stole more
when out of work, their crimes being predominantly pilfering
of objects displayed in shops or markets or carelessly exposed
outside houses, etc.

61. This group will later be further subdivided – see p. 185.
62. *Morning Chronicle*, 29 Oct. 1849; cf. 25 Oct. 1849.
63. L. Faucher, *Etudes sur l'Angleterre*, Paris 1845, vol. i, pp. 330–31.

There was, of course, a group of hardened thieves of the type described earlier; as the quotation in the previous paragraph shows, Captain Willis regarded this group as the largest part of the criminal population of the town. These people did not seek work in the mills but lived entirely by crime – earlier descriptions of the hardened thieves and their prostitutes drew partly on Manchester evidence. There was frequent movement of such people between Manchester and Liverpool. To the door of this class can no doubt be laid the more skilled crimes, such as the theft of lead and other materials from new buildings which was said to be prevalent in Manchester. They were presumably also responsible for the garrotting outbreak in 1850. Manchester had its Fagins, too; 'One-armed Dick' kept a shop near the Oldham Road in the early 1850s and employed a number of youngsters in stealing lead and other metals and articles.[64]

As in other towns, Manchester's criminals tended to gather in rookeries. The worst of these, and the yardstick by which the others were judged, was that called Angel Meadow or, from its main thoroughfare, Charter Street – or even just 'the Street'. Charter Street, Blakeley or Bleakley Street and Dantzig Street were names used at various periods for sections of what is now known by the last-mentioned name; in 1826 it did not extend south of Hanover Street. The street was said in 1849 to be 'entirely composed of lodging-houses, and is well known to the police throughout the kingdom'.[65] The Dog and Duck in Charter Street was 'the house of call for the swell mob of Manchester and the superior class of "prigs" '. In 1897 Angel Meadow was defined[66] as being bounded by Rochdale Road (the former St Georges Road), Miller Street, Cheetham Hill Road (the former York Street) and Gould Street, but earlier in the century it extended south of Miller Street to include the streets and alleys between Long Millgate and Smithfield Market.

64. See p. 119.
65. *Morning Chronicle*, 12 Nov. 1849.
66. J. E. Mercier, *The Conditions of Life in Angel Meadow* (read to Manchester Statistical Society, 28 April 1897), Manchester n.d., p. 161.

Deansgate was the core of the second criminal area, the streets and alleys on either side of it from Bridge Street southward having an evil reputation. The building of the Central Station and its lines in the 1870s led to the demolition of the south-eastern corner of this rookery, and the widening of Deansgate which began in the same decade eliminated many of the interconnecting courts and alleyways which had made the area so suitable from the criminal point of view. Other criminal areas of the town included Canal Street, London Road and the Ancoats district, together with Gaythorn Street, Salford. However, by the 1870s only Charter Street, Deansgate and Canal Street still contained a criminal population, and even these rookeries were not what they had once been.

Liverpool resembled London most closely of all the towns in most respects, though it was apparently second to Birmingham in the number of its juvenile delinquents. The juvenile thieves of Liverpool were hardened professionals, and they were supported by a criminal area which approached the level of the worst parts of London. Abraham Hume, an incumbent of a poor district of the city and an indefatigable pamphleteer with a passion for detail, declared that the parish (as opposed to the borough) of Liverpool could be divided into an upper and a lower part by a line along Scotland Road, Byrom Street, Lime Street, Renshaw Street, Berry Street and Great George's Street. The lower part, that nearer the river, contained 'the worst characters of every kind: the convicted felon, the professional thief, the receiver of stolen goods, the drunken blasphemer'. It contained streets

which are a terror to a solitary policeman, and into which a respectable person rarely ventures. One street contains very few families who pursue lawful occupations; and others are an annoyance not only to the town but to the surrounding neighbourhood.

In such streets, said Hume, a convict returned from transportation was 'a young man that has been abroad, God help him', a captured burglar 'a poor boy who got into trouble', the most wicked among the gentler sex 'an "unfortunate girl" '. Hume

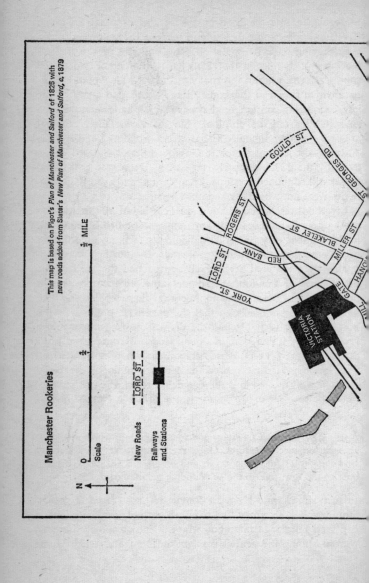

Manchester Rookeries

This map is based on Pigot's *Plan of Manchester and Salford* of 1825 with new roads added from Slater's *New Plan of Manchester and Salford, c. 1879*

N

Scale

0   ¼   ½ MILE

New Roads — — LORD ST

Railways and Stations

YORK ST.

LORD ST

RED BANK

ROGERS ST

BLAKELEY ST

MILLER ST

HANOVER

GOULD ST

ST GEORGES RD

VICTORIA STATION

GATE

MILL

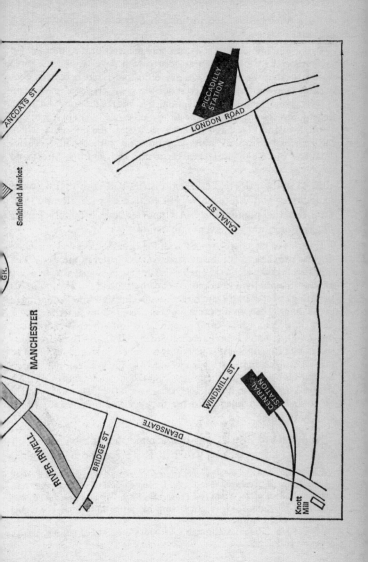

had no doubt about the distinction between the poor and the criminal districts.

Crime and immorality, but especially the class of the latter known as the Social Evil, are often associated with poverty, and the three centres usually lie not far distant; but there is no necessary connection between them. In Liverpool the great artery of pauperism is Marybone and its continuation, on both sides of which the poorest streets are found. The artery of crime, again, is Scotland Road, Scotland Place, and Byrom Street; while the line along which the principal streets of houses for immoral purposes lies, reaches from the old Zoological Gardens to the end of Lime Street and Copperas Hill.

In 1858 the principal criminal district had been that between Dale Street and Whitechapel, but clearances were already thinning out the population.[67] An undated but probably earlier description of the area went into details:[68]

Entering Whitechapel from the Old Haymarket, we find ourselves in close proximity with the most notorious district in the town. The first street on the right is Spitalfields – a name associated with every phase of depravity and crime ... Crosshall Street ... also pours its polluting streams into Dale Street at one end, and into Whitechapel at the other. Then, in the same line, comes notorious Peter Street – a dark *cul de sac*, which can be approached only from Whitechapel, or by a little outlet from Crosshall Street. All these streets are intersected by so many alleys, open into so many courts, and lead into so many passages, that a stranger would have the greatest difficulty in finding his way out of them. . . . There is a whole cluster of dark streets crowded with inhabitants unsurpassed for their proficiency in crime and almost unequalled for the depth of infamy into which they have fallen.

Another bad district was that around Ben Jonson Street, off Scotland Place, and the Vauxhall Road ran through criminal

67. A. Hume, *Missions at Home, or a Clergyman's Account of a Portion of the Town of Liverpool*, 1850. pp. 15–16, *Condition of Liverpool* ..., Liverpool 1858, p. 24, *State and Prospects of the Church in Liverpool* ..., Liverpool 1869, pp. 26–8; the 1858 work has a Booth-like map classifying the streets of the town.
68. P. Knib, 'Rambles Through Liverpool', unidentified cutting, British Museum 10,352 1 9.

districts – Bevington east of it, around Ford Street and Maguire Street, and the Vauxhall district, around Chisenhale Street. One may guess that those driven out from the Dale Street area found their homes here, where, it was said in 1862, the 'genuine Liverpool rough' was to be met with.[69] Liverpool was the entry-port from Ireland and the exit-port for America, and it thus had a higher population in transit than other places. It attracted, too, bad characters from other parts of the country; it offered the advantages of obscurity that London presented and doubtless attracted some who would not undertake the journey to London.

The dock area was, of course, the scene of much crime, and it was indeed its maritime nature that determined the two main features of Liverpool's crime. Throughout the century larcenies of goods from the docks or in transit through the streets formed a major part of it. One of Henry Mayhew's colleagues on the *Morning Chronicle* described the scene at mid century.[70]

Cotton bales lie in immense heaps on the quays, where, in defiance of the utmost vigilance of the police, swarms of children prowl around during the day and the night to abstract it by handfuls, and conceal it amid their rags until they can transfer it to a depraved mother or father, who watches in a dark alley or in the shade of a large warehouse to receive it from them. Sacks of meal, corn, beans, rice, and coffee – all equally tempting to dishonest poverty – invite young thieves to learn their trade. . . . Cotton picking is, however, the principal source of plunder for the juvenile criminals of Liverpool . . .

Women are often seen to follow the lorries or carts laden with bags of Indian corn or bales of cotton, to rob them on their way to the warehouses. It is their practice to make a hole, either with a knife or a pair of scissors, in one of the bags of Indian corn, and hold up their aprons to catch the contents as they are jolted out by the movement of the vehicle. When their aprons are full, they squat down under the vehicle just as it approaches the dock gate on its way out, and, creeping under the feet of the horses, get clear off, although the police may be standing at the gate. . . . The women

69. H. Shimmin, *Liverpool Sketches*, 1862, p. 122 (cf. pp. 107–8, 130–31).
70. *Morning Chronicle*, 27 May 1850.

stuff cotton into their bosoms and under their clothes, until they look quite corpulent ... and they wear dresses made on purpose for this kind of robbery, with large receptacles or inner flounces, which they stuff with cotton.

The prostitutes who were as numerous as one would expect in a major port were, in Liverpool as elsewhere, frequently engaged in crime. 'Drunken and incautious strangers ... commercial men, and sometimes an Irish member or two of parliament,' runs one list of their victims,[71] and emigrants awaiting passage to America were of course a target both for them and for their male associates.

Bristol seems in a small way to have shared the characteristics of London and Liverpool. A high proportion of its youngsters maintained themselves by crime alone. As in Liverpool, stealing from the docks was a prevalent crime; the Lloyd's Agent in the town spoke of rigging and warps being stolen from vessels in the port.[72] Until the establishment of a reformed police in 1836 there seems to have been much disorder in the streets of Bristol. The town's criminals were closely linked with those of nearby Bath, criminals from both towns being blamed for much of the crime of the surrounding countryside.

Bath had a criminal class of its own, said in 1828 to comprise sixty per cent of the boys of the town.[73] Stealing from shops and picking pockets were the principal crimes. The attraction of the town was of course the number of wealthy invalids and retired people who lived there or visited it, although the town had lost something of its former position even by 1815. The establishment of a reformed police after the Municipal Corporations Act of 1835 reduced crime in the town; one resident made a vivid contrast between life in the town and life outside it which is testimony to the efficacy of the force.[74] However, complaints that criminals from Bath committed crime in the surrounding districts continued.

71. H. Brandon (ed.). *Poverty, Mendicity and Crime* ... , 1839, pp. 57–8.
72. Chadwick Papers, box 128 (statement of E. Drew).
73. s.c. on Criminal Commitments, P.P. 1828, vi, pp. 457, 464–70.
74. See p. 273.

Birmingham was regarded by one authority as second only to London for the number of its juvenile delinquents.[75] Most of the juvenile criminals of Birmingham had or were prepared to take jobs, and indeed the most prevalent crime was larceny from their masters or from shops and so forth committed by youngsters who had an honest job. Many Birmingham boys stole fairly consistently whether they were in work or out of work, and several features of the town's trades facilitated larceny. It was easy to steal a worthwhile quantity of the valuable metals which were their raw materials. The metal could seldom be identified, and was quite untraceable once it had been thrown into the furnaces which the receivers kept hot in readiness. The large number of small workshops meant that many opportunities for theft existed, particularly because much material had to be carried through the streets to and from out-masters working for the master-manufacturers. Amongst other things this provided opportunities for boys to be waylaid by receivers and tempted into the all-important first theft; to this end a high price might be given for a worthless file or other tool or piece of metal. A further feature of the town's trades was the high proportion of outdoor (i.e. non-resident) apprentices, who were able to dispose of portions of their master's property on their way home.

Another feature of Birmingham crime was the predominance it appears to have enjoyed in the earlier part of the century in the forging of bank-notes. In 1838 Sir George Stephen, a solicitor concerned with these matters, on whose knowledge of the subject the Royal Commission on a Constabulary Force relied heavily, wrote that by far the greatest quantity of forged Bank of England notes emanated from Birmingham, whence most of the notes passed in London came. Two decades earlier forgery was mentioned as a speciality of the town.[76] Two members of

75. s.c. on Juvenile Offenders, p.p. 1847, vii, p. 46 (q. 227).
76. Sir George Stephen's comments on the draft report of the R.C. on Constabulary Force, H.O. 73/4, Part I (MSS. loose sheets), Public Record Office; J. E. Eardley-Wilmot, *A Letter to the Magistrates of Warwickshire on the Increase of Crime . . .*, 1820, pp. 8–9.

the Hill family told of a forger, William Booth, who was active during the boyhood of Frederic Hill (who was born in 1803). Booth, who operated on a large scale, lived and worked in a specially constructed fortified house in a deserted spot outside the town. There was no staircase in the part where the forging was done, access being by a ladder drawn up while the work was in progress. The point of these precautions was to delay the entry of the police so that the evidence could be destroyed. This was long successful, but eventually in a sudden raid the police, who were accompanied by a detachment of the Scots Greys, broke in through the roof and managed to seize a few scraps of half-burnt notes. This evidence was sufficient to secure Booth's conviction and execution. Booth also engaged in counterfeiting, and as proof of his effrontery it was related that he would send his metal to be rolled out in the ordinary course of trade. On one occasion his messenger used the coin he intended to counterfeit as an indication of the thickness required.[77]

Leeds appears to have followed the pattern of Manchester, though of course its problems were much smaller in scale. Its crime seems to have been largely pilfering by juveniles who lived by honest work when they could, though the evidence is rather scanty. Prostitutes were active in theft here as elsewhere.

In general terms the pattern of crime in these provincial towns followed that of the country as a whole. In particular they participated in the decline in juvenile crime in and after the late 1850s. Some of the evidence already quoted in support of the view that this decline occurred was drawn from descriptions of the provincial towns, but one writer in particular paid attention to the provinces. T. B. L. Baker, the Gloucestershire magistrate, declared in 1860 that the regular, habitual, skilful boy-thief with half a dozen convictions or more had almost ceased to exist outside London. He had earlier spoken of reductions of crime in Liverpool, Bristol and Birmingham. His strongest claim was made in relation to his own county, and in

77. H.O. 73/3 (statement of E. Hill, pp. 23–4), P.R.O.; F. Hill, *Crime, its Amount, Causes and Remedies*, 1853, pp. 5–6.

particular Cheltenham, the area of operation of the Hardwicke
Reformatory School of which he was a sponsor. The capture of
'two young master-thieves' in 1856, coupled with the introduction in the same year of an automatic sentence to reformatory school on second conviction, led to a reduction by half or
more of the number of juvenile criminals brought before the
courts of Cheltenham; when the sentencing policy was altered in
1861 the number of juvenile offenders rose again, and a reversion to the automatic sentence brought it down once more.[78]
This enthusiast for the reformatory school is not a disinterested
witness, but his views are broadly consistent with those of others.
There seems good reason to accept that the crime of the provincial towns in the last forty years or so of the century was at a
lower level than it had earlier been.

78. T. B. L. Baker, *War With Crime*, 1889, pp. xxiii, 44–5, 185, 210,
229–30, and his 'On the Official Criminal Statistics of England and Wales,
1854–9', *Journal of the Statistical Society*, vol. xxiii, Dec. 1860, p. 429. His
account was perhaps the basis for the similar remarks in ibid., vol. lxiii,
June 1900, p. 192.

Part Three

Factors affecting crime

8. Poverty and population growth

Poverty

It will perhaps seem natural to a twentieth-century reader that a discussion of the effect of economic and social conditions on crime in the nineteenth century should commence with poverty. However, the first point to note is that in fact poverty, in the sense of the immediate pressure of want, was not throughout the century regarded as a prime cause of crime. It may be said in general terms that it was only in the years immediately after Waterloo that such a view was held.

At that time, indeed, poverty was readily put forward as a cause. Robert Owen said in 1816:[1] 'If the poor cannot procure employment, and are not supported, they must commit crimes, or starve,' and his remark was echoed by others at the time and later. However, the Royal Commission on a Constabulary Force which reported in 1839 took a different view. Crime, it said, was not caused by want but by the superior attractions of a criminal life.[2]

> We have investigated the origin of the great mass of crime committed for the sake of property, and we find the whole ascribable to one common cause, namely, the temptations of the profit of a career of depredation, as compared with the profits of honest and even well paid industry. . . . The notion that any considerable proportion of the crimes against property are caused by blameless poverty or destitution we find disproved at every step.

The Commission's Report was written virtually single-handed

1. s.c. on Police, p.p. 1816, v, p. 234. cf. ibid., pp. 33, 66; ibid., p.p. 1817, vii, pp. 330, 434; ibid., p.p. 1828, vi, pp. 7, 84, 194–5.
2. r.c. on Constabulary Force, p.p. 1839, xix, p. 73 (para. 65).

by Edwin Chadwick, and Professor S. E. Finer says[3] that he used a 'smoke-screen of "evidence" ' as a means of re-presenting in 1839 his proposals for police reform made in 1829. Whatever use Chadwick made of it, the evidence was there. Enough of it survives to testify to the thoroughness of his investigations and to show that, on this issue as on many others, the view put forward in the Report is a fair reflection of the opinions of the witnesses.[4] The Report either transformed the views of the general public about the effect of want on crime (which is by no means impossible, for it had a profound influence on thought on criminal matters) or is the expression of a new attitude just making itself felt; from 1839 we hear much less about the effect of want. From this time contemporary opinion plays down the effect of poverty in the direct sense.

Cyclical fluctuations in trade were none the less still thought to have an effect on crime. At mid century there were those who argued that committals to prison were correlated with the state of trade and with wheat prices.[5] This was by no means a unanimous view, however. Then and later there was a well-informed body of opinion which felt that any connection between trade fluctuations and crime worked the other way. Crime was thought to be higher in good times, because of the greater quantities of drink consumed. Matthew Davenport Hill, the Recorder of Birmingham, in 1857 wrote: 'In the manufacturing districts a flush of prosperity, which suddenly enhances the rate of wages, overwhelms the working classes with temptations to indulge in liquor – a cause of crime which is

3. S. E. Finer, *The Life and Times of Sir Edwin Chadwick*, 1952, pp. 164–5.

4. Some of the supporting evidence on this issue is in the Report, loc. cit.; see also Chadwick Papers, boxes 129 (statement of M. I. Whitty) and 131 (printed evidence, pp. 3, 5, 6, 18, 96), University College, London. Some of the Commission's papers are in the Public Record Office.

5. A. Alison, *The Principles of Population* ... , Edinburgh, 1840, vol. ii, pp. 197–8; J. C. Symons, *Tactics for the Times, as regards the Condition and Treatment of the Dangerous Classes*, 1849, pp. 51–6; J. T. Burt, *Irish Facts and Wakefield Figures in Relation to Convict Discipline in Ireland*, 1863, p. 64. cf. K. K. Macnab, *Aspects of the History of Crime in England and Wales between 1805–1860*, PH.D. thesis, University of Sussex, 1965, pp. 295–394.

more potent for its increase than the diffusion of plenty is for its diminution.[6] The Rev. J. W. Horsley, a prison chaplain, found the same thing in London in the 1880s: 'Our prison population rises with prosperity and the consequent power of getting drink. Bad times and the slackness of work in winter produces less crime, and not more.'[7]

The view that crime was not as a rule the result of want appears to have been generally correct. However, an analysis of the connection between the two must begin by making a distinction between the commission of crimes by those who were already members of the criminal class and the commission of crimes by those hitherto honest.

For members of the criminal class crime was a bread-and-butter matter. When funds were low they went out to raise more, in the spirit of the frontiersman taking down his gun when the time came to fill the pot. They stood little chance of meeting their needs in any other way, for there is ample evidence that even those who wished to 'go straight' would have found it virtually impossible to do so. In some cases people in this class would take honest work for a brief while, if opportunity presented itself, and therefore they stole less in busy times, when employers were less particular. Apart from this, however, and from the opposite effect that opportunities for theft may have been greater in times of prosperity, these people were more or less detached from the economy on which they preyed and immune from its fluctuations.

Discussion of the effect of want on the entry into crime of the honest poor must again be divided, this time on the basis of age. So far as the adult poor is concerned, there is ample descriptive testimony to back up the view that want played little part in causing crime. People of honest habits would suffer the most extreme hardships before descending to crime – if a man is honest to twenty he is honest all his life, it was said in 1839.[8] This generalization suffers the weaknesses of all generalizations, no

6. M. D. Hill, *Suggestions for the Repression of Crime . . .* , 1857, p. 109.
7. J. W. Horsley, *Jottings from Jail . . .* , 1887, p. 57.
8. Chadwick Papers, box 129 (statement of M. I. Whitty).

doubt. There were surely many who stole a little here or there without being detected; there were those, honest whilst in work, who soon succumbed to temptation when times were bad; there were those who turned to crime part way through life. But the impression gained from studying the evidence is that stated – on the whole honest people remained honest despite appalling suffering and often great temptation. To misquote Clive, one is astonished at their moderation.

If we thus accept as correct the view held after 1839, what of the contrary view common before that date? We cannot dismiss the possibility of a reduction in the effect of want on crime having taken place in or by the 1830s. Such a reduction could have occurred if the connection between the two had in some way been associated with the long wars which had just ended. Perhaps men discharged from the services stole when forced to do so by distress, reverting to their former practice of 'living off the country', while later generations were less likely to switch from an honest life to crime and (if possible) back again. Or perhaps there is truth in the notion that long wars have an unsettling effect on society, an effect which would lead men to steal more readily and which twenty-five years after the end of the war had worked itself out. A decline in the effect of want on crime could also have been caused by a decline in employment opportunities, but in this case it would have affected the young rather than the adult poor. We do not, of course, have to believe any of these explanations. It is quite easy to accept that the simple and naïve view that crime and poverty were directly correlated was widely held among the general public until it was denied by the Royal Commission on a Constabulary Force in 1839. The Commission's Report, on this view, would be the means of bringing the ideas of the informed before the uninformed.

On the whole, therefore, there is little ground to think that the immediate pressure of want was a major cause of adult crime, or that cyclical changes in this pressure altered its level.

The general question of the causes of juvenile crime is discussed later (see pp. 190 ff.); it suffices here to say that want is recognized as a cause of crime for orphans, runaways and deserted children, for whom crime must often have been the only alternative to starvation. Homeless children were of course not the only ones to enter the criminal class. For many other children, too, their own or their parents' poverty must often have been a cause of entry into a criminal life. But other factors surrounding the lives of urban juveniles led many of them into crime, and these other factors turn not on individual poverty but on society's poverty, the poverty of social institutions. It is this latter type of poverty which declined in the nineteenth century, a decline that was in large measure responsible for the decline in juvenile crime.

However, the large towns were not all alike in the prospects which they presented to their juvenile population, or in the effect on crime of fluctuations in the state of trade. In Birmingham crime was not usually thought to be increased by cyclical poverty or unemployment. M. D. Hill is a leading exponent of the general view.[9] He did indeed make reference in 1847 to the number of juveniles thrown out of work when trade was bad, but his later denials that there was a general connection between want and crime were emphatic. He told the Select Committee on Juvenile Offenders in 1852 that 'very few crimes indeed' were committed under 'the actual pressure of want', which was a 'much smaller cause of crime' than usually thought. In his book he stated his case more fully:

I have compared the prices of corn from year to year with the criminal statistics published by the Corporation without being able to establish any connection of cause and effect between dearth and high numbers; and I have been equally unsuccessful when attempting to trace an increase in the calendar to deficiency of employment when such deficiency existed.

It must indeed be admitted that J. T. Burt was basing himself on recent experience in Birmingham when in 1863 he wrote[10] of

9. s.c. on Juvenile Offenders, p.p. 1847, vii, p. 52 (q. 281); ibid., p.p. 1852, vii, pp. 44 (q. 391), 69 (q. 547); M. D. Hill, op. cit., pp. 109, 437-8. cf. s.c. on Criminal Commitments, p.p. 1828, vi, pp. 445-6, 462.

10. Burt, op. cit., p. 14.

changes in the state of the labour market and the cost of food determining the fluctuations in the behaviour of those who were honest if honesty was easy, criminal if they were tempted. However, temptation in Birmingham came to those in work as well as those out of it.

Observers discussing conditions in London (after the 1830s) seldom suggest bad times lead to an increase of crime. Manchester's experience was, however, different, and it was generally accepted there that crime was highest in times of bad trade.[11] The rather scanty evidence from Leeds points to a similar state of affairs.[12]

Thus cyclical fluctuations in the state of trade were thought to have an effect on the level of crime in Manchester and Leeds, but not in Birmingham or (for most of the century) London; and though it is unsafe to argue from the absence of evidence it is tempting to think that Liverpool and Bristol too may be added to the list of places where the effect did not occur, for their crime was discussed as much as Manchester's but no references to the point have been noted. Yet all these towns had a population of habitual criminals, the especially depraved town criminals. Why then did this difference occur? The answer may lie in differences in the employment opportunities for juveniles in the various towns. It has been suggested[13] that the major towns fell into two distinct groups. In London, Liverpool and Bristol (and Bath) the youngsters of the criminal class looked to crime alone for their support. In Manchester, Birmingham and Leeds there were, in addition to youngsters of the type found in the first group of towns, juveniles who combined theft and honest work as convenience dictated. (Once again it must be stressed that we are here talking in broad generalities. It would be absurd to suggest that no one in the first group of towns

11. s.c. on Criminal Commitments, p.p. 1828, vi, pp. 493, 498; Chadwick Papers, box 126 (statement of J. E. Foster, f. 28); s.c. on Juvenile Offenders, p.p. 1852, vii, p. 15 (q. 83); F. Hill. *Crime, its Amount, Causes and Remedies*, 1853, pp. 30–32; W. H. Dixon, *The London Prisons . . .*, 1850, p. 310.

12. s.c. on Criminal Commitments, p.p. 1828, vi, pp. 486, 491.

13. See p. 164.

combined work and theft; the point is that, according to contemporary evidence, a recognizable section of the youngsters of the towns of the second group behaved in this way.)

The towns of the second group shared the characteristic that there was in good times enough work for all their youngsters, most of whom took an honest job from time to time. However, the three differed from one another in some respects. Manchester and Leeds were textile towns, factory towns, dependent on the export trade and affected by the swings of the trade cycle. When labour was in demand in Manchester, employers would wait outside the House of Correction to engage boys on their release, but when trade was slacker they would not take those who had been in prison. When trade was bad the disreputable characters who lived partly by honest work and partly by petty crime were the first to be discharged, and hence they had more time and more need to steal. Crime therefore increased in bad times because these people who were part textile operative and part criminal concentrated on the latter side of their lives. Perhaps it was at such times easier to recruit new members to the criminal class as well. Much the same course of events probably occurred in Leeds.

Things were different in Birmingham. Its principal industries were of course the metal and jewellery trades, and the organization of its industries facilitated the theft of materials by youngsters at work in them.[14] Opportunities for theft would obviously be more frequent in busy times; and in quiet times the reduction in thefts by those in work would offset any increased crime by those dismissed. Birmingham's trade was organized more in small workshops than in large factories, and in any event it was not until the 1870s that the Factory Acts applied to the industries pursued in the town. In consequence there was more employment of juveniles than in the textile towns where the acts came into operation from the 1830s onwards. It is possible also that Birmingham was less affected than the textile towns by swings in the demand for exports.

These three towns of the second group can now be contrasted

14. See p. 173.

with those of the first group. The latter did not offer enough work for all their juveniles even in good times. London, Liverpool and Bristol were ports, and though they were thus connected with foreign trade they were subject to seasonal variations in employment at the docks as well as cyclical variations. Casual employment was more frequent than in the other towns. In Liverpool, moreover, a similar mechanism was at work to that in Birmingham. A principal form of theft was stealing goods at the docks or in transit through the town,[15] and these activities were easier in busy times. A further complication in Liverpool, of course, was the immigration of Irishmen, which was not (or at any rate not primarily) governed by conditions in Liverpool. Though the effect on crime of the Irish immigration is not certain, it might well have played its part in complicating the situation in Liverpool.

It must be admitted that in the twenty years or so after Waterloo people in London regarded fluctuations in the state of trade as leading to fluctuations in crime, and this does not fit in with the analysis just made. There are a number of possible explanations. First, those concerned could be seeking to prevent blame falling on the authorities responsible for law enforcement by ascribing fluctuations in crime to external forces. However, there are enough people uttering these views, and their ideas on other matters differ sufficiently, for this to be unlikely. Next, the comments could be a reflection of a general view that want is the main cause of crime and hence must be responsible for any fluctuations. Their dying out would on this view be the result of the work of the Royal Commission on a Constabulary Force. The third possibility is that the change in the general view really did reflect a change in conditions. In some towns cyclical variations in trade had little effect on the level of crime because (amongst other things) even in good times there was not enough work for all the available workers; in other towns everyone who wished to do so found work in busy times and crime was in some cases laid aside for honest work. If the employment situation in London in the 1820s and early

15. See p. 171.

1830s approximated to the latter situation and from the later thirties onwards to the former situation, this would have resulted in changes in the state of trade having more effect on the level of crime in the earlier period. London witnesses in the years in question would in this case have been right in suggesting that cyclical fluctuations in the state of trade affected crime.

The relationship between crime and poverty was thus by no means a simple one. The two were often closely linked, but it is necessary to look below the surface to see the connection between them. In many cases it was not poverty alone that was the cause of crime, but poverty amid all the pressures of the overcrowded and expanding towns.

Population growth

The expansion of the towns played an important part in the development of a criminal class. That expansion had begun in the eighteenth century, and continued in the nineteenth century. The population of England and Wales at the census of 1811 was just over ten million, and in 1861 just over twenty million – the population thus virtually doubled itself in fifty years. By 1901 the total was over thirty-two million, a lower proportionate increase but still a rapid one. The rate of increase in the large towns, moreover, was for much of the century even greater than in the country as a whole. Four of them had in 1821–31 growth-rates of over forty per cent a decade, and Liverpool and the combined town of Manchester and Salford actually achieved this for two successive decades (1821–41 and 1811–31 respectively).

Contemporaries were of course conscious of this rapid growth, and the mere increase of population was given as a cause by some of those who believed that crime was increasing in the period after Waterloo. Some of them were content merely to think in terms of an increase of crime which matched the increase of population, leaving the ratio of crime to population unchanged. Others, however, saw the growth of the population,

187

and above all the growth of the towns, as a factor likely to increase the ratio of crime to population and hence to cause a more than proportionate increase in crime. They were conscious of the different atmosphere of the large towns. The *Eclectic Review* declared in 1854:[16]

There is no longer any dispute that the aggregation of the population in large towns and cities is accompanied by the development and rapid growth of certain forms of crime; nor is it less [sic] a question of dispute that a criminal class, *per se*, is one distinctive feature of all such populations.

Fifteen years later *St Paul's Magazine* said that a criminal class 'can only exist in communities whose condensation is great and whose civilization is complex'.[17] John Wade in 1829 spelled out the problem:[18]

The differences observable between small and moderately-sized towns, consisting of a settled population, and great capitals, a large proportion of whose inhabitants are migratory, are very striking. In the former, the retreats and opportunities for delinquency are few and limited; the pursuits and even character of each person are matters of notoriety and interest; not to be known is to be an object of inquiry or suspicion: in a word, every one is the police of his neighbour, and unconsciously exercises over him its most essential duties. But this is widely different from the mode of living in a great city, especially London. Here there is no such thing as vicinage – no curiosity about neighbours – every one is engrossed in his own pursuit, and neither knows nor cares about any human being except the circle to which he has been introduced and with which he is connected by ties of business, pleasure, or profit. It is from this circumstance London affords so many facilities for the concealment of criminality. ... The metropolis is like an immense forest, in the innumerable avenues of which they [offenders] may always find retreat and shelter ...

The magnitude of the place, and consequent ignorance of individuals of many by whom they are necessarily surrounded,

16. *Eclectic Review*, new ser., vol. vii, April 1854, p. 387.
17. *St Paul's* vol. iii, Feb. 1869, p. 600.
18. J. Wade, *A Treatise on the Police and Crimes of the Metropolis ... by the Editor of 'The Cabinet Lawyer'*, 1829, pp. 6–7.

precludes all nice scrutiny into motives and purposes; even the distinctions of wealth and rank are almost lost in the crowd; and all that can be relied upon are certain external indications and appearances which may be either genuine or counterfeit. Many have no fixed domicile: they live in lodging-houses, hotels, or taverns, and, forming moving bodies with no determinate orbits, are removed from the restraint and observation which a settled abode and known circle of acquaintance impose on individual conduct.

One of Henry Mayhew's colleagues on the *Morning Chronicle* observed in 1849 that 'the temptation to crime and the facility of its commission increase together'.[19] The great characteristic of all large towns, it was said in 1837, is that the lower classes 'do not feel towards each other any of those kindly emotions which are so visible . . . in small towns'.[20]

The exodus of the middle class to the suburbs was a further crime-producing factor. On the one hand it meant that City shops and warehouses were more frequently unoccupied at night and week-ends – the Select Committee on Police of 1828 was told that this had 'increased wonderfully' in the previous twenty years. On the other hand it resulted in an increase in the number of houses without the protection of a male during the day – a resident of Camberwell told the same Committee that 'one half of our places belong to gentlemen in business in town and they go and leave their families, and the trampers and beggars commit depredations, and frequently insult ladies, and they are obliged to give them something from fear'.[21]

The nation's response to these difficulties was in the first half of the nineteenth century inadequate. Surveying the scene at the end of the century a prison doctor wrote that in towns 'we have lost the personal interest we ought to have in our neighbours; we have gone out from among them; we have cast on officials duties we ought to undertake ourselves as citizens, and the result is an increase in the number of offences'.[22] However, in the first half of the nineteenth century the duties had not yet

19. *Morning Chronicle*, 18 Oct. 1849.

20. J. D. Grant, *The Great Metropolis*, 2nd ed., 1837, vol, i, p. 324.

21. S.C. on Police, P.P. 1828, vi, pp. 65, 189.

22. J. Devon, *The Criminal and the Community*, 1912, pp. 93–4.

even been cast on officials. In or about 1839 one contemporary warned the rival groups concerned with the moral welfare of the lower classes of the difficulties ahead, in terms which are clear enough, even though some of the people to whom he addressed his advice are no longer familiar names:[23]

In no country, (excepting perhaps Ninevah, Babylon, and Rome), did masses of population ever grow up so rapidly as in London and the manufacturing and commercial cities of the empire. And we have done nothing to carry out our institutions, civil or religious, to meet them. Sir R. Inglis, the Bishop of London, and Mr Baines, must not expect that they can maintain civil virtues by religious means alone; churches and schools without commensurate and harmonious civil institutions will not succeed. Lord Melbourne, Lord J. Russell, and quakers, and philanthropists, and philosophers, must not expect that schools and policemen will succeed without churches, much less in opposition to them.

It was to be some time before the 'institutions, civil or religious', were to be in a condition to cope with their problems.

Thus many people in the early nineteenth century realized that the increase in population was causing severe social strain. They were no doubt right in thinking that this would tend to increase crime. If crime had merely increased in proportion to population, it would have thrown such an additional burden on courts and police as to justify all the complaints that were made. But truth probably lies with those who felt that the matter went deeper than this, that an increase in the number of those living together as one community actually increased the proportion of the population who were criminals. This point is important enough to warrant further examination.

The effects of increased population were felt mainly in relation to the children, and population growth and juvenile crime

23. C. D. Brereton, *A Refutation of the First Report of the Constabulary Force Commissioners*, n.d., 3rd part, pp. 28–9. The first group are of course opponents of State intervention in education; those in the second and rather motley collection are regarded as opponents of the claims of the Church of England.

were so closely linked that it is convenient to survey here the views of contemporaries on the causes that led youngsters into crime. As far as the children of the criminal class were concerned, contemporaries knew that they need not look far for an explanation. The Governor of Westminster House of Correction told W. A. Miles in the 1830s that 'Boys brought up in a low neighbourhood have no chance of being honest, because on leaving a gaol they return to their old haunts, and follow the example of their parents or associates.'[24] The Rev. W. D. Morrison in 1891 wrote: 'In some instances these unfortunates have lived all their lives in criminal neighbourhoods, and merely follow the footsteps of the people around them.'[25] John Wade observed that, as with other trades, children usually followed the trade of criminal parents.[26] It was also known that bad results were even more likely to occur when the mother was a criminal than when the father alone broke the law. Miss Mary Carpenter in 1852 declared: 'I have known numerous instances in which a family has been well brought up, with a bad father and a good mother, but I have never known an instance of a family being otherwise than vicious with a bad mother.'[27] From start to finish of the century there is recognition of the likelihood of criminal parents bringing up criminal children.

There was another group of children which ran a high risk of ending up as members of the criminal class. These were the orphans and deserted children and the runaways who joined them and lived with them in the streets and lodging-houses. The Superintendent of the Hulks told the Select Committee on Police of 1828 that of 300 boys in the *Euryalis* hulk 101 were fatherless; thirty-five of them had lost their mother as well. Another committee a few years later was told that of 600 juvenile delinquents under seventeen years of age, over forty per cent were fatherless; twelve-and-a-half per cent had lost both

24. H. Brandon (ed.), *Poverty, Mendicity and Crime* . . . , 1839, p. 44.
25. W. D. Morrison, *Crime and its Causes*, 1891, p. 88.
26. Wade, op, cit., pp. 158–9.
27. s.c. on Juvenile Offenders, P.P. 1852, vii, p. 144 (q. 1078).

parents by death or desertion. Such statistics no doubt to a large extent rested on the mere assertion of the children concerned, and the Select Committees on Juvenile Offenders of the middle of the century were warned that youngsters would often make false claims to be orphans.[28] But the high birth-rates and death-rates of the period increased the proportion of orphans, and children who had lost their parents were likely enough to end up in the criminal class.

It was often difficult for such children to get relief from the Poor Law authorities, even though a high proportion of Poor Law funds went on the relief of orphans and dependent children (about one-third of those being relieved at any time were under sixteen years of age). Miss Carpenter recounted the story of two boys who appeared at a Bristol Ragged School and told the teacher that[29]

they were utterly destitute of food and shelter. . . . [One boy had a father living in Manchester; the other, an Irish lad, thought himself to be an orphan.] They had applied at the Poor-house the preceding evening, but were refused relief or shelter, and had passed the night in the streets; a teacher went with them to renew their application, but they were again refused any help, though directed to appear the next day before the committee. Then one loaf was given to the English lad, and he was told with that to make his way to Manchester! The Irish lad was peremptorily refused all help, for Bristol claims a right to treat all Irish as aliens.

She quoted the following case-history from a report of the Chaplain of Manchester Gaol, who offered it 'as a sample of many others':[30]

A boy, only twelve years of age, who had already been eight times in the New Bailey, was committed to the Borough Gaol. His father was dead; his mother lived in a cellar in one of the lowest streets of the town, and endeavoured to earn a scanty subsistence by selling

28. s.c. on Police, p.p. 1828, vi, p. 105; s.c. on Gaols, p.p. 1835, xii, p. 252; s.c. on Juvenile Offenders, p.p. 1847, vii, pp. 58–9 (q. 345); ibid., p.p. 1852–3, xxiii, p. 227 (q. 2245).

29. M. Carpenter, *Juvenile Delinquents, their Condition and Treatment*, 1853, pp. 187–8.

30. ibid., pp. 202–3.

pipeclay. She could just support herself, and left the boy to pick up a living as he best could. ... Going into his cell one day shortly before his term of imprisonment expired, I inquired into his condition and prospects, and feeling painfully how hopeless they were, and how impossible that the lad could escape the life of misery and crime to which his very circumstances seemed to oblige him, I . . . said to him, 'If I could obtain some sort of situation for you, where you could earn an honest living, would you try to do better?' The boy, who was never known to give way to any softened feelings before, burst into tears and sobbed convulsively, as he assured me I should never have cause to repent it. ... My hope was to have got him into an institution for destitute children near London, but £20 was required; and after an unsuccessful appeal to two or three individuals, I was unable to obtain it, and the boy was discharged. Two days after I opened the door of a cell, and to my surprise found him again an inmate. ... Looking at me with an appealing and hopeless expression of anguish I can never forget, he said, with an almost passionate emphasis, 'Sir, what *could* I do?' and then told me his tale. ... On leaving the gaol, he went directly to look for his mother, in the cellar where he had left her. She was not there, gone, the neighbours said, into the workhouse. Penniless and houseless, he wandered about all day and all night in the streets, and the next day, driven by hunger, he stole some bread, and was committed for the offence. He said he knew not what to do, and everything was better than his condition outside. Shortly after, an officer looked into his cell, one Sunday afternoon ... and found the unhappy boy suspended by a hammock girth to the gas-pipe – and *dead!*

Henry Mayhew described the many honest ways in which the children of the streets could gather a living in London – his finders of coal and gatherers of dog-dung, for example – and no doubt similar opportunities existed in the other large towns. But Mayhew and other observers made it clear that many of the youngsters, unwilling to adopt these ways or, more probably, unable to do so, drifted into crime or were taken in hand by a thief and shown how to steal.

That the children of the criminal class were likely (one might almost say 'were bound') to become criminals in their turn hardly needs argument. Equally, it can easily be accepted that orphans and runaways, in an age when virtually no one else would or could do anything for them, would soon drift willy-nilly into the ranks of the criminal class. Homeless children still existed at the end of the century, but provision for them improved over its course, and this played its part in the reduction of juvenile crime in the second half of the century.

Orphans were not necessarily much worse off than some of those with one parent still living. The Chaplain of Redhill School, a farm school for delinquents run by the Philanthropic Society, told the Select Committee on Juvenile Offenders of 1852 that half the juvenile criminals had a step-parent – 'the altered state of the family, the altered state of the home, does seem a very powerful' cause of crime. The step-mother favoured her own child in the 'struggle for bread', said a London judge, who felt that criminal children with step-parents were a disproportionately large part of the total.[31] Another committee ten years later was told that step-children 'lead the life of dogs at home'.[32] Miss Carpenter recorded the remark of a step-mother whose husband told her he was going to drown his two eldest children to get rid of them:[33] 'If you are going to drown them, you might as well leave the shoes for Johnny'; but the actual parent (one can hardly say 'the natural parent') was the prime mover in this case.

Some children, whilst neither brought up as criminals nor completely deserted, were left to bring themselves up. In the post-Waterloo years commentators tended to blame the parents, regarding them as uninterested in the children's welfare or too drunken to take any part in their upbringing, but later observers drew attention to the parents' difficulties. Even if they were completely honest and well-meaning and genuinely interested, it was realized, they were not always able to keep their children from harm. Youngsters, it was believed, were easily contaminated by the life of the streets, and once this had happened parents often found it impossible to keep them at

31. s.c. on Juvenile Offenders, p.p. 1852, vii, pp. 39 (qq. 364–5), 217 (q. 1825).
32. s.c. on Gaols, p.p. 1863, ix, p. 182 (q. 1584).
33. Carpenter, op. cit., p. 60.

home. Magistrates before the Select Committees on Police explained the problem. In 1816 one said:[34]

I have frequently sent for the parents of such as have been brought before me, and on their solemnly promising they will take care of the children, and punish them themselves for the offences they have committed, I have given them up to them; but it seldom happens to any good purpose, for they get out, and again associate with their thievish comrades, and continue their practices.

In 1828 another lamented that parents frequently brought their children before the magistrates for repeated offences: 'it is one of the most distressing things that occurs to a magistrate in London. The parents come and say that they have done every thing to bring up their children well, but that they have got into bad associations, and are ruined.'[35] He did not blame the parents, and was not accusing them of neglect.

It is really a difficult thing to keep children constantly in the house; they must be allowed by poor parents to go about, even for air and exercise. ... [The magistrates] are placed in this painful situation, that we cannot counsel a parent to prosecute a child to conviction and yet, by not prosecuting, we know that they must go on till they become hardened in crime.

Poverty accentuated the difficulties which all parents faced in controlling children. A prison inspector described the case of a boy who was put to bed in a locked room with no clothes on but who made his escape through the window after making a garment with some hemp left in the room. Other prison inspectors drew attention to the difficulties which arose when both parents had to work.[36] This was to become a common view-point, for the mother who went out to work was often cited as a crime-producing factor. Mayhew, for example, wrote:[37]

Our artificial state of society ... and the scanty remuneration

34. S.C. on Police, P.P. 1816, v, p. 63.
35. ibid., P.P. 1828, vi, p. 172.
36. Report of Prison Inspectors, Home District, P.P. 1836, xxxv, p. 87, S.C. on Juvenile Offenders, P.P. 1852–3, xxiii, p. 220 (q. 2225).
37. H. Mayhew and J. Binny, *The Criminal Prisons of London* ..., 1862, p. 387.

given to many of our forms of labour, as well as the high price of rent and provisions among us, render it now almost impossible for a family to be supported by the man alone, and hence most of the wives of the unskilled portion of our work-people have, now-a-days, to forego their maternal duties, and to devote themselves to some kind of drudgery by which they can add to the petty income of the house. . . . If, then, the mother be away from home the greater part of her time, and the children, consequently, left to gambol in the gutter with others as neglected as themselves, what reward, think you, can society look for from such a state of moral anarchy and destitution? . . . This constitutes the real explanation of juvenile delinquency.

The stress laid here on the inevitable lack of proper control was a common theme throughout the century.

Contemporaries were probably right in these views. We can believe that the criminal class received recruits from the ranks of youngsters who were neither the offspring of criminals nor orphans or runaways, and that the children of honest parents became criminals in large numbers. Here we return to the question of the growth of the towns. Those who came into the large towns from the countryside, from Ireland or from smaller towns found themselves in a bewildering place, in which many of their former standards did not apply and in which they lacked the support of a small, cohesive community to which they were accustomed. The census returns show that many in the large towns were first-generation residents. In 1851 over half of those aged twenty and above in London had been born elsewhere, and in Birmingham, Bristol, Manchester and Salford and Liverpool even higher proportions of the adult population had been born outside the city or borough in which they were counted. In Manchester and Salford, for example, over seventy per cent came into that category, even though those born in Manchester but counted in Salford, and vice versa, are reckoned as having been counted in the town of their birth. For all these people life had changed drastically.

Moreover, the growth of the large towns did not only affect those who moved into them from outside. Even the town-bred children of town-bred parents must have been bewildered by the changes. Someone born in Liverpool in 1821 was born in a city of 138,000 people, passed his twentieth birthday in a city of 286,000, and his fortieth in a city of 444,000. Homes, shops, streets, hospitals, law-courts and prisons – all must have been engulfed by the new flood and must have been inadequate for the new tasks. Professor Chevalier regards the growth of the population of Paris and the consequent 'remplacement d'une société ancienne, lentement mûrie au cours des âges par une société nouvelle et brutalement renouvelée, aux caractères étrangement différents,'[38] as the main fact of its social history during the first half of the nineteenth century, and much the same can be said of the major English towns.

All this is obvious enough, perhaps, but it is worth stating and worth proving, for the people in these various categories, like detribalized Africans or rootless dwellers in a New Town or council housing estate, must have been a fertile spawning ground for crime. We can easily accept the contemporary view that many turned to drink and that many abandoned the effort to look after their children. Moreover, though poverty did not often drive into crime those who had remained honest in youth, the constant struggle to make ends meet engaged the attention of the parents and reduced the time they could devote to looking after their children, and the grandmothers, the traditional mother's help of the poor, were not so readily at hand in the new age of movement. We can easily believe that many who made a genuine attempt to do so were unable to find solutions to the manifold problems of raising honest children amidst the temptations of a nineteenth-century city with none of the supporting agencies of the twentieth century. In this situation, finding that their old habits and norms of behaviour were inapplicable, many migrants into the towns would adopt the habits and norms of the district in which they found themselves, and if it was a criminal one they would become criminal.

38. L. Chevalier, *Classes laborieuses et classes dangereuses à Paris pendant la première moitié du 19ème siècle*, Paris 1958, p. 184 – for the full discussion see pp. 180–84, 213–14, 311–12.

Factors affecting crime

The effects of the movement to the towns were, moreover, sharpened by the youth of those concerned. A substantial portion of the migrants must have consisted of unattached youngsters in their 'teens or earlier twenties. Throughout the century almost half the population of the country was under twenty years of age – the proportion of those aged nineteen or under to the total population of England and Wales was between forty-two and forty-seven per cent in the 1841–1901 censuses. Though the large towns tended to have a lower percentage of their population under the age of twenty than did the country as a whole, the corresponding figure for each of them was forty per cent or more in the 1841–91 censuses, and in the 1821 census in the cases in which the figures exist. (As a standard of comparison, the proportion of the population under the age of twenty in England and Wales in 1961 was just under thirty per cent.) A further factor inducing us to believe that the townward drift contained a high proportion of people in their 'teens or early twenties was the fact that jobs in the country districts tended to go to married men with families to support.

One qualification must be made. Some of the young newcomers to the towns were of course domestic servants living with their employers. (In 1851 the proportion of female domestic servants under twenty years to the total number of girls aged ten to nineteen years in the large towns other than London varied from just over ten per cent to just over twenty per cent.) However, it must not be thought that those in this category were not exposed to the risk of becoming criminals. There is ample testimony, from London in the first decades of the century and later from the country as a whole, that domestic servants were often involved in criminal enterprises against their masters. A City policeman waxed indignant in 1816:[39]

That is a thing that wants very much looking into; the easy mode servant girls have of turning anything they can bring away into money. There is scarcely what is called a chandler's shop in any part of the Metropolis ... but buys old bottles or linen, or anything that

39. S.C. on Police, P.P. 1816, v, pp. 261–2.

a servant girl, when she goes there to purchase things, can take with her. The green-stalls will purchase things of them, and they find a facility of raising money upon anything they take to these kinds of shops; and many girls lose their reputation by the encouragement women keeping these shops give them. This is not a suspicion, it is a thing proved and known. ... This species of domestic robbery ... is increasing still greatly. ... Servants ... have become vile in the extreme; servant girls in particular; they are infamous.

In 1828 the Select Committee on Police was told: 'There is no more dangerous person upon earth than a discarded gentleman's servant.'[40] They generally became thieves – 'we have had a great many of them'.

Something must be subtracted from such remarks because of the obvious prejudices of their authors; but not everyone thought the blame lay only in one quarter. In the 1850s a prison chaplain wrote:[41]

Looking at the less noticed causes of crime, we are not to pass over the luxurious habits of the wealthy, who multiply attendants beyond all possibility of moral control; and who expose them by their own habits, in the pursuit of pleasure, to so manifold temptations beyond what is unavoidable in the condition of a servant.

An earlier writer had complained: 'It is too often the case that servants are looked upon as little better than slaves.'[42] On the other hand, he felt that:

Another evil in society that is pregnant with mischief, is giving a false character to servants, which ladies are constantly in the practice of doing to avoid being plagued ... thus a pilferer having once had the luck to start off in a private family with a good name, is from this shameful habit let loose upon the public to commit his depredations at leisure and convenience, with the chance of blame falling upon an honest individual.

Some employers, however, dismissed their servants and denied

40. ibid., P.P. 1828, vi, p. 45.
41. J. Kingsmill, *Chapters on Prisons and Prisoners, and the Prevention of Crime*, 3rd ed., 1854, pp. 76–8.
42. Brandon, op. cit., p. 16.

them a character too readily; in 1816 the Select Committee on Police was told: 'The Magistrates have lamented that they have not had it in their power to compel masters or mistresses to give a reason why they dismiss their servants.'[43] There was, too, a constant emphasis on the proportion of domestic servants amongst the young girls who became prostitutes.

To some extent these remarks bear witness to their authors' views on moral and social questions rather than to the underlying facts; and the high proportion of the age-group which was in service no doubt explains why the failings of young domestic servants were so much in the public mind. But there remains enough evidence to prove that domestic servants, and especially the younger ones, were much exposed to temptation. This conclusion is sufficient for our purposes here, for the object of this discussion has been to argue that the inflow of young people into the large towns, even though inflated by a large number of female domestic servants living with their employers, increased the number of potential young criminals. There was in most towns a body of youngsters living apart from their families, who, even if they went into domestic service, were exposed to the risk of becoming criminals. We can thus note the inflow of young people and regard it as a crime-producing factor.

It is worth paying particular attention to one group of migrants, the Irish. There is abundant testimony that the worst juvenile criminals were the Irish cockneys, or more generally the English-born children of Irish families. (The young Irish immigrants who came to England in their 'teens and left their families behind them in Ireland and those who came over as infants with their parents were in contemporary comments doubtless lumped in with the English-born.) That this was not, or was not merely, prejudice is shown by the general comment that the Irish themselves, apart from their addiction to drink and violence, were on the whole law-abiding citizens. Where there were complaints of crime by adult Irish, it was usually in relation to thefts from gardens and fields.[44]

43. s.c. on Police, P.P. 1816, v, p. 229.
44. s.c. on Police, P.P. 1816, v, p. 100; ibid., P.P. 1828, vi, pp. 61, 94–5, 193,

These comments on the Irish immigrants in the nineteenth century fit in well with subsequent experience elsewhere and with criminological theory.[45] Adult immigrants are thought as a rule to stick to the types of crime familiar to them in their place of origin, while the second generation, the first to be born or brought up in their new homeland, are often unusually prone to crime. They reject the ideas and standards of their parents, it is argued, and enthusiastically adopt those of the people of the area in which they live. In the nineteenth century as in later times, immigrants were likely to end up in the poorest and most disreputable part of the town. Hence the standards they adopted with such vigour tended to be those of the criminal class.

To sum up, then, it may be concluded that the rapid growth of the towns in the earlier part of the nineteenth century was a major factor in causing or maintaining a high level of crime, and in particular juvenile crime. A flood of migrants, and especially young migrants, entered the towns and bewildered themselves and those who had been there before they came. A new way of life was called for, and many must have given up the struggle to adapt themselves to meet the new requirements and turned instead to the apparently easier life of crime. After the middle of the century conditions in the towns were eased by various governmental and non-governmental actions. They were also eased by a slowing-down of the rate of growth itself. The towns were of course larger than they had been earlier in the century; they were still growing; but they were not growing so quickly, and the problems were not so great. We must not go too far. The absolute increase in the size of the towns was

---

198; Report on the State of Irish Poor in Great Britain, R.C. on Poor (Ireland), P.P. 1836, xxxiv, pp. 446–8; Chadwick Papers, boxes 127 (statements of J. S. Thomas and T. Fellows), 128 (statement of E. Davis); W. B. Neale, *Juvenile Delinquency in Manchester* . . . , Manchester 1840, p. 8; Reports received by Poor Law Commissioners, P.P. 1846, xxxvi, pp. 341–3; S. P. Day, *Juvenile Crime, its Causes, Character, and Cure*, 1858, p. 57.

45. E. H. Sutherland, *Principles of Criminology*, 5th ed., revised by D. R. Cressey, Chicago 1955, pp. 143–9.

greater in the latter part of the century, and in some cases the rate of growth was higher in the second half of the nineteenth century. But still the changes were not so great; life in the large cities had by mid century acquired the pattern it was to retain for the rest of the century. This point is taken up again in the concluding chapter, but for the time being we can register the conclusion that the rate of increase of the population was a major factor affecting the level of crime.

9. Other economic and social change, I

Education

In 1815 few poor children had much chance of regular weekday schooling; in the last quarter of the century most of them received some sort of elementary education. A movement to educate the poor by Sunday and evening classes had started in the eighteenth century, and by the time of Waterloo such schools were providing the beginnings of an education for a large number of children. Though attention was increasingly directed to the need for day schools, agreement could not be reached on the establishment of a system of State schools, for the Church of England claimed rights in schools provided by public funds which some others were not prepared to grant. Hence the provision of weekday schools for the children of the poor was for much of the century left to charitable bodies. Foremost among these were the two school societies, the British and Foreign School Society and the National Society for Promoting the Education of the Poor in the Principles of the Established Church. Founded in 1808 and 1811 respectively, the societies provided on an increasing scale schools where education of a sort was given for a modest weekly charge. They received grants from public funds from 1833. State supervision followed in 1839, and was made more effective by the Revised Code of grant regulations adopted in 1862. In 1870 the State at last began to provide schools itself. School Boards (which were to become Local Education Authorities in the twentieth century) were set up by the Education Act of 1870, with the task of establishing, at the expense of the rate-payers, schools in those areas where the societies had not been able to provide sufficient places. The School Boards were from the beginning allowed to make local by-laws for compulsory attendance; in 1880 they were required to make such by-laws, and effective measures for compulsion came into existence over the whole country.

Perhaps more important, to the kind of youngster with whom we are concerned, was the increased provision of three other types of school, the Ragged School, the workhouse school and the prison school. The Ragged School movement, which started about 1840, catered for those for whom the societies' schools were unsuitable, for reasons explained by Miss Carpenter:[1]

The weekly payment, however small, would be an insuperable obstacle to those who required every farthing to supply their physical wants, or would be unwilling to spend it for what they did not value. But would any good Day Schools receive these children? ... We know that the masters or superintending committees of such would generally exclude, as undesirable associates for those under their care, the outcast or vicious children, young in years, old in all the arts of crime. ... Nor would these ill-clad children feel at ease in the company of the clean and neat ones. ... They *will not* come to be looked down on by those whom they feel superior to themselves in external advantages only.

In any event, she said, even if these difficulties could be overcome, they would not attend with sufficient regularity; a school 'can, of course, do little or nothing for those whose attendance is so irregular that they unlearn one week in the streets all that they have gained the preceding one in the School'.

The workhouse school catered for those who accepted the assistance of the Poor Law authorities. There was a steady improvement in the handling of these children, from the pre-1834 practice of accommodating them in the general ward of the workhouse to the post-1850 system of district schools. The prison school started merely as a boys' ward, but education became steadily more important until finally the reformatory school and the industrial school provided places of detention and education distinct from the prisons.

1. M. Carpenter, *Reformatory Schools for the Children of the Perishing and Dangerous Classes and for Juvenile Offenders*, 1851, pp. 33-4, 224.

How far did this increased provision of education help to reduce crime? We cannot estimate its effects with any precision. Views on the efficacy of education as a preventative of crime were often coloured by their holder's views on the great school question – National Society or British Society, church schools or lay schools – which agitated the country for so much of the nineteenth century. Often enough, it must be admitted, what starts as a discussion of education and its effect on crime ends by praising or attacking a particular type of school.

Making what allowance one can for this, it may be said that, though lack of education was regarded as a cause of crime throughout the century, contemporaries were not always agreed that the effect of the schooling currently being provided was to reduce crime. The balance of opinion in 1816–18 was that the provision of further schools would help to reduce crime, both by the direct effect on the children and by the indirect effect on their parents and others with whom they came into contact.[2] By 1828, however, people had begun to examine the effects of increased schooling more closely. Some spoke of the dangers of 'over-education' – indeed, one police magistrate, H. M. Dyer, ran into difficulties on the subject. 'You think this makes people run the risk of being hanged, and other punishments?' a committee-member asked sarcastically; 'No,' he replied, 'I do not think that; but I think it makes fine gentlemen of those who would have been content with a more inferior situation, and who are led to supply their artificial wants by undue means.' They continued to press him closely, and he found it difficult to express more fully what he meant and to justify what had only been a casual after-thought.[3] But another witness put the point in a nutshell: 'I confess I think the over-education of the lower class of the people has done harm. I do not mean to say that it is not desirable that children should be educated, but if they are to be educated, and afterwards have no employment, you have merely given them expertness to become thieves.'[4] At mid-

2. See, for example, s.c. on Police, P.P. 1816, v, pp. 29–30, 168.
3. ibid., P.P. 1828, vi, pp. 170–71.
4. ibid., p. 57.

century a prison chaplain too felt that instruction merely served to make the boys more skilful criminals; education changed the character of the crime but not of the man, he observed.[5]

In general terms it may be said that from the late 1820s onwards there was an articulate body of critics of education as then prevalent. On the whole, however, official circles took a more optimistic view, and the belief that education was a great factor in eliminating juvenile delinquency is generally regarded as one of the main reasons for the sharp rise from the 1830s onwards in public expenditure on schools. Bearing these views in mind, and having regard to the types of schools in existence up to and including the 1840s, we may perhaps conclude that the provision of educational facilities is unlikely to have had a significant effect on crime in the earlier part of the century, but that in the second part of the century improved schooling is likely to have been increasingly effective. It is true that the Rev. J. W. Horsley commented in 1887 that[6]

One can get no clear evidence or trustworthy statistics to prove that the greater attention to educational matters has largely diminished even juvenile crime. There are fewer boys and girls sent to prison happily, but this arises from various causes, and not entirely from their increased virtue and intelligence. On the other hand, we find boys swindle and forge in a precocious manner, which is attributable not to ignorance, but to instruction.

However, another prison official writing in 1910 said that compulsory education led to a decrease in crime because it swept off the streets 'hundreds of neglected waifs and strays who were criminals-in-the-making'.[7] This latter view seems preferable. Improved education must have helped to raise the general standards of the poor and to equip them to take advantage of the increasing opportunities for employment. In both these ways it helped to reduce the inflow into the criminal class.

5. J. Kingsmill, *Chapters on Prisons and Prisoners, and the Prevention of Crime*, 3rd ed., 1854, p. 468.

6. J. W. Horsley, *Jottings from Jail* . . . , 1887, p. 57.

7. R. F. Quinton, *Crime and Criminals, 1876–1910*, 1910, p. 38.

The effect of the special types of school mentioned earlier was also important. The Ragged Schools certainly did not stop their pupils from committing crime. One writer[8] spoke of 'children who thrive [sic – 'thieve' was perhaps intended] and beg all day, rush to school in the evening, have two hours' instruction, and rush out to beg and steal again'. Others described how Ragged Schools would empty at particular times as the children rushed off to take advantage of some favourable opportunity for theft.[9] Mayhew made more thorough-going criticisms. He said that he could not but arrive at[10]

the conclusion that, however well intentioned such institutions may be, they are, and must be, from the mere fact of bringing so many boys of vicious propensities together, productive of far more injury than benefit to the community. If some boys are rescued – and that such is repeatedly the case is cheerfully and fully conceded – many are lost through them.

This conclusion was of course disputed by those connected with the schools. Though Mayhew had some justification for what he wrote, the Ragged Schools probably did good on balance. They provided education for those who would otherwise have received it only in gaol. The teachers took an interest in those in whom no one else was interested. They had kind words for those for whom most other people had only harsh words or blows. It was probably from this social side of their work that the main benefits came.

The workhouse schools were the subject of severe criticism in the earlier part of the century, but the district schools which were provided on an increasing scale after the middle of the century were much more satisfactory. It can readily be accepted that as a result children in the care of the Poor Law

8. M. Hill and C. F. Cornwallis, *Two Prize Essays on Juvenile Delinquency*, 1853, p. 220.

9. T. Beames, *The Rookeries of London*, 1850, pp. 127–8; *Once a Week*, vol. xii, Jan. 1865, p. 64.

10. *Morning Chronicle*, 29 March 1850 (cf. 25 March, 22 April and 25 April 1850).

authorities had a better chance of avoiding a life of crime. The reformatory schools and industrial schools achieved favourable results, and though the explanation of this again rests principally on factors other than educational success, they too played their part in the general spread of education.

Rookeries and housing

Like adequate education, adequate housing is a reflection of the wealth of the community, and came low in the list of priorities in the initial stages of economic growth. Slums and rookeries were not the creation of an industrial society, but formed part of the 'nightmare of ancient slums' long associated with the growth of cities. The criminal area played an important part in perpetuating crime in the large towns. During the course of the nineteenth century the rookeries were affected by clearances to make room for railways, new roads and additional offices and shops. Sometimes the population of a rookery was increased because such works elsewhere drove more people into it; sometimes the size of the rookery was reduced by works affecting part of the original area; and sometimes a rookery was eliminated by major works going through its centre.

One contemporary writer was not sure that any benefit flowed to society from such happenings. The criminals had to go somewhere, he observed,[11] and perhaps it would be better if they were all together in a known place; the railways had cut through the criminal districts, but this had not made any real difference. Most people, however, took a different view. Indeed, the destruction of rookeries was sometimes seen as an incidental advantage of works of the type in question, and the final line of at least one new street was chosen so as to cut through a rookery – Victoria Street was deliberately run through the worst part of Westminster.[12]

11. T. Archer, *The Pauper, the Thief and the Convict* . . . , 1865, pp. 64–6, 92–3.
12. H. J. Dyos, 'Urban Transformation: a Note on the Objects of Street Improvement in Regency and Early Victorian London', *International*

There can be little doubt that the destruction of the rookeries did help to reduce crime. In the criminal area every facility for crime was to hand, and the whole atmosphere was one in which crime was normal. As rookeries were destroyed some of the people displaced did, no doubt, merely crowd in on others in existing rookeries or even start new ones; but some moved to less tainted spots. Moreover, it was not only the police who knew where the rookeries were; criminals from other areas, and those attracted to the criminal life, knew where to find assistance and companionship. The ending of this state of affairs was beneficial. It can thus be concluded that the clearances for railways, roads and rebuilding, which gathered pace in the 1840s and later decades, by breaking up the rookeries helped to reduce crime and played a part in the improvement of conditions by the end of the century.

Of course the criminal area was not necessarily worse than some of the districts occupied by the honest poor in terms of housing, and this latter topic demands attention. Contemporaries did not at first realize that the low quality of the housing available to the honest poor could in itself be a cause of crime. The first reference to the point that has been noted was in W. B. Neale's study of juvenile crime in Manchester; he regarded an improvement in the quality of housing as essential.[13] Even so zealous and so kind-hearted a friend of the poor as the Rev. John Clay did not realize the importance of this point until 1842, when Edwin Chadwick's Report on the *Sanitary Conditions of the Labouring Poor* called attention to the problem and led to a number of further investigations.[14] Thereafter a fierce light played on housing in the large towns, and its impact on crime was not neglected. The effects of bad housing, it was

Review of Social History, vol. ii, 1957, part ii, pp. 262–4. For similar arguments in relation to Haussmann's clearances in Paris, see L. Chevalier, *Classes laborieuses et classes dangereuses à Paris pendant la première moitié du 19ème siècle*, Paris 1958, pp. 99–100.

13. W. B. Neale, *Juvenile Delinquency in Manchester; its Causes and History, its Consequences* . . . , Manchester 1840, pp. 52, 55.

14. W. L. Clay, *The Prison Chaplain; a Memoir of the Rev. John Clay* . . . , Cambridge 1861, pp. 496–7.

said, were to cause the men, and often the women, to prefer the gin-shop to a return home, to cause the children to be turned out into the streets to play – and hence to get into bad company – and to lower the moral atmosphere because whole families had to live in single rooms. It was argued that improved housing and sanitation, by improving the self-respect of the poor would help to reduce crime. The Rev. W. D. Morrison put the point well: 'Insufficient food, insufficient shelter, insufficient clothing, degrade men in their own eyes ... and in many case their conduct eventually falls to the same miserable level as their economic surroundings.'[15]

The effect of housing conditions on crime was undoubtedly quite as important as contemporaries suggested. The towns could not provide enough homes for their rapidly growing populations, and bad housing was an aspect of that general degradation of the poor which helped to turn many youngsters into criminals. Though some of the remarks cited in the previous paragraph applied to many areas at the end of the century (or even apply today), there was a trend to improved housing and sanitation over the century; and though there is no means of assessing the effect of this on general behaviour or on entry to the criminal class, it may well have been a considerable force for good.

Drink

One response to bad housing was to turn to the public house or the gin-shop. Drink of course played a very important part in the life of the poor, honest and criminal, in the nineteenth century; and there were at all times commentators who regarded drink as a major or even the major cause of crime. The volume of such statements seems if anything to increase in the 1820s and 1830s; but it is certainly true that the same sentiments are expressed at the beginning and the end of the century, and in between.[16] Contemporaries said that a taste for drink led

15. W. D. Morrison, *Juvenile Offenders*, 1896, p. 173.
16. See, for example, s.c. on Police, P.P. 1816, v, pp. 89, 116; s.c. on

many people to enter the criminal class, and that it was the want of a drink or the spending on drink of the price of food or lodging that often caused the first step into crime. Not only was here the crime committed by the drinker himself. Attention was often called to the disastrous effects on the family when the father, and even more the mother, was addicted to drink.

One is bound to look suspiciously on ideas so redolent of Victorian morality as these; yet they may well have had more than an element of truth in them. There is little doubt that crime and drink were often associated. Some members of the criminal class said that they needed a drink before they went out to work, others that they needed drink afterwards to help them forget their miseries (but these were usually prostitutes, who were probably making a routine play for sympathy or free drink). It is certainly clear that most of the proceeds of crime went on drink, for the criminal himself or his associates. It was probably true that, as was often said, criminals went out to steal when they ran short of the price of a drink.

Drink also played its part in leading people into the criminal class. Assaults and other minor offences were at times the result of excessive drinking and a consequent loss of self-control. Honest workmen imprisoned for the offences thus caused would all too often become criminals either because of the advice and example received in gaol or because of their loss of reputation. Moreover, contemporaries may have been right in suggesting that crime was often committed by hitherto honest people in order to obtain the price of a drink. John Burns said that the tragedy of the working man was the poverty of his desires; in a state of life in which the one indulgence accessible to the poor is drink, drink will often be the target for desire. We may perhaps conclude that in many cases drink was one cause in a complex of social causes of crime. It was a symptom of a society, and of an individual condition, in which crime was very likely to occur.

Drunkenness, P.P. 1834, viii, p. 320 (para. 18), 341 (q. 127), 615 (q. 3408), 533 (qq. 3684–7); W. Hoyle, *Crime in England and Wales in the Nineteenth Century*, 1876, pp. 91, 95–9, 105–14; Horsley, op. cit., p. 27.

Because of this connection between drink and crime, it is relevant to our purpose to consider contemporaries' views about fluctuations in the amount of drunkenness. On the whole there seems to have been a view just after 1815 that drunkenness among the lower classes was on the decline, but there had been a switch from beer to gin as a result of a fall in the quality of the beer and a cheapening of the more potent spirit.[17] This switch was intensified by the lowering of the spirit duty in 1825. The Beer Act of 1830 (11 Geo. IV, 1 Will. IV, c. 64) was designed to bring about a reverse movement by making beer more easily obtainable, and to this end it allowed beer-houses to be opened without a justices' licence. The result was, however, merely an increase of drunkenness (especially in the rural areas) – it was this act which inspired Sydney Smith's famous remark that 'the sovereign people are in a beastly state'. There were amending acts in 1834 and 1840 (4 & 5 Will. IV, c. 85 and 3 & 4 Vict., c. 61), but there was no real reduction in the number of beer-houses until control of them was restored to the justices in 1869 (by 32 & 33 Vict., c. 27). Special conditions obtained in some places, of course. Licensing policy was particularly lax in London between 1817 and 1825, for instance, and in 1869 Manchester obtained a local act which was thought to have reduced drunkenness. Surveying the country as a whole and looking back in 1876, L. O. Pike saw a marked reduction in drunkenness over the previous half century; nevertheless drunkenness remained, to him, as to his contemporaries, a grave evil.[18]

The decline in drunkenness towards the end of the century may be largely attributed to the steady growth of real incomes. This did not much affect the lower classes before 1850, but it supported a drive towards temperance and a 'reformation of

17. See, for example, S.C. on Police, P.P. 1816, v, pp. 59, 68, 77; ibid., P.P. 1817, vii, pp. 113, 150–51, 338, 350; S.C. on Drunkenness, P.P. 1834, viii, pp. 317–18.

18. L. O. Pike, *A History of Crime in England* . . . , 1876, vol. ii, pp. 431–4 J. W. Horsley, *Prisons and Prisoners*, 1898, pp. 74–94; S. and B. Webb, *The History of Liquor Licensing in England*, 1st ed. reprinted 1963, pp. 84–5, 123–34, 139–44.

manners' which gradually had an effect in the second half of the century. The Chartist movement of the 1830s and 1840s had its temperance wing, and the trade unions joined in the work after the formation of the 'New Model' unions in the early 1850s. The Evangelicals and nonconformists entered the temperance movement in force in the second half of the century. Sidney and Beatrice Webb spoke of the 'wonderful story of the growth of Temperance organizations', which began to have an effect on public opinion after 1860.[19] Though it was not the public opinion of the poor to which they were referring, the evidence suggests that the temperance movement had begun to have an effect in the third quarter of the century.

One very practical expression of the temperance movement was the drive to provide some more desirable alternative to the public house. The need for this began to attract attention in the 1830s. Edwin Chadwick, in evidence to the Select Committee on Drunkenness in 1834, argued for the provision of 'public parks and zoos, museums and theatres' as a means of reducing liquor consumption, as did a less famous witness, John Finch of Liverpool. William Lovett wrote to Francis Place in similar terms in the same year.[20] Some progress was made. The London Zoo had opened in 1828. The 'best consequences' flowed from the opening of the British Museum on public holidays, and a public meeting was held in 1837 to petition for an extension of the process by the free opening of Westminster Abbey, the National Gallery and similar places.[21] Ten years later there were demands for evening club-houses and public gardens and cricket grounds – 'I know it would be almost a sin to say Hyde Park,' said someone in 1852.[22] The movement had, however, by then gone far enough for another witness before the same

19. S. and B. Webb, op. cit., p. 144; cf. K. Heasman, *Evangelicals in Action* . . . , 1962, pp. 128–9, 132.

20. s.c. on Drunkenness, P.P. 1834, viii, pp. 360 (q. 325), 643 (qq. 3785–6); letter dated 17 Nov. 1834, Place Papers, Add. MSS. 27,827, ff. 29–31, British Museum.

21. J. S. Taylor, *Selections from the Writings* . . . , 1843, pp. 269–71.

22. s.c. on Juvenile Offenders, P.P. 1852–3, xxiii, pp. 231 (qq. 2302–4), 300–301 (qq. 3085–92).

committee to point to the beneficial effects of the parks and gardens which had already been provided in the larger towns. The significance of the provision of playing fields was heightened by the fact that the children of the criminal class did not play games; it was reckoned to be a good sign when boys in reformatory schools began to join in games of cricket, football or 'bounders'.[23] The provision of places where the poor could meet in pleasant surroundings and without having to buy drink began with the opening of a coffee-house in Dundee in 1854. The earlier coffee-houses had become the resorts of the rich or had fallen into disrepute, but there was from this time onwards a revival of respectable and cheap eating-places for the poor.[24]

Viewing the movement to provide alternatives to drink as a whole, some of the improvement in manners can be put to its credit. It would be foolish to think that it resulted in dramatic changes, but the effects, however small, can only have been beneficial. As a prison chaplain remarked in 1853, the Crystal Palace was better than a gin palace, a museum or zoo better than a theatre or jerry shop.[25] The pattern of life of the poor was moved a little nearer to that of the well-to-do.

The gulf between the classes

The gulf between the classes came frequently to mind when the people of the nineteenth century sought to explain the prevalence of crime, as we should expect of the age of the Two Nations. Over much of the century observers were prepared to lay part of the blame for crime on the upper classes' lack of interest in and consideration for the poor. Though a Frenchman comparing Paris to London drew attention to the advantages the latter city derived from the presence of a middle class to act as intermediary between rich and poor,[26] native com-

23. *Good Words*, vol. vii, April 1866, p. 281.
24. Heasman, op. cit., pp. 137–44.
25. H. S. Joseph, *Memoirs of Convicted Prisoners . . .*, 1853, p. 117.
26. Gerando, *De la bienfaisance publique*, 1839, quoted Chevalier, op. cit., p. 155.

mentators on the British scene were less impressed. W. L. Clay in 1861 wrote of his father, the Rev. John Clay, that[27]

> He was one of the first to preach the doctrine, common enough now, that the heartless selfishness of the upper classes, their disgraceful ignorance of, and indifference to, the brutal degradation in which they suffer the poor to lie, is the primary cause of almost all the crime in the country. ... Nothing filled him with more anger and disgust than to hear selfish cowardice crying for indiscriminate vengeance on all sorts and conditions of criminals, as if the comfort and ease of the vocal, self-asserting respectability, which rides paramount on the surface of society, was altogether to outweigh the rights, temporal and eternal, of the helpless inarticulate mass that lies below ...
>
> In common with most practical philanthropists, he considered that almost all crime was traceable to three closely linked causes, drunkenness, ignorance, and the habit of living in filthy, overcrowded dwellings. But he maintained that these, in their turn, were due, in a great measure, to the want of sympathy and intercourse between the upper and lower classes.

Others deplored the bad example set the poor by the self-indulgent and sometimes dishonest rich and the way in which low-paid people were at times led into crime by the temptation to ape the habits of their employers.[28] Not only moral failings were alleged; the victims of crime were often criticized for not taking due care of their property – but we need hardly be surprised at this or look for any change in this perennial failing.

Others saw a more impersonal cause. John Wade in 1829 was sure that a cause of crime was to be found in[29]

> the avarice of trade, and avidity of mercantile speculation. In no country are there so many worshippers of the *golden calf* as in England, where virtue and worth of every kind is measured by the standard of wealth. Every pursuit is chiefly valued as it conduces to

27. Clay op. cit., pp. 211–12, 492.

28. H. Brandon (ed.), *Poverty, Mendicity and Crime* ..., 1839, pp. 14–15; *Eclectic Review*, new ser., vol. vii, April 1854, pp. 396–8; *Reformatory and Refuge Journal*, July 1866, no. 32, p. 158.

29. J. Wade, *A Treatise on the Police and Crimes of the Metropolis* ... *by the Editor of 'The Cabinet Lawyer'*, 1829, p. 218.

the *accumulation of capital* . . . all are excited into emulation, into pursuits of pride and ambition, and a rivalry of property, display, and ostentation.

He is clearly not talking here about the poorest classes, but he suggests that the impact of ideas like these spread through the whole nation. Another writer went so far as to speak of the hatred of the poor for the rich and their detestation of the existing laws and institutions.[30] Others felt that industrialization, large-scale organization and the factory system were demoralizing the nation. It is well known that in the nineteenth century fears were entertained for the moral welfare of factory employees; that they might descend into actual crime, as distinct from immoral but non-criminal conduct, was part of these worries.

The charges against the rich summarized in the preceding paragraphs, though vague and generalized, could no doubt have been substantiated at the individual level in some cases. No doubt some youngsters were led astray by the example of the rich, and some were driven into crime by thoughtlessness and callousness. Moreover, it can be accepted that industrialization and its consequences were widening the gulf between the classes. One consequence of the growth of the large towns was a reduction in social cohesion. Mr J. M. Prest, in his study of Coventry during the Industrial Revolution, found that the growth of the town in the 1840s and 1850s contributed to the dissolution of the public opinion which had earlier assisted the 'majority of honourable masters and men in their attempts to impose the accepted standards upon the whole trade'.[31] He suggests that people were much less concerned with one another's conduct in business.

It would, however, be wrong to accept completely the con-

30. *Old Bailey Experiences, Criminal Jurisprudence . . . by the Author of 'The Schoolmaster's Experiences in Newgate'*, 1833, pp. 14, 264. cf. H. Worsley, *Juvenile Depravity*, 1849, pp. 73–115.

31. J. M. Prest, *The Industrial Revolution in Coventry*, 1960, pp. 79–80, 92–3, 140–41.

temporary ideas set out earlier and to condemn the rich in general for contributing to the sins of the poor – to begin with, because the nation cannot be divided so easily into just two groups. There was in truth a number of labouring classes, and not just one. This point is of particular relevance when crime is under consideration, for, as Frederic Hill, a former prison inspector, said, there were few 'skilled artisans or well-trained husbandmen' among the criminals. He went on:[32]

A really good carpenter, shoemaker, or blacksmith is seldom to be found in prison, and still less frequently a good machine maker, watch maker, or mathematical instrument maker. I know several large, well-ordered factories which scarcely ever produce a criminal; and rarely indeed is a member of that highly-respectable class of skilled agricultural labourers engaged from term to term in the north of England and the Lowlands of Scotland to be found in prison.

Even if allowance is made for this, of course, it is still possible to regard the upper classes as having failed in their duty to the lower classes. However, we must take account of the grave difficulties which would have faced them had they sought to do much more than they did to relieve the distress of the lowest classes. The magnitude of the townward drift has been demonstrated; the towns were swamped by the influx. The settled and employed working people were not in a strong position: even the well-to-do artisan walked on a narrow tightrope and the merest trifle could with ease plunge him into disaster. The people of the nineteenth century lacked the resources to cope with these problems. They lacked the technical knowledge – Edwin Chadwick had a long, hard struggle to win acceptance for oval sewers rather than square ones. They lacked an administrative machine capable of carrying out the work. They lacked too the attitude of mind that might have led them to remedy some of these deficiencies, for it was only gradually that the people of the nineteenth century as a whole came to regard problems of this sort as soluble and to regard government as having the duty to find a solution.

32. F. Hill, *Crime, its Amount, Causes and Remedies*, 1853, p. 41.

Moreover, the great majority of contemporaries did not see their duty in the terms in which it was seen by those quoted earlier and those who thought like them. Many held the philosophy that work was the sole road to salvation, and that indiscriminate charity, and above all State aid, was in the long run harmful to those whom it sought to help. To a great extent, then, the rich did no more because they believed, sincerely if conveniently, that it would have been wrong to do more.

It would moreover be unfair not to stress how much was in fact being done. There is no need to recapitulate here the work of public authorities and voluntary bodies, or to examine the philosophies, religious or secular, which provided so much of the inspiration; but clearly the contribution thus made was far from negligible. The reduction of crime towards the end of our period was in part attributable to an improved administration of the towns and an increase in what the twentieth century calls welfare services, and to the growth in the scale of voluntary action;[33] and to say this is in a way an admission that in the first half of the nineteenth century the provision of these things was inadequate. But the people of the early nineteenth century faced an overwhelming task; and, despite the strictures that some contemporaries placed on them, they can hardly be criticized for having been overwhelmed by it.

33. See p. 290.

10. Other economic and social change, II

Transport

Some of the most far-reaching changes of the nineteenth century were improvements in the means of transport, and naturally these changes had repercussions in the field with which we are concerned. It was not always the most dramatic and best-known steps forward that were the most important in relation to crime, however, and we have to deal first with a little-remembered development, the provision of docks in London. The considerable reduction of crime on the River Thames which occurred just before the end of the Napoleonic Wars was due in large part to the establishment of the West India and other docks which reduced the number of ships lying at anchor in the open river. Reforms in the naval dockyards after 1806 also played their part. A reduction of the plundering from lighters and barges had been one of the principal reasons put forward in 1796 for the construction of docks,[1] and though much good resulted from the establishment in 1798 of the Thames Police, wrote someone in 1842, 'the source of the evil was still untouched, the temptation remaining undiminished so long as the exposure of property was rendered unavoidable by the absence of sufficient accommodation in quays and warehouses'.[2] A modern writer echoes the thought: 'the only real remedy' for the thieving and the congestion that was its cause

1. J. G. Broodbank, *History of the Port of London*, 1921, vol. i, pp. 82–3, 99, 134, 138, 143; cf. J. Wade, *A Treatise on the Police and Crimes of the Metropolis . . . by the Editor of 'The Cabinet Lawyer'*, 1829, p. 349.
2. C. Knight (ed.), *London*, 1842, vol. iii, pp. 67, 70.

was the provision of docks.[3] The West India Dock was opened in 1802, the London Dock in 1805 and the East India Dock in 1806; the Commercial Dock, the Surrey Canal Dock and St Katherine's Dock were added by 1828. There is no doubt that this improvement in facilities was the main factor in the reduction in theft from shipping in the Port of London and from goods in transit. (The lack of adequate warehousing facilities at the docks was at mid century said to be a major cause of crime in Liverpool.[4])

We must not overestimate the effect of such a change, of course. As was only to be expected, the river thieves were equal to the challenge, and were able to switch their field of activity to the new area and adapt their techniques to the new conditions. Charles Dickens described the river thieves in 1853 in terms not very different from those used at the end of the eighteenth century. The 'tier-rangers', he said,[5] listened for snores and stole the property of captains of anchored vessels while they slept; the 'lumpers', unloaders with large concealed pockets, stole small packages and smuggled goods ashore for the crew; the 'truckers' were less thieves than smugglers; the 'dredgermen' lay around barges on pretence of dredging coal and when occasion served threw overboard parts of the cargo to be dredged up later; and 'a vast deal of property' was stolen from wharves, and barges were sometimes cut adrift and looted.

The steamship was becoming a factor by the time Dickens was writing. It had won the short-haul traffic in the 1820s, and was by the 1850s beginning to show its worth in the Atlantic trade. Steamships provided only about six per cent of the total tonnage on the British register in 1853, but were increasing in number rapidly; and the *Great Eastern,* the wonder-ship of its day, was on the drawing-board. Dickens said that unloaders were able to steal more from steamers than from sailing ships,

3. A. Bryant, *Liquid History: to commemorate Fifty Years of the Port of London Authority, 1909–1959,* 1960, p. 21.

4. *Morning Chronicle,* 27 May 1850.

5. Dickens, *Reprinted Pieces: Down With the Tide,* 1853; cf. Mayhew, *London Labour and the London Poor* . . . , 1861–2, vol. ii, p. 149.

because of the greater number of small packages and the need for a quicker turn-round.

Soon after Dickens wrote his account the Victoria Docks were opened (in 1855), and the Millwall Docks followed in 1868; extensions to the existing docks were also taking place about this time. However, the prevalence of crime does not seem to have been a motive in this later spurt of building – J. G. Broodbank makes no reference to theft from vessels or docks later than 1838 in his exhaustive account of the building and extension of the docks.[6]

Land transport similarly experienced some reduction of crime from improvements less dramatic than many of the inventions of the nineteenth century. Once again there was one conspicuous change, again attributed by many to the creation of a new police force: highway robbery (i.e. the operations of the mounted robber, as opposed to the foot-pad) had more or less disappeared from the environs of London by 1815. The influence of the Horse Patrole, established in 1805, must not be ignored. However, contemporary observers stressed the importance of such factors as the enclosure of Hounslow Heath and similar places, the introduction of mail-coaches, the increase of traffic on the roads and of dwellings alongside them, and the extension of the turnpiking of the roads around London. We can agree with these views, especially the last point. Though toll-gate keepers were said to be often in league with criminals, every additional toll-gate keeper meant either another accomplice to be paid or another potential informer to be feared – or of course both of these things together. Furthermore, the better roads that turnpike trusts were able to maintain out of toll-revenue, by speeding travel, reduced the need to be out after dark. By 1839 highway robbery was regarded as virtually extinct throughout the country, and the turnpikes were given much of the credit.[7]

In much the same way, though the police improvements of

6. Broodbank, op. cit., vol. i, p. 207.
7. R.C. on Constabulary Force, P.P. 1839, xix, pp. 52–4 (para. 51); S.C. on

the early 1820s were decisive in obtaining the reduction in crime in the London streets which then occurred, they were assisted by gaslighting, which was becoming general in London in that decade. 'We are so familiar with well-lighted streets', wrote John Wade in 1829,[8] going on to stress that they formed 'no inconsiderable branch of the police by guarding both persons and property from violence and depredation. ... Every improved mode of lighting the public streets is an auxiliary to protective justice.' As gaslighting spread – and most of the streets of the larger towns were lit by gas by 1838 [9] – it must have been a potent factor in making criminal activities more difficult. As the various new streets were cut during the century, too, life became more difficult for the pickpockets, as congestion was reduced and movement speeded. Londoners, it was said in 1856,[10] seldom had property stolen from them in the streets, for they walked too quickly.

The freedom of movement which had been attained by the beginning of our period was not, of course, an unmitigated blessing from the point of view of its effect on crime. Criminals too could now travel more easily. The Select Committee on Criminal Commitments of 1828 regarded improved communications as one of the factors which had led to the growth of an 'organized [criminal] society'.[11] One example of the effect of increased mobility is provided by the complaints, frequent until about 1840, of the depredations of London thieves in the surrounding districts. They would set out from town in the early evening with a light cart and rapid horses hired for the occasion, burgle and steal in the country parishes, and return to London in the early morning, being safely back in the obscurity of the large city before the alarm could be raised. One Bow

Police, P.P. 1822, iv, p. 152; ibid., P.P. 1834, xvi, pp. 108–9 (qq. 1372–84); G. Stephen, *A Letter to ... Lord John Russell ... on the Probable Increase of Rural Crime ...* , 1836, p. 9.

8. Wade, op. cit., pp. 268–9, 286.

9. Information kindly supplied by Mr M. E. Falkus.

10. *Quarterly Review*, vol. xcix, June 1856, p. 184.

11. S.C. on Criminal Commitments, P.P. 1828, vi, p. 423.

Street Runner, in his evidence to the Select Committee on Police in 1816, set precise limits to their sphere of operation: he said it covered the area from eight or ten to twenty miles around London. Another witness spoke of the thieves going even to Brighton.[12] Whatever the area covered may have been, there can be no doubt that the practice was common. The police would sometimes check carts at night; the criminals would often claim to be 'only resurrection-men' in the hope of avoiding a search.[13] To avoid these checks, the stolen goods were sometimes hidden for later collection and transfer to London by an innocent-looking woman coach-passenger.[14] The Metropolitan Police seems to have carried out night checks of carts on a greater scale than had its predecessors – it was of course a more numerous body. This may eventually have borne fruit, for the thieves' use of the river as a means of transport was said to have increased[15] and we hear no more of the use of horse and cart until 1872. In that year a writer in a magazine spoke of it in a rather different context, describing thieves in light carts with fast horses who went down country lanes in search of open windows, sheep or anything else which presented an opportunity for theft.[16] But in any event, of course, other means of transport were now becoming available.

The railway age began in 1830 with the success of the Liverpool and Manchester Railway. Railways spread rapidly in the 1830s and 40s, and by 1850 the foundation of the country's network of lines was completed. It was not long before the railway made its impact on the activities of the criminals. It conferred upon them an increased mobility which enabled them to take much greater advantage of the opportunities presented by special occasions such as race-meetings and Royal visits, and to extend their area of operations. Criminals had always liked

12. s.c. on Police, p.p. 1816, v, p. 176; ibid., p.p. 1828, vi, pp. 190–91.

13. Wade, op. cit., pp. 196–7; H. Cole, *Things for the Surgeon*, 1964, pp. 16, 90.

14. s.c. on Police, p.p. 1828, vi, p. 94; r.c. on Constabulary Force, p.p. 1839, xix, pp. 141–2 (para. 190).

15. s.c. on Police, p.p. 1838, xv, p. 415 (qq. 428–9).

16. *Dark Blue*, vol. ii, Feb. 1872, p. 697.

working in one place and living in another, even if still within the confines of a large town, and the railway facilitated this. It made it easier for people to escape from the scene of their crime; the more frequent departures aided planning, and the greater anonymity conferred by the increased number of passengers made pursuit more difficult. The steamships – which had also taken over the short-haul passenger traffic in the 1820s – helped as well, because the new-found certainty of departure made it possible to time an escape accurately and to be sure of leaving the country before pursuers could catch up.[17] On the other hand, as is well known, the transfer of goods traffic from canal to railway much reduced pilferage.[18] Of course, property on the railway was not immune from attack. An example of what went on is the ingenious system of stealing baggage in transit which was in use from the 1850s onwards. A case placed in the guard's van by a passenger travelling from London to Dover, for example, would have a label for an intermediate station such as Croydon stuck over the rightful one; the article would be claimed, returned to London and sold almost before the owner had discovered his loss.[19] Furthermore, trains, and buses as well, were a favourite scene of operations for pickpockets and other thieves.[20] We cannot strike a balance of gains and losses, but on the whole the criminals' operations seem to have been favoured by the new means of transport.

The more rapid communication of news was more of a disadvantage to criminals, though the penny post and the electric telegraph were of course convenient to them at times. But these

17. Chadwick Papers, box 126 (statement of M. M. Dowling), University College, London. The note in similar terms but without indication of source in H.O. 73/4, Part I, Public Record Office, is perhaps based on this statement.

18. For the misdeeds of the canal boatmen see R.C. on Constabulary Force, P.P. 1839, xix, pp. 54–61 (paras. 52–6). There is much supplementary evidence in the Chadwick Papers.

19. *Convict Life . . . by a Ticket-of-Leave Man,* 1879, pp. 39–40.

20. Chadwick Papers, box 127 (statement of J. Gattley, senior); R.C. on Constabulary Force, P.P. 1839, xix, pp. 61–2 (para. 57); W. L. Clay, *The Prison Chaplain; a Memoir of the Rev. John Clay . . .,* Cambridge 1861, pp. 527, 530.

two inventions did much to facilitate the rapid circulation of information about thefts and thieves – something which since the days of Henry Fielding has been recognized as a most important step in fighting crime. The photographing of prisoners, introduced in Bristol in the 1850s and gradually extended over the rest of the country, was a much more satisfactory method of recognizing old offenders than the previous elaborate arrangements for policemen and gaolers to see those arrested. The use of photography was endorsed and recommended by the Select Committee on Gaols in 1863.[21] If criminals could move around the country more easily, then there was at least the recompense that word of their doings could be spread more easily as well. Furthermore, the general improvement in communications, both railways and posts, helped to reduce the burden on the private prosecutor, and in this way too it helped to combat crime and hence to reduce its volume.

Improved machinery and improved methods

A general trend to improved machinery and improved methods was of course a marked feature of the nineteenth century. A writer in 1852 said happily that criminals adopted new methods only slowly, and that all 'great discoveries, from printing down to the electric telegraph, have aided detection rather than the accomplishment of crime.'[22] Few would have agreed with this optimistic statement. The Select Committee on Criminal Commitments of 1828 took a very different view:[23] 'It must be confessed that of late years the art of Crime, if it may be so called, has increased faster than the art of Detection.' Viewing the period as a whole, however, the truth was more complex than either statement would suggest. Counterfeiters, for

21. s.c. on Goals, P.P. 1863, ix, p. 17 (para. xv). cf. R. and F. Davenport-Hill, *The Recorder of Birmingham: a Memoir of Matthew Davenport Hill* . . ., 1878, p. 207.

22. J. H. Burton, *Narratives from Criminal Trials in Scotland*, 1852, vol. ii, pp. 1–2.

23. s.c. on Criminal Commitments, P.P. 1828, vi, p. 423.

example, in the 1820s faced difficulties as a result of improvements in minting which made it harder to make a good counterfeit coin, as well as from better methods of testing suspect coins. At the lower end of the trade, those who made poor imitations which could only hope to gain acceptance in a crowd or in bad light were hit by a decline in the metal-button trade, whose processes were used for two types of cheap counterfeit coin. However, electroplating had by the 1850s come to the coiner's aid; it made his equipment light and portable where previously it had been heavy and cumbersome, and the production of good imitations thus became easier and safer.[24]

On the other hand, the same process of electroplating worked against the house-breaker, for the general substitution of plated ware for solid silver in the middle-class home had by the latter part of the century reduced the value of a principal target. House-breakers had already suffered from the improvement of locks, though this did not proceed so far or so fast as might be thought – as late as 1866 it was complained that few houses were built with reliable locks, that in many rows one key opened all the houses, and that a few pick-locks would open most doors. However, house-breakers had benefited from sophistication in manufacture in at least one respect – the standardization of shutter-bars made it easier to learn how to break them.[25]

And so the struggle went on, first one side and then the other gaining from a new technique. A classic instance was the tussle between safe-breakers and safe-manufacturers. A writer in 1863 listed eight changes of method, by breakers and manufacturers alternately, each side finding a way to circumvent the last improvement introduced by the other. The advantage, he said, was at the time he wrote with the manufacturers, but we can be sure that it did not stay with them for long.[26] In much

24. S.C. on Police, P.P. 1817, vii, p. 496; Wade, op. cit., pp. 182–5; M. D. Hill, *Suggestions for the Repression of Crime . . .* , 1857, pp. 46–7.

25. *Good Words*, vol. vii, Dec. 1866, pp. 848–9; *The Times*, 26 Aug. 1884.

26. *Cornhill Magazine*, vol. vii, Jan. 1863, pp. 82–7; cf. R.C. on Constabulary Force, P.P. 1839, xix, p. 223.

the same way, though the forgery of cheques was in the 1820s made much more difficult by an improved ink – forgers used to remove all writing save the signature with an ink-eradicating fluid, until the printers altered the ink of the background so that this too was affected by the fluid – no doubt more sophisticated methods of forgery were soon forthcoming.[27]

Perhaps the only generalization that can be made is that as a result of technical progress more skill was required by the criminal. Criminals normally worked for themselves, and had no need to worry about gild restrictions or patent rights or to fear a Luddite-like protest against the adoption of new techniques. There was thus a rapid response to changing conditions and a rapid adoption of all that new technology had to offer. In general this could be expected to give criminals an advantage over their less flexible opponents, official and unofficial, but changes did not always favour the wrongdoer. New methods might for a time present new opportunities to those with the ability to use them, or might for a time make crime more difficult; but the cumulative effect was in many cases to increase the level of ability required without affecting the amount of criminal activity. The changes put a premium on skill, and this was one cause of the trend to more skilled and less violent forms of crime. To some extent, of course, this reduction of violence was a reflection of a general trend; sports and the code of punishment, to take two diverse examples, were becoming less bloody. But the Sheffield 'outrages' – the violent treatment of non-unionists – of 1866, for instance, act as a warning against over-emphasis on this, and there is thus some reason to think that the need for skill was a principal factor in bringing about a reduction in violence. A criminal can of course be both skilful and violent, but – in the nineteenth century at any rate – this seems to have been an unusual combination.

Sometimes, of course, changes took place in technology or other aspects of life without having much effect on criminal activity. For example, the crowds which gathered in 1820 on Queen Caroline's route to her trial were in many ways different

27. *London Review*, col. i, Feb. 1829, p. 272.

from the crowds which gathered in 1852 for the Duke of Wellington's funeral – but to the pickpockets both occasions represented a wonderful opportunity. Whether people went to Drury Lane Theatre or 'Spurgeon's New Tabernacle', whether they flocked to executions or exhibitions, gathered round coaching-inns or railway stations, the pickpockets would take their crowd where they could find it. In much the same way, burglars and safe-breakers, shop-lifters and sneak-thieves would adapt readily to new circumstances.

It is convenient to deal here with changes in the techniques of retail distribution. At the time of Waterloo the glass-fronted shop had just established itself in London and all save the most old-fashioned towns. Shopkeepers, in the poorer parts of town at any rate, retained something of the former habit of displaying goods where customers could touch as well as see them, and would suspend great festoons of their wares outside their door as a further bait to purchases. The effect may be readily imagined. The practice resulted in an increase both of the temptation to young passers-by and of the ease with which they could succumb to temptation. Many commentators complained about the habit, and judges frequently refused to refund to these shopkeepers the expenses of prosecution. However, the practice continued, and even increased, as a result, we are told, of increased competition during the greater part of the century. The latest reference which has been noted was in 1858, when it was inaccurately described as 'this modern practice of exposing goods for sale at shop doors'.[28] One may suspect that the comment dies out after that date, not because the practice ceased, but because the decline in the number of juvenile offenders reduced the resultant thefts.

The rise of the shop was associated with a change in the role of the fair, which had earlier been a form of retail or wholesale

28. By S. P. Day, *Juvenile Crime, its Causes, Character, and Cure*, 1858, pp. 50–52. For the earlier remarks which prove him wrong, see, for example, s.c. on Police, P.P. 1816, v, p. 29; ibid., P.P. 1828, vi, pp. 57, 67; s.c. on Criminal Commitments, P.P. 1828, vi, p. 443; s.c. on Juvenile Offenders, P.P. 1852, vii, pp. 43 (q. 388), 86 (q. 681); ibid., P.P. 1852–3, xxiii, p. 300 (q. 3085).

distribution but which, though still retaining some aspects of that role at times, was now primarily an occasion for jollification. (The sale of beer at fairs, it may be noted, was free from all regulation until 1874.) In 1816 there were, it was said, eighty fair-days a year within 10 miles of the metropolis, and in London and elsewhere fairs were a source of worry to magistrates and police officers. They attracted thieves and prostitutes from many miles around. Moreover, contemporaries were convinced, rightly or wrongly, that young people were all too often led astray while at the fair. They might, it was feared, lose all their money and turn to crime or prostitution to replace it, or be seduced by the apparent attractions of a life free from the cares and labour of a normal existence. Thieves were believed to be constantly on the look-out for likely recruits, and the fairs were felt to be good places for this purpose. As a result of these beliefs, efforts were made to deal with the evil. Some fairs held without authorization were suppressed, and police supervision reduced the dangers of those that continued. However, even at mid century the harmful effects of fairs were still a subject of complaint.[29]

Money

There were during the nineteenth century a number of changes in the form of money in circulation. In 1815 the main currency of the country consisted of notes of the Bank of England and other banks, which had replaced gold coins during the Napoleonic Wars. Gold re-entered active circulation upon the resumption of cash payments by the Bank of England in 1821, and the return to earlier conditions was completed by the withdrawal of £1 and £2 notes by 1829. After this date the £5 note was the smallest in circulation, and the sovereign and half-sovereign formed the main part of the active currency.

These changes had their effect on crime. The wartime sub-

29. s.c. on Police, p.p. 1816, v, p. 170; ibid., p.p. 1817, vii, pp. 376, 403–4; ibid., p.p. 1822, iv, pp. 148, 153–4; Report of Prison Inspector, Northern and Eastern Districts, p.p. 1841 (sess. 2), v, p. 139; s.c. on Juvenile Offenders, p.p. 1852, vii, pp. 21 (q. 154), 86–7 (qq. 683–6).

stitution of bank-notes, which were at any rate sometimes traceable, for the completely anonymous gold coins must have made life more difficult for thieves – it was given some of the credit for the elimination of highway robbery. However, it had as its main effect in our field a considerable enlargement of the opportunities for forging bank-notes. Moreover, the tokens issued by some provincial manufacturers to eke out the supply of currency were an easier target for counterfeiters than the coins issued from the Royal Mint. The withdrawal of the smaller notes after 1829 meant that bank-notes were more rarely handled and more readily examined on presentation, and these changes virtually eliminated, for a time at any rate, the forgery of Bank of England notes. Gold coins were the hardest of all to counterfeit, so a double blow was struck in defence of the currency.[30]

The banking habit grew throughout the nineteenth century, and the consequent reduction in the amount of cash kept in offices and houses and carried about the person reduced the opportunities presented to thieves. However, the persistence of the practice of paying dividends publicly gave thieves an opportunity which they did not neglect of spotting people who were carrying large sums of money. Dividend Day at the Bank of England was long famous as a rendezvous for pickpockets, and Townsend, the great Bow Street Runner, was always engaged to go there to discourage at least the known criminals from attending.[31] The payment of dividends publicly on Exchange was the subject of criticism as late as 1866.[32]

The ways in which wages were paid also underwent improvement in the nineteenth century. At its beginning the vicious system of paying wages in public houses was prevalent. These 'pay-tables' were responsible for much drunkenness, if nothing else, for the men were kept waiting late for their money (by

30. Wade, op. cit., pp. 182–9; Sir G. Stephen's comments on the draft report of the R.C. on Constabulary Force, H.O. 73/4, Part I (MSS. loose sheets), P.R.O.

31. P. Pringle, *The Thief-Takers*, 1958, p. 167.

32. Chadwick Papers, box 132 (reprint of article); s.c. on Juvenile Offenders, P.P. 1847, vii, p. 218 (q. 1822); *Good Words*, vol. vii, Dec. 1866, p. 851.

agreement with the publican, if he was not himself the employer) and had usually run up quite a score by the time that they were paid. The system was beginning to decline by 1840, but its evil effects were still sufficiently strong for Parliament to have to give attention to the matter. As was so often the case, special cases were dealt with first. An act of 1842 (5 & 6 Vict., c. 99) prohibited the payment of miners' wages in public houses, and a local act of the following year (6 & 7 Vict., c. ci, s. xxiv) had a similar effect in relation to coal-whippers in the Port of London. This latter act, however, expired in 1856, when payment in public houses was said to have been revived, with disastrous consequences.[33] It was not until 1883 that a general prohibition of the practice was imposed, most trades having to wait for the Payment of Wages in Public-Houses Prohibition Act (46 & 47 Vict., c. 31).

An even more prevalent system in the earlier years of the century, and an equally unsatisfactory one, was the practice of paying wages late on Saturday night. This tempted men to drink much of their wages even if they did not receive them in a public house, made Sunday trading inevitable despite attempts to suppress it, and forced working-men's wives to buy at the last minute and in an uneconomical way. By the middle of the century Saturday payment was usually avoided in London, Friday was the customary pay-day in Leeds, and apparently payment on Saturday was becoming less usual everywhere. The regular weekly pay-day, instead of fortnightly or monthly pays or the 'long-pay' system (a subsistence payment with an occasional settling-up), had also become usual by this time. It is not suggested that these unsatisfactory methods of paying wages were often a direct cause of crime; but they contributed to that general degradation of the poor which led many youngsters to adopt a life of crime.[34]

33. Mayhew, op. cit., vol. iii, pp. 236, 240, 285 (a highly coloured account); Chadwick Papers, box 131 (reports of Metropolitan Police superintendents, 1840); J. E. Ritchie, *Here and There in London*, 1859, pp. 127–34.

34. S. Neal, *Special Report on the State of Juvenile Education and Delinquency in . . . Salford . . .*, 2nd ed., Salford 1851, appendix, pp. 6–10; F. Hill, *Crime, its Amount, Causes and Remedies*, 1853, pp. 80–81.

11. Punishment

Capital punishment

The great reliance on capital punishment in the eighteenth century has often been described.[1] Though the exact number of capital offences is probably impossible to compute, it is often said that there were over 200 at the end of the century. The process of demolition of this vast structure began in 1808, when Sir Samuel Romilly managed to persuade Parliament to remove the death penalty from the offence of picking pockets ('privately stealing from the person'). The work of repeal continued by stages until 1837. The campaign against capital punishment did not end then, but it took on a new complexion, for in that year the use of the death penalty was limited to a fairly narrow list of offences. This was in law wider than the later list, but the only difference in practice was that executions for attempted murder took place in 1838, 1839, 1841 and 1861. In 1861 the number of capital offences was reduced to four, and thence it remained unchanged until 1957.

It must be stressed that by no means everyone who was sentenced to death was in fact executed; Professor Radzinowicz estimates that by the end of the eighteenth century not more than one in three of those sentenced to death in London and Middlesex were executed.[2] The proportion was even lower for certain offences, and it dropped as the nineteenth century progressed. Thus none of the eighty people convicted at the Old Bailey in the years 1805–14 of the offence of stealing privately in a shop

1. L. Radzinowicz, *History of the English Criminal Law*, 1948–56, vol. i, *passim*.
2. ibid., p. 151.

was executed; and of the 8,483 sentenced to death in England and Wales in the years 1828–34, only 355, or less than five per cent, were executed.[3]

What was the effect of capital punishment and of these reductions in its use? Capital punishment for offences other than murder was generally thought undesirable, even if we leave out of account the views of those who were in principle opposed to capital punishment for any crime. Most people thought that the death penalty tended to promote crime, believing that it did not deter the criminal, who regarded it as a risk of the calling and accepted it as a soldier accepted the risk of death in battle, but that it did deter prosecutor, magistrate, jury and judge, who were tempted to strain the law to avoid the risk of what was felt to be an unjust penalty. In support of this view, the Statistical Branch of the Home Office pointed out that in some cases the proportion of convictions to committals fell in the years after the death sentence had been carried out for the offence concerned, rising again when the memory of the executions had begun to fade.[4] This opinion was of course not a unanimous one. Some police officers, magistrates and judges in the period before 1837 argued that the capital penalty did act as a deterrent to seasoned criminals. Some of these defenders of capital punishment called for more stringent and more stringently enforced laws; others asked that executions should be carried out quickly to increase the deterrent effect. However, the main weight of opinion was against the death penalty for offences other than murder.[5]

Opportunities to test these theories occurred as various offences were removed from the list of capital crimes. Most people, including the Statistical Branch of the Home Office, believed that there was no increase, and perhaps even a decrease, in the number of crimes of each type as the change was

3. s.c. on Police, P.P. 1816, v, p. 251; minute dated 19 Oct. 1835, Criminal Register Letter Book, pp. 118–19, Home Office.

4. Minute dated 11 Feb. 1841, ibid., p. 183.

5. s.c. on Police, P.P. 1816, v, pp. 144, 223, 229–30, 250–51; ibid., P.P. 1817, vii, p. 420; ibid., P.P. 1818, viii, pp. 174–5, 182; ibid., P.P. 1822, iv, pp. 147–8; R.C. on Criminal Laws, P.P. 1836, xxxvi, pp. 230–31, 233.

made, and it was shown that for some offences the abolition of capital punishment had had the beneficial effect of increasing the proportion of convictions to committals. Some opponents of capital punishment sought to prove that abolition reduced crime by pointing to a decline in the number of committals for trial for certain offences, while others sought to use an increased number of committals to prove that abolition had increased the public's willingness to prosecute. Even at the mid-point of the century, however, some people claimed that the effect of the drastic limitation of capital punishment had been to increase crime.[6]

By mid century the debate about capital punishment was substantially a debate about murder, and thus it is not directly of interest here. However, people occasionally wondered whether professional criminals were deterred from adding murder to other crimes by fear of the death penalty. One judge felt that the penalty had no effect on unpremeditated crimes but saved life in premeditated and carefully planned ones. Confirmation of this view may perhaps be found in the statement made before capital punishment was confined to murder cases that pistols were occasionally taken to major crimes by those who knew they stood a good chance of being hanged if they were caught.[7]

It is certain that the wide use of capital punishment before 1837 did not have a significant deterrent effect. There is little doubt, of course, that criminals did try to avoid capital crime. This was the view of experienced police officers, and it is sup-

6. s.c. on Criminal Laws, p.p. 1819, viii, pp. 37, 45, 52, 232–3; Introduction to Criminal Returns for 1840, p.p. 1841, xviii, pp. 260–61; J. S. Taylor, *Selections from the Writings . . .* , 1843, pp. 234–7, 243; J. C. Symons, *Tactics for the Times, as Regards the Condition and Treatment of the Dangerous Classes*, 1849, pp. 75–9; J. Kingsmill, *Chapters on Prisons and Prisoners, and the Prevention of Crime*, 3rd ed., 1854, p. 381; Introduction to Criminal Returns for 1854, p.p. 1854–5, xliii, pp. 4–5; Society for the Abolition of Capital Punishment, *Analysis and Review of the Blue Book of the Royal Commission on Capital Punishment*, 1866, pp. 8–9.

7. s.c. on Juvenile Offenders, p.p. 1847, vii, p. 601; r.c. on Constabulary Force, p.p. 1839, xix, p. 219.

ported by a wealth of evidence of attempts by criminals to persuade youngsters to perform the actual criminal act in the hope of avoiding the death penalty. But the general conclusion remains valid despite this qualification.

It is equally certain that capital punishment operated to deter prosecutor, magistrate, jury and judge. At first one is tempted to argue that by the commencement of the period under review executions for crimes other than murder had decreased in number so far that they had reached a level which, though shocking to our twentieth-century susceptibilities, was unlikely to have had the same effect on our tougher forbears. The annual toll for England and Wales varied between thirty-five and ninety-seven between 1815 and 1829, when the wave of abolitions gathered pace, and this might not be expected to seem too large in the context of the time.[8] But the evidence must be accepted that capital punishment affected the actions of many of those concerned in bringing malefactors to justice.

It should not be thought that this effect was confined to the more serious cases in which a sentence of death was likely to be carried out, or even to those crimes for which the death sentence could in fact be passed. The story was told that, 'many years' before 1840, a Grand Jury took the unjustified and contradictory course of rejecting a bill of indictment for a capital charge and sending the prisoner for trial on a non-capital charge only, in a case in which the evidence was the same for both charges and was sufficient for both or for neither. They justified this action by saying that 'they had not had an execution in their own for thirty years, and please God, they never would – nor even run the chance of it!' The petty jury then acquitted the prisoner on the non-capital charge for the same reason, explain-

8. Evidence of the difficulty of using nineteenth-century statistics, even for something as definite and as noteworthy as an execution, is provided by the fact that one source for these figures – Statements about Criminals, P.P. 1830, xxiii, pp. 171, 179 – gives the total of executions for offences other than murder in 1828 as 61, while another – Return of Executions, P.P. 1846, xxxiv, p. 746–70 – gives it as 41. There are other, less marked, differences between the two returns.

ing that they had not been quite sure whether the charge was a capital one and had decided not to take any chances.[9] How typical such a train of events was we cannot say, but feelings of this sort must have helped many criminals to escape punishment.

It can therefore be concluded that the removal of capital punishment from a wide range of offences, carried out principally between 1808 and 1837 but completed only in 1861 constituted a marked improvement in the law and tended to reduce the amount of crime.

Secondary punishment

Contemporaries used the term 'secondary punishment' for all non-capital punishment. It is convenient to deal first of all with punishments other than those involving some form of detention, for we can say very little about them. Both fines and whipping were in use during the nineteenth century (the latter sometimes as well as imprisonment, sometimes instead of it) but because they were used for the more trivial offences it is impossible to establish with what frequency they were inflicted or what effect they had.

Informal systems of probation developed in the nineteenth century. The pioneering work of the Warwickshire Quarter Sessions in the 1820s and of Matthew Davenport Hill when he became Recorder of Birmingham in 1839 is well known;[1] London magistrates were handing children over to parents or guardians after a warning in the post-Waterloo period.[11] It is however, impossible to say much about the effects of these systems. We may suspect that youngsters who were given the benefit of one or other of them were less likely to commit further crime than those exposed to the contamination of

9. Taylor, op. cit., p. 418n.

10. The work of these pioneers is described and documented in United Nations Department of Social Affairs, *Probation and Related Measures*, New York 1951, pp. 23–4 (para. 19), 42–7 (paras. 32–43).

11. See p. 195.

prison; but we have no means of assessing the importance of this factor.

For practical purposes, then, our examination of non-capital punishment is confined to the various forms of detention. In the early part of the century those undergoing detention of course included many who had been sentenced to death and reprieved; nearly all of them were transported to the penal settlements overseas or served their sentence in the hulks or prisons in this country. They thus shared the fate of those sentenced directly to transportation or imprisonment.

What that fate was varied considerably as a result of the changes in the prison system which went on throughout the century. Prisons for much of the nineteenth century fall into two categories: the national prisons, in which were confined the 'convicts', those sentenced to death or transportation or, later in the century, to penal servitude, and the local prisons, in which other sentences of imprisonment were served. The former were under the control of the Secretary of State for the Home Department, the latter of the local justices in Quarter Sessions. In 1877 both groups of prisons were transferred to the administration of the Prison Commission, a central body responsible to the Home Secretary.

At the time of Waterloo many of the abuses described by John Howard in his *State of the Prisons* of 1777 still persisted. In some gaols the prisoners of all categories were confined together in wards or yards with no attempt to prevent conversation or the contamination of the innocent. In some the boys were not separated from the men, nor the males from the females. The Gaols Act of 1823 (4 Geo. IV, c. 64) was the first major step forward; it made it the duty of justices to classify prisoners and to submit regular reports to the Home Secretary. This duty of classification gave rise to one of the most bitter battles of the nineteenth century, that between advocates of the two rival systems of transatlantic origin, the separate system and the silent system. Both aimed at preventing the corruption of the good by the bad prisoner, the former by eliminating any contact at all between prisoners and the latter by punishing all attempts at conversation though the prisoners spent the day in association. The conflict was finally won by the separate system, and the Prison Act of 1865 (28 & 29 Vict., c. 126) ordered that all local prisons should have separate cells. The years 1878–94, the years of the 'Du Cane régime', were years of rigorous treatment. Under their Chairman, Sir Edmund Du Cane, the Prison Commissioners prescribed, say the Webbs,[12] 'a uniform application of cellular isolation, absolute non-intercourse among the prisoners, the rule of silence, oakum-picking, and the tread-wheel'.

Our concern is of course merely with the effects of these changes on the course of crime. The unreformed prisons had few defenders; contemporaries were familiar with the evil effects of the indiscriminate herding together of all kinds of prisoners. Though each of the various reformed systems had its convinced adherents, criticisms of the prisons were not silenced. The failure of prison as a reformatory measure was often mentioned as in itself a cause of crime, and when the reformatory school movement started in the 1850s a criticism of the effect of prison was often the starting-point for advocacy of the new-found alternative. Furthermore, a positive harmful effect was noted from reformed as well as from unreformed prisons. Certainly until the mid 1850s, and to a lesser extent much later, prison was alleged to be the great training ground of crime. The briefest acquaintanceship with the inside of a prison, even on remand, was regarded as likely to ruin for ever those for whom there would otherwise have been hope. Both victims and magistrates were very reluctant to send to prison anyone of apparent good character, and especially youngsters. A London magistrate set out his feelings in 1816:[13]

12. S. and B. Webb, *English Prisons Under Local Government*, 1st ed., reprinted 1963, p. 207. The proceeding account of developments in prison administration is largely based on the Webbs' survey.

13. S.C. on Police, P.P. 1816, v, p. 57; cf. ibid., pp. 110, 216; ibid., P.P. 1817, vii, pp. 538–40; ibid., P.P. 1828, vi, p. 40; B. Waugh, *The Gaol Cradle: Who Rocks It?* ..., 3rd ed., 1876, *passim*; *Convict Life ... by a Ticket-of-Leave Man*, 1879, pp. 6–7, 34, 38–9, 41, 163–5.

I have seen instances of children that I have been under the painful necessity of committing to prison, shew marks of contrition at the time he [sic] has been under examination (as far as one can look into the human mind;) ... but from the present system of mixing children with the most depraved characters, I consider them as lost to society for ever. ... When a child has been committed for further examination, we do not tell the prosecutor himself, but we find the means of giving him a hint, that if he does not wish to prosecute, he may afford us an opportunity of discharging him, being fully aware that it would be the ruin of that child, and that he would be lost for ever.

The attempts of the separate system to prevent prisoners from recognizing one another in later life were defeated by the mixing allowed before trial, at the court awaiting trial, and during the process of discharge.[14]

This picture fits in well enough with the generally accepted view of nineteenth-century prison administration and its effects; it is very much what we should expect; it is supported by an impressive weight of evidence. Though the various reformed régimes, and even the old unreformed prisons and the hulks, no doubt had their occasional successes, they can have done little positive good to reclaim criminals (after all, we still do not know how to do this). That prisons were training-grounds for criminals, schools of crime, is only too easy to believe. There is ample evidence of the ingenuity of prisoners, and doubtless they were able to triumph over all the apparatus of masks and individual stalls in chapels and on treadmills, over silence rules and separate confinement. It can be accepted that neophytes in crime furthered their training in prison, though it is reasonable to suppose that in the reformed prisons opportunities to learn were more restricted than under the old system.

If, then, prisons failed to reform their inmates and served only as schools of crime, what success did they have as a deterrent? The advocates of the silent and separate systems claimed deterrent powers for their favoured régime. It was, for example, said that criminals had been driven from Berkshire to

14. *London Review*, vol. i, Feb. 1829, p. 302; cf. *Fraser's Magazine*, vol. vi, Aug. 1832, p. 21n.

Buckinghamshire by the separate system at Reading Gaol,[15] where the redoubtable Rev. John Field was Chaplain – prisoners in the 'Read, Read, Reading Gaol' had only a Bible for company. The treadmill and the cell-crank were highly regarded as deterrents in the earlier part of the century, but they eventually fell out of favour.[16] On the whole, however, few contemporaries believed that prison deterred criminals.

On the other hand, there were many who felt that conditions in prison were so favourable as actually to induce crime. There was a belief that some petty crime was committed with a view to gaining admission to prison. W. L. Clay wrote, with reference to the 1830s,[17] 'The prison was worse than useless; it tempted to, rather than deterred from, crime. Diseased and starving wretches frequently committed offences for the avowed purpose of benefiting by its abundant rations and comfortable infirmary.' Greenwood quoted a boy who, on leaving gaol, said:[18] 'It's the most comfortable crib as ever I was in. I wish I'd a got three months 'stead of three weeks. I'll do summat wot'll make it hot for me next time, no fear.' A firm denial that such things happened came from Sir William Crofton in 1863, but as a prison administrator he was not a disinterested witness.[19]

It was a general belief over most of the nineteenth century that prisoners got better food than many free labourers. Sir Robert Peel himself wrote in 1826 that when the prisoners in the General Penitentiary on Millbank[20]

lived well, their lot in the winter season was thought by people outside to be rather an enviable one. We reduced their food, and

15. s.c. on Juvenile Offenders, P.P. 1847, vii, p. 492 (q. 4920).

16. W. L. Clay, *The Prison Chaplain; a Memoir of the Rev. John Clay . . .*, Cambridge 1861, pp. 132–3, 270; Capt. Cartwright, *Criminal Management* 1865, p. 123.

17. Clay, op. cit., p. 116.

18. J. Greenwood, *The Wilds of London*, 1876, p. 244; cf. M. Carpenter *Juvenile Delinquents – their Condition and Treatment*, 1853, p. 176.

19. s.c. on Gaols, P.P. 1863, ix, p. 337 (qq. 3267–8); but cf. ibid., p. 98 (q. 755).

20. Letter dated 24 March 1826, C. S. Parker, *Sir Robert Peel . . .*, 1899 vol. i, p. 402.

from the combined effect of low but ample diet, and the depression of spirits which is the frequent attendant on the dull unvarying punishment of imprisonment for years, there arose a malignant and contagious disorder. ... The present occupants are therefore again living too comfortably, I fear, for penance.

William Cobbett and Edwin Chadwick also drew attention to the disparity between free labourers' conditions and those of prisoners, and the point is frequently made later.[21] The definitive statement seems to be that of W. A. Guy, Medical Superintendent of the General Penitentiary, Millbank. In 1863 he said that prisoners in all categories received more than the general mass of labourers throughout the country and that those in convict establishments received at least as much as the 'well-off' labourers.[22] Convicts sentenced to penal servitude (introduced in 1853), and in general all those sentenced to long terms of imprisonment, received better treatment, and especially a more generous diet, than those committed for a few weeks, and this put a premium on the more serious forms of crime. Prisoners not only were better fed than free labourers; they often did less work as well. For instance, the task for ten hours' hard labour in Holloway in 1868 was the picking of 3 lb of oakum, but an honest woman had to pick over 6 lb. to earn 1s., a very modest daily wage.[23]

One consequence of the New Poor Law of 1834 can conveniently be dealt with here. That law was founded on the doctrine that life in a workhouse had to be 'less eligible' than life as a free labourer if the morale of the nation was not to be sapped; but this had the unfortunate side-effect that life in a workhouse also became less eligible than life in prison. The prisoner was better treated than the pauper; this was particularly true in the case of illness. After all, to be governor of a

21. S. E. Finer, *The Life and Times of Sir Edwin Chadwick*, 1952, p. 83; V. Cobbett, *Rural Rides*, Everyman ed., 1953, vol. i, p. 296.

22. s.c. on Gaols, P.P. 1863, ix, pp. 394–5 (qq. 3854–68); cf. s.c. on Criminal Commitments, P.P. 1828, vi, pp. 433, 461; s.c. on Juvenile Offenders, P.P. 1847, vii, p. 347 (qq. 3168–70); *Five Years Penal Servitude, by One Who Has Endured It*, 4th ed., 1878, pp. 299–301.

23. *Journal of the Statistical Society*, vol. xxxi, Sept. 1868, p. 320n.

gaol was a position for a gentleman, whilst a Bumble could be master of a workhouse. It was widely believed that crime was sometimes committed to acquire the status of prisoner rather than that of pauper. Miss Carpenter wrote of 'old and experienced thieves and vagabonds' staying in a workhouse but 'committing, if it is not according to their taste, such acts of mischief and insubordination as will entitle them to a week's lodging in a favourite gaol, where it is known that every attention will be paid them'.[24] The Rev. W. D. Morrison spoke of elderly workmen having a year or two of crime before entering 'the House'.[25] But the last word belongs to an old lady whom the Rev. J. W. Horsley was trying to persuade to end her days in a workhouse rather than in prison:[26] ' "Excuse me, sir," she said, "have you tried both places? No? Well, I have, and I know where I am best off." '

Thus R. W. Emerson's famous remark that in England 'the pauper lives better than the free labourer; the thief better than the pauper; and the transported felon better than the one under imprisonment'[27] was merely one expression of familiar ideas. In 1865 Thomas Archer wrote:[28] 'The health and physical comfort of the British felon is better cared for than that of the ordinary British pauper, and receives far more earnest attention than that of the British soldier or the British sailor.' In the general belief, then, both the unreformed and the reformed prisons actually tempted people into crime. But one must be on one's guard against accepting such views; not only do they represent a constantly recurring criticism of prison administrations which has often been refuted,[29] but they are likely to have

24. M. Carpenter, *Reformatory Schools for the Children of the Perishing and Dangerous Classes, and for Juvenile Offenders*, 1851, p. 239.

25. W. D. Morrison, *Crime and its Causes*, 1891, p. 89.

26. J. W. Horsley, '*I Remember*' – *Memories of a 'Sky Pilot' in the Prison and the Slum*, 1911, p. 85; cf. his *Jottings from Jail* ..., 1887, pp. 212–15.

27. R. W. Emerson, *English Traits*, Everyman ed., 1919, p. 48; the lectures were delivered in 1847 and first published in 1856.

28. T. Archer, *The Pauper, the Thief and the Convict*, 1865, p. 218.

29. For example, by G. B. Shaw in his preface to S. and B. Webb, op. cit. pp. xii–xiii.

sprung fairly readily to the lips of Victorian believers in the virtues of self-help. Yet there is a ring of truth in the evidence, which is impressive in its bulk and one-sidedness; and the story is not without plausibility. The honest poor did not turn to crime, as a general rule, to meet hard times, and the sort of person we are considering here is the petty criminal, dishonest enough to have some acquaintanceship with the inside of a prison and to have lost any fear of it, but not dishonest enough, or more probably not skilful enough, to maintain himself above the level of prisoners or of honest folk. It is probably true that people of this class would, when it suited their book, deliberately get themselves sent to prison; and there are no grounds for thinking that this was less prevalent at the end of the nineteenth century than at the beginning (or indeed today).

Contemporaries were not so naïve as to blame the state of the prisons alone for the high rate of reconvictions; they realized that in many cases released prisoners reverted to crime for want of a better alternative. Throughout the century the difficulty – some said the impossibility – of discharged prisoners obtaining honest work was stressed. It was sometimes said that prisoners committed new crimes on the very day of their release – Mayhew indeed said within an hour, but then he was a journalist.[30]

One reason for employers' reluctance to employ ex-prisoners was said to be the objection of other workmen.. A London magistrate in 1838 said[31] that a strike would be the result of an attempt to employ a convicted felon, and in 1863 an Inspector of Prisons put forward[32] the objections of other workmen in factories as one reason why it was more difficult for discharged prisoners to find work in towns. Agricultural

30. Note (n.d., ?1826), Place Papers, Add. MSS. 27,826, f.209, British Museum; s.c. on County Rates, P.P. 1834, xiv, p. 171 (q. 1305); Mayhew, *London Labour and the London Poor* . . . , 1861–2, vol. iii, p. 383; Archer, op. cit., p. 239; Waugh, op. cit., pp. 32, 40, 43, 49–50, 131–2.

31. s.c. on Police, P.P. 1838, xv, p. 553 (qq. 2191–3).

32. s.c. on Gaols, P.P. 1863, ix, p. 68 (q. 440). cf. W. C. Osborn, *A Lecture on the Prevention of Crime delivered . . . Nov. 26th, 1849*, Ipswich, n.d., pp. 10–11.

labourers, he said, did not mind – we may surmise that they were in no position to voice any objections. The ticket-of-leave men complained in the 1850s and 1860s of police interference preventing them from keeping honest jobs, and they found some people to believe them.[33] The Commissioner of Police for the Metropolis did indeed tell a Royal Commission in 1863 that he objected to ex-prisoners holding certain jobs – cab-driving, for instance – because they presented a particular temptation to crime.[34] However, the Rev. J. W. Horsley was quite firm on the point:[35] he said that he had frequently examined the statements of ex-prisoners that they had lost jobs through being hounded down by the police, 'but I have never found one to be true. The story is usually quite baseless; but where work has been lost it has usually been by the man himself opening his mouth.'

Discharged prisoners must clearly have found it difficult, and very often impossible, to obtain honest work. This was probably a more permanent state of affairs in London than in the northern and midland industrial towns, where the occasional periods of boom conditions and shortages of labour would from time to time relieve the situation. It is probable also that the difficulty was more acute in the first part of the century than after its mid-point; this is to some extent supported by the tone of contemporary comment, which is particularly hopeless in the earlier years, but is primarily based on the consideration that the lot of the common man in general, and his employment prospects in particular, improved a little in the second half of the nineteenth century.

Even at the end of the century, however, though a network of Discharged Prisoners' Aid Societies had been established, the difficulties of the many honest poor placed an obstacle in the way of remedial action. Thomas Holmes observed in 1908[36] that 'For every situation that is vacant, or is likely to be vacant,

33. Mayhew, op. cit., vol. iii, pp. 430–39.
34. R.C. on Transportation, P.P. 1863, xxi, p. 423 (q. 1684).
35. Horsley, '*I Remember*' . . . , op. cit., p. 107.
36. T. Holmes, *Known to the Police*, 1908, p. 112, and chs. viii–xiv.

where skill and experience are not required, a hundred honest men are waiting – waiting to fight each other for a remote chance of getting it.' He devoted several chapters of his book to describing the sufferings of poor but honest people. In such circumstances, if discharged prisoners were helped to find jobs – or at any rate if this was done too energetically or too publicly – a premium was put on crime, which became the passport to employment.

Attempts to relieve the immediate post-discharge needs of prisoners, to avoid the pressing necessity which led to so rapid a relapse, met a similar difficulty. When the magistrates of Warwickshire decided to give a shilling to all juvenile prisoners on their discharge, for example, the young criminals on their summer peregrination made Birmingham workhouse a port of call – and tore their clothes or committed some other minor offence in order to be sent to Warwick Gaol. The policy had to be changed – it was soon reported that the youngsters no longer tried Warwick, as the shilling had been stopped for those who had been there before, and few had not been. When clothes were given to those discharged from Cold Bath Fields Prison in the 1820s, prostitutes were said to have found that the commission of a trifling offence was a good way to get a new outfit. And, of course, any gift in cash or kind was said to be often turned into drink; and doubtless this was often true.[37] Difficulties of this sort are of course perennial and probably in essence unchanging.

Much of what has been said about the prisons in general applies also to the hulks and to transportation to Australia or elsewhere. The hulks – old warships moored round the coasts and serving as prisons – received convicts on their being sentenced to transportation. Some prisoners (as a rule those with the longest sentence to serve or the worst record) were sent to the penal settlements, most going to Australia, a few to Bermuda and Gibraltar; but many served their time in the hulks

37. G. L. Chesterton, *Revelations of Prison Life*, 2nd ed., 1856, vol. i, pp. 168–70; Mayhew, op. cit., vol. iii, pp. 401, 406; Horsley, *Jottings . . .*, op. cit., pp. 59–60, 70.

and were released in this country. The term 'transport' was applied to those who remained in the hulks as well as to those who were sent overseas.

There seems to have been a general acceptance for most of the period that some criminals, perhaps even most criminals, welcomed transportation, or at any rate did not fear it – it will be remembered that Charley Bates's reflections on the Artful Dodger's fate did not include any expression of surprise or regret that he was in fact likely to be transported. It was of course pointed out from time to time that some people feared the separation from connections and the move into the unknown, but for the most part glowing reports from some of the transports had made transportation an attractive idea. A magistrate in 1828 referred to the 'letters which we are frequently in the habit of seeing written by persons under transportation at Botany Bay to their friends here, in which they speak of their very comfortable situation, and express their desire that their friends should some how or other find means of following them'.[38] Some people, indeed, were thought to have taken the obvious means of following them and to have committed crimes in the hope of so doing. The Ordinary of Newgate named one man who had done this, and Mrs Elizabeth Fry told a Select Committee that 'Charlotte Newman, I believe, was induced to commit the crime she did from the great desire she had to follow her husband to Botany Bay . . . but it was thought proper to make an example of her, and she was executed.'[39]

However, in the late 1820s doubts began to creep in. J. H. Capper, the Superintendent of the Hulks, who had said in 1816 that most convicts preferred transportation overseas to remaining in the hulks, in 1828 reported a change of view:[40] 'They

38. S.C. on Police, P.P. 1828, vi, p. 172.

39. ibid., P.P. 1816, v, p. 233; ibid., P.P. 1818, viii, p. 177.

40. ibid., P.P. 1816, v, p. 219; ibid., P.P. 1828, vi, p. 108. cf. S.C. on Gaols, P.P. 1835, xi, p. 238; S.C. on County Rates, P.P. 1835, xiv, p. 320; R.C. on, Criminal Laws, P.P. 1836, xxxvi, p. 227; S.C. on Transportation, P.P. 1837 xix, pp. 676–8; ibid., P.P. 1837–8, xxii, pp. 19–21; A. Alison, *The Principles of Population* . . . , Edinburgh 1840, vol. ii, pp. 137–8; J. Mirehouse,

would rather stay on board the hulks than go to New South Wales, with some few exceptions; that was not so three years ago, because since Governor Darling has been governor, he is carrying on the discipline of New South Wales more strictly.' In the 1830s and 1840s the balance was rather in favour of the idea that transportation had become a matter of fear to most criminals, who had by this time more information about conditions in the settlements. In 1849 gold had been discovered in Australia and after 1853 transportation was confined to Western Australia, where much milder conditions prevailed. Thereafter the view once again predominated that criminals welcomed the journey to a new land. One transport wrote home from Western Australia, in the early 1850s: 'This is quite a different country to Old England. There is no such things as pawn-shops and poor-houses here; there is plenty of money, food and raiment for them that will work.'[41]

It seems reasonable to accept that for the most part criminals did not fear transportation to Australia. In the earlier part of the period it was doubtless no particular misfortune to most people, and throughout the life of the system there must have been those who welcomed the chance of a fresh start. The fate of a transport in Australia was very much a matter of luck; some ended up on the dreaded Norfolk Island (where Alexander Maconochie's brief rule was an interlude in a history of brutality) or in the chain-gangs, but others, finding a good master under the assignment system, lived as trusted servants and on the expiry of their term or on receiving a ticket-of-leave were able to set up as farmers on their own account. Those who wrote cheerful letters home may have been putting a bold front on things for their families' sake, but true or not the tale was likely to be believed. It is well known that when the final

Crime and its Causes ..., 1840, pp. 24–5; s.c. on Juvenile Offenders, P.P. 1847, vii, pp. 59–61 (qq. 356–85).

41. H. S. Joseph, *Memoirs of Convicted Prisoners* ..., 1853, p. 45, cf. s.c. on Transportation, P.P. 1856, xvii, pp. 109 (qq. 1136–7), 324 (q. 3344); W. L. Clay, *Our Convict Systems*, Cambridge 1862, p. 12; R.C. on Transportation, P.P. 1863, xxi, p. 639 (qq. 4248–50, 4253).

outcome of a course of action may be very good or very bad, individuals will take an unduly favourable view of their own chances. We can believe that many transports, particularly the young ones, had high hopes of the future and, as was said in 1818, looked forward to the kangaroo hunts at Botany Bay.[42]

When the use of hulks and of transportation came to an end in 1853, they were replaced by penal servitude in this country, though in fact convicts continued to be sent to Western Australia on a modified basis and a reduced scale until 1867. Just as transports in the colonies had been eligible for tickets-of-leave after a certain time, so now were those serving their sentences in convict prisons in this country. The public did not take so kindly, however, to the premature release of criminals in Britain itself. People had not realized that systems of this sort had operated for many years. Convicts in the hulks could be, and often were, released after serving only $3\frac{1}{2}$ years of a seven-year sentence, and all those who had served six years of such a sentence 'with order and regularity' were released. A similar system had been tried in the 1840s with prisoners in the General Penitentiary, but was abandoned as a failure.[43] Despite these precedents, the ticket-of-leave system under the Penal Servitude Acts was the subject of a great public outcry. The first of the acts, that of 1853 (16 & 17 Vict., c. 99), made release on licence more or less automatic, and very little was done to see that the stipulations made about the behaviour of the ticket-of-leave man were observed. Police powers of supervision were limited in order not to prejudice the man's chances of taking an honest job. The Act of 1864 (27 & 28 Vict., c. 47) made it more difficult to get a licence, and supervision after release was made more stringent.

Some well-informed commentators regarded the outbreaks

42. s.c. on Police, P.P. 1818, viii, p. 171.
43. s.c. on Police, P.P. 1816, v, pp. 217–19; J. Wace, *A Treatise on the Police and Crimes of the Metropolis ... by the Editor of 'The Cabinet Lawyer'*, 1829, pp. 365–6; s.c. on Juvenile Offenders, P.P. 1847, vii, p. 78 (qq. 545–7). cf. Clay, op. cit., p. 33.

of violent crime about this time as unconnected with the ticket-of-leave, but others of equal authority felt that it was at least partly to blame, especially in its pre-1864 form.[44] On the whole there seems no reason to associate the two features – as was pointed out at the time, the term 'ticket-of-leave man' probably became attached to all criminals in the public mind. It was of course true that criminals who would previously have been shipped off to Australia and released on licence there were now being released in this country, so that the proportion of them who committed further crimes committed them here and not ten thousand miles away. However, it was not the ticket-of-leave system but the ending of transportation which was responsible for this change. If the ending of transportation increased crime in this way (as it undoubtedly increased the average age of criminals),[45] there was something in the opposite scale, for the nineteenth-century criticisms of transportation appear to have been justified. The closing of the hulks, too, must have been beneficial in the long run.

Reformatory schools and industrial schools

The introduction of reformatory schools and industrial schools about the middle of the nineteenth century was widely regarded as having brought about a startling reduction in juvenile crime. The distinction between the two was that reformatory schools received those who had committed crimes punishable with imprisonment, while industrial schools took children who had committed less serious offences or indeed had not committed offences but lived in such circumstances that they seemed in imminent danger of becoming criminals. The reformatory schools received legislative sanction in 1854 (by 17 & 18 Vict., c. 86); industrial schools were so blessed in 1857 (by 20 & 21 Vict.,

44. W. L. Clay, *The Prison Chaplain; a Memoir of the Rev. John Clay* ... Cambridge 1861, pp. 409–18; R. and F. Davenport-Hill, *The Recorder of Birmingham: a Memoir of Matthew Davenport Hill* ... , 1878, pp. 194–8, 202.

45. L. O. Pike, *A History of Crime in England* ... , 1876, vol. ii, p. 456.

c. 48). From the late 1850s there was a swelling body of opinion testifying virtually unanimously to the beneficial effects of the new schools. The Royal Commission on the Reformatories and Industrial Schools in 1884 said that they were[46]

credited, we believe justly, with having broken up the gangs of young criminals in the larger towns; with putting an end to the training of boys as professional thieves; and with rescuing children fallen into crime from becoming habitual or hardened offenders, while they have undoubtedly had the effect of preventing large numbers of children from entering a career of crime.

Nearly all those who described the sharp drop in the level of juvenile crime and the elimination of the hordes of young but expert thieves gave the credit to the new schools, and this seems an inescapable conclusion.

It is possible to surmise how these beneficial results came about. Those who were sent to reformatory schools, those actually convicted of the more serious crimes, were less likely to commit further offences thereafter. This was partly because of less opportunity – having been confined for two years or more, as opposed to the sentences of one or three months' imprisonment which had previously been common, the youngsters would lose their connections. Two years was a long time to wait, even for the key member of a gang of pickpockets. More important – for connections could be re-formed or a new gang found – was the fact that youngsters lost their skill. 'Twelve months' hard work in a reformatory ruined for ever the delicacy of finger necessary for a pickpocket.'[47] If opportunities for criminal activity were poorer, opportunities for honest employment were better. Contemporaries were conscious of the danger of helping those who had, as it were, qualified themselves by misconduct, but it was obviously the right thing to do, and those running reformatory schools naturally wanted to get

46. R.C. on Reformatories and Industrial Schools, P.P. 1884, xlv, p. 10 (para. 3).

47. T. B. L. Baker, *War with Crime* . . . , 1889, p. 23; cf. S. Cave, *Prevention and Reformation: the Duty of the State or of Individuals*, 1856, p. 23.

the best results from their training. And anyway, boys from reformatory schools had acquired, it could be hoped, habits of work, and perhaps some skills, which would be useful in a labour market which was now not quite so overcrowded as before. Miss Carpenter, indeed, said that employers were not only willing but eager to employ those who had 'undergone a steady, regular training' in the reformatory schools.[48]

Nor was this all. The boys sent to reformatory school, particularly when this became the routine course on second conviction, were removed from the scene of criminal life before they could become fully hardened. Contemporaries were convinced that most juveniles followed a progression from minor offences to major ones, and that prison played an important part in the process. Now, instead of the brief spell in prison and a return to old haunts, youngsters were removed from the possibility of further contamination, save in so far as reformatory schools themselves contained more expert boys to continue the lessons. Those sent to industrial schools were similarly interrupted in the traditional progression of juvenile criminals, though at a slightly earlier stage. That some of the benefits came from this removal from bad surroundings is perhaps borne out by the fact that recidivism was highest when boys went back home on release.[49]

One part of the benefit of the reformatory and industrial schools was, then, that those sent to them were less likely to remain or to become criminals. Even when a boy's conduct was not altered, sending him to one of the schools led to a reduction in the number of juvenile criminals appearing before the courts, for many of the boys who spent two years in the schools would otherwise have made a number of court appearances in that time. However, the most important effect of the schools was that the removal for long periods of the more skilled juvenile criminals operated to check the corruption of other youngsters and so to cut down recruitment to the ranks of juvenile de-

48. M. Carpenter, *Our Convicts*, 1864, vol. i, p. 170.
49. *Good Words*, vol. vii, April 1866, p. 283; Horsley, *Jottings* . . . , op. cit., p. 90.

linquents. The effect of the Borstals (in operation after 1902) was summed up in a phrase which can be applied to the reformatory schools as well:[50] 'The removal of the heads, or of the leading spirits, to other spheres of industry at once damps the energies of the remainder, and leads to the disbandment of the whole gang.' In this way the introduction of the reformatory and industrial schools helped to break the vicious circle which perpetuated the existence of the criminal class.

Sentencing

One aspect of the penal system remains to be examined: what use was made of the various forms of punishment? To put it another way, can we detect in our period any changes in sentencing practice? The generalization can be made that throughout the nineteenth century there was a trend to shorter sentences for a given crime. M. D. Hill, the Recorder of Birmingham, in 1863 set out what his experience had been.[51]

The administration of even secondary punishments, on the scale of severity which universally prevailed when I began to practise in criminal courts forty years ago, would after the lapse of twenty years from that date have filled the audience with disgust and even consternation; while prosecutors, witnesses and juries would, by their reluctance, and in many instances by their absolute refusal to act, have so impeded the course of justice as to compel a relaxation of rigour. And now, after a second interval of twenty years, punishments awarded at the commencement of that second interval, with the approbation of society, would shock the sensibilities of all classes, even while this *epidemic* of anger and alarm is still raging.

Thirty years later the Rev. W. D. Morrison remarked that sentences were shorter than twenty years previously.[52] An examination of the statistics supports these views.

50. R. F. Quinton, *Crime and Criminals 1876–1910*, 1910, pp. 124–5.
51. Paper to Law Amendment Society, 12 Jan. 1863, quoted Carpenter, op. cit., vol., i, p. 84; cf. R.C. on Transportation, P.P. 1863, xxi, pp. 24 (paras. 33–4), 438–9 (qq. 1845–65), 441–2 (qq. 1900–5).
52. W. D. Morrison, *Crime and its Causes*, 1891, pp. 16–17.

TABLE 1. *England and Wales 1834–96; sentences being served by those convicted of burglary*

Year	Number convicted	CUMULATIVE PERCENTAGE SERVING			
		Life sentence	Sentence of transportation or penal servitude	Sentence greater than imprisonment for one year	Sentence greater than imprisonment for six months
1834	163	66·2	91·4	93·9	97·6
1835	193	67·9	85·0	90·7	96·4
1836	185	74·6	93·5	94·6	98·4
1844	354	9·0	69·8	77·1	93·2
1945	307	4·9	70·7	75·9	92·1
1846	264	1·5	67·4	72·7	88·3
1854	384	0·8	47·7	55·5	87·0
1855	392	2·0	52·6	62·2	86·7
1856	515	1·8	50·5	64·5	86·4
1864	412	0	36·4	51·0	78·2
1865	403	0	33·3	52·6	83·4
1866	352	0·3	26·1	41·5	79·0
1874	226	0·4	32·2	46·7	76·7
1875	187	0	32·6	47·1	81·3
1876	280	0	30·7	44·3	77·1
1884	390	0	16·2	28·2	58·5
1885	309	0	16·2	33·7	64·1
1886	316	0	16·1	28·8	58·5
1894	434	0	19·4	not available	
1895	404	0	14·6	,,	,,
1896	414	0	15·9	,,	,,

SOURCE: Returns of Criminal Offenders and Judicial Statistics.
NOTE: the figures for 1834–6 are not strictly comparable with the later figures, for they include a number of prisoners sentenced to death; indeed, the 1835 and 1836 totals each include one prisoner who was executed.

Factors affecting crime

Table 1 sets out the sentences being served by those convicted of burglary throughout England and Wales in each of three consecutive years in each decade from the 1830s to the 1890s. (The phrase 'sentences being served' is used because the figures for the years 1834–6 include a number of prisoners who were sentenced to death; in all but two cases the sentences were commuted, and the table takes account of the sentences substituted by the King-in-Council.) Two thirds or more started life sentences in the 1830s; the proportion in this plight dropped below one tenth in the 1840s and was negligible or nil thereafter. Over four fifths began sentences of transportation in the 1830s; the proportion dropped to two thirds in the 1840s; one half began sentences of transportation or penal servitude in the 1850s, and about one third began sentences of penal servitude in the 1860s and 1870s; the proportion was below one fifth in the 1880s and 1890s. The proportion serving sentences greater than imprisonment for one year, over ninety per cent in the 1830s, was around one-half in the 1860s and 1870s and below one third in the 1880s, and in the latter decade around one third received sentences of six months imprisonment or less.

Table 2 contrasts the years 1838–40 and 1873–5 in respect of sheep-stealing (which had until 1837 carried an automatic sentence of transportation for life). The most revealing comparison is between the proportion sentenced to transportation in the earlier years and the proportion sentenced to more than six months' imprisonment in the later years; the former figures are the higher. The earlier emphasis on transportation can be stated another way: the courts in the earlier period sentenced about three quarters of those convicted to transportation, while courts in the later years sentenced less than one quarter to penal servitude.

Statistics for other offences would tell a similar story. This reduction in the length of sentence was to some extent the result of legislation, for Parliamentary activity in this field was not confined to removing capital punishment. From time to time the punishment specified for a particular offence was reduced or the range widened by a lowering of the minimum sentence. In

1846 a general act (the Central Criminal Court Act, 9 & 10 Vict., c. 24) removed all minimum periods of detention: thenceforward courts could for any offence pass a sentence of transportation or imprisonment (the minimum period of transportation remained at seven years and the maximum

TABLE 2. *England and Wales 1838–40 and 1873–5; sentences being served by those convicted of sheep-stealing*

Year	Number convicted	Life sentence	Sentence of transportation or penal servitude	Sentence greater than imprisonment for one year	Sentence greater than imprisonment for six months
		CUMULATIVE PERCENTAGE SERVING			
1838	332	4·2	85·2	88·0	97·0
1839	332	5·4	74·1	84·0	93·1
1840	427	3·3	73·5	84·1	94·9
1873	115	0	20·9	42·6	73·0
1874	94	0	23·4	30·9	60·6
1875	111	0	23·4	41·5	70·3

SOURCE: Returns of Criminal Offenders and Judicial Statistics.

period of imprisonment under this act was two years). The effect of this act was striking. Rape, for example, no longer carried the fixed sentence of transportation for life attached to it in 1841 (in place of the death penalty).[53] The sentences prescribed for sheep-stealing give a more extended example of change. Until 1832 the only sentence courts could pass was death, and between 1832 and 1837 it was transportation for life. From 1837 the offence was punishable by transportation for a term of ten to fifteen years or imprisonment for not more than

53. The acts governing the punishment for rape were:
18 Eliz., c. 7   1575
9 Geo. IV, c. 31   1828
4 & 5 Vict., c. 56   1841
24 & 25 Vict., c. 100   1861 Offences Against the Person Act

three years, and the act of 1846 thus made a reduction of three years in the minimum sentence of transportation.[54]

Legislation was not of course the whole story, and the judges and magistrates appear to have adapted themselves to the new attitude evidenced by the legislative changes. As Samuel Redgrave, the Home Office statistician, put it,[55] 'the effect of any diminution of the severity of punishment has not been confined to the offences to which it has immediately referred . . . it has in practice operated as a reduction of the whole scale of punishment'.

Professor Burn, it must be admitted, detects a hardening of attitudes towards criminals in the 1860s.[56] This is not apparent in the figures of Table 1, but this neither disproves his point nor invalidates the conclusions drawn from the statistics. The argument presented here is that in the nineteenth century as a whole the attitude of Parliament and judiciary towards the sentencing of prisoners became less severe; it is not inconsistent with this that on a closer examination of shorter periods a more complex ebbing and flowing is perceived.

It is tempting to speculate on the causes of this change of heart in Parliament and on the bench. To some extent it represents a continuation of the movement against capital punishment, which of course had the wider impact to which Redgrave referred. To a large extent, no doubt, it may be attributed to the general reforming and liberalizing spirit of the age. Perhaps it is also to some extent a consequence of the improvement in society's apparatus for catching and convicting offenders; and this idea is explored later (see pp. 289 ff). In the Du Cane era it was no doubt to some extent merely a response

54. The acts governing the punishment for sheep-stealing were:

14 Geo. II, c. 6	1740
7 & 8 Geo. IV, c. 29	1827
2 & 3 Will. IV, c. 62	1832
7 Will. IV. & I Vict., c. 90	1837
24 & 25 Vict., c. 96	1861 Larceny Act

55. Introduction to Criminal Returns, P.P. 1854–5, xliii, p. 5; cf. ibid., P.P. 1841, xviii, p. 262.

56. W. L. Burn, *The Age of Equipoise*, 1964, pp. 183–4.

to the increased severity of the prison régime. One year's imprisonment then must have been far more of a punishment than a longer sentence earlier in the century (or today). Lord Goddard commented in 1950 on the effect which the severity of prison discipline had on sentencing practice:[57]

Of late years the courts have been very reluctant to impose a penalty more severe than that of two years' imprisonment, but that was because, until the reforms which took place during the latter part of the nineteenth century [i.e. after 1895], imprisonment was a severe punishment. In the days when shot drill, crank drill and the tread mill were common everyday accompaniments of imprisonment, at least of imprisonment with hard labour, a sentence of two years' imprisonment was, no doubt, regarded as a very severe sentence.

It remains to consider what effect the reduction in the length of sentences had on crime. If the removal of capital punishment from a wide range of offences increased willingness to put the law into operation, it seems reasonable to think that the similar movement with which we are concerned should have had the same effect. It is one thing to prosecute a forger when two thirds of those convicted are transported, as in 1838, and another when not more than one third are being sent to penal servitude, as in 1875. When courts had received greater power to discriminate between individuals when awarding punishment and when the prevailing levels of punishment fell, it became easier for juries and all who preceded them in the long process of prosecution and conviction to dissociate themselves from the punishment suffered by the prisoner and to discharge their duty firmly. Hence the reduction in the length of sentence would tend to improve law enforcement and thus reduce crime.

Of course the greater discretion possessed by the courts to some extent increased the possibility of very different punishments being imposed for similar offences, and this was not entirely desirable. One of the complaints against the penal code at the beginning of the century had indeed been that the uncertainty of application which resulted from its harshness had in-

57. R. *v.* Morris, [1951] 1 K.B., pp. 396–7.

duced criminals to hope that, even if caught, they would 'this time' be punished lightly. It had been the arbitrary and unpredictable nature of the application of the punishment which had done the damage – no one had been able to assign a reason why one had been hanged or been transported while another had been let off more lightly. Such problems persisted later in the century[58] – they are of course perennial and inevitable – but when more discretion was left to the courts there was at any rate a chance that the criminals would understand the principles upon which discretion was being applied.

It is of course not possible to argue that the shorter sentences were better from a reformative point of view, for we still do not know how to reform prisoners. The change in policy necessarily led to an increase in the number of the very brief periods of imprisonment which were believed by contemporaries (and of course by present-day thinkers) to be of little use;[59] however, the coming of the reformatory schools reversed this trend in relation to juveniles, and one factor in their success was the longer period of confinement.

It is difficult to sum up all these points; but it seems that the movement to shorter sentences tended to encourage the enforcement of the law and in this way reduced crime.

58. J. C. Symons, *Tactics for the Times, as Regards the Condition and Treatment of the Dangerous Classes*, 1849, pp. 85–8.

59. R. and F. Davenport-Hill, op. cit., p. 203; *Fraser's Magazine*, vol. v, June 1832, pp. 523, 527.

12. Some other new laws and new systems

Changes in the criminal law

During the course of the nineteenth century there took place a number of legal changes which have the common factor that they made the prosecution of offenders cheaper and easier. One very important series of improvements dealt with the system for refunding the expenses of prosecutors and witnesses.

Until 1818 prosecutors and witnesses could look to the Parliamentary Reward for a return of the money they had spent. These rewards, of £40 in most cases and £10 in others, had been attached to various felonies by a series of statutes, and were payable on the conviction of an offender for the felony concerned. The system was almost universally disliked and regarded as harmful. It was commonly alleged that criminals were not interfered with by police officers until they committed offences to which the £40 reward was attached – until they 'weighed forty pounds', in the cant phrase. The officers hotly denied that this 'nursing' took place, and on the whole they were supported, albeit in somewhat guarded language, by the police magistrates, though not always by those less committed to the system.[1] Be that as it may, all who discussed the matter were certain that the Parliamentary Reward led juries to discredit the evidence of police officers, whom they thought to be concerned merely to get their blood-money.[2] Indeed, the juries were right, for police officers agreed that the system led to over-anxiety on their part (or rather, on their colleagues' part) to secure a conviction and could lead to their straining the

1. s.c. on Police, P.P. 1816, v, pp. 46–7, 55, 148; ibid., P.P. 1817, p. 327.
2. ibid., P.P. 1816, v, pp. 43, 123–4, 173; ibid., P.P. 1817, vii, pp. 423, 427.

evidence – they would 'give them a little one in', the phrase ran. Townsend, the great Bow Street Runner, mused on the point:[3]

> Officers ... are dangerous creatures; they frequently have it in their power (no question about it) to turn that scale, when the beam is level, on the other side; I mean against the poor wretched man at the bar: why? this thing called nature says profit is in the scale; and, melancholy to relate, but I cannot help being perfectly satisfied, that frequently that has been the means of convicting many and many a man. ... Whenever A. is giving evidence against B. he should stand perfectly uninterested.

The Parliamentary Reward system was generally thought to defeat its own object and to increase crime, and few on the right side of the law can have mourned its abolition in 1818 (by 58 Geo. III, c. 70).

This same statute of 1818 sought to put a more flexible system in the place of the fixed Parliamentary Reward. Eighteenth-century statutes[4] had already made provision for the payments of expenses in cases of felony, and the 1818 act provided that courts could pay expenses and an additional reward at their discretion. Despite these provisions, the expense involved remained an important cause of reluctance to prosecute offenders – though in some places, for example Birmingham, the generous attitude of the magistrates was said to lead people to prosecute for the sake of the expenses.[5] One reason for this general failure of the act of 1818 was that, like its predecessors, it applied only to felonies and not to misdemeanours; but we may perhaps infer a general ineffectiveness as well.

One of the many acts of law reform introduced by Sir Robert Peel in the 1820s (the Criminal Law Act, 1826, 7 Geo. IV, c. 64) swept away all the earlier acts, and established in more explicit terms a system of payment of expenses for felonies and misdemeanours alike. Courts retained some power to pay rewards,

3. ibid., P.P. 1816, v, p. 139; cf. ibid., pp. 214, 264.

4. 25 Geo. II, c. 36 (1751), 27 Geo. II, c. 3 (1754) and 18 Geo. III, c. 19 (1778).

5. J. E. Eardley-Wilmot, *A Letter to the Magistrates of Warwickshire on the Increase of Crime* ... , 1820, pp. 17–26.

and Professor Radzinowicz quotes a complaint (in 1836) that some prosecutions were still being instituted for the sake of the reward.[6] Whether for that reason or, more probably, for the more respectable reason that most of the expense could now be recovered, the act was successful in increasing the general willingness of the public to prosecute. However, the expense involved continued to be cited as a deterrent to prosecution until the middle 1840s.[7] Its dying out then appears to be attributable to other improvements in the enforcement of the criminal law.

Expense was not the only cause of reluctance to prosecute. In the earlier part of the century considerable trouble had to be taken by prosecutors, who were entirely responsible for the preparation of the case and for seeing it through the various stages of the procedure; much time was needed. Most indictable offences were tried at Assizes (or, in London, at a similar court); Quarter Sessions dealt only with petty larcenies and misdemeanours for the most part, and few charges could be disposed of summarily by magistrates 'out of sessions' – i.e. sitting alone or in small groups. The prosecutor required a considerable amount of persistence to see his case through to trial. Even when that stage had been reached, he and his witnesses had to hang around from the opening day of the Quarter Sessions or Assizes until their case was called, ready to appear at short notice on penalty of having the verdict go against them by default. At the beginning of the century no indication was given of the order in which cases were to be taken; Alderman Wood said that at the Old Bailey: 'I have known persons from Brentford, from Uxbridge, and from the districts around, as far as Middlesex extends, kept a fortnight, and I have known them kept so long that they have been quite worn out.'[8] Furthermore,

6. L. Radzinowicz, *History of the English Criminal Law*, 1948–56, vol. ii, pp. 81–2.

7. Chadwick Papers, box 126 (statement of J. Bishop, pp. 57–65, 78, 85–6), University College, London; R.C. on Criminal Laws, P.P. 1845, xiv, p. 491.

8. S.C. on Police, P.P. 1828, vi, p. 83.

there was a real fear that reprisals might be taken against the prosecutor and his family by the criminal's friends, and by the criminal himself if the prosecution failed.[9] Finally, people were, it was said, reluctant to prosecute because there was so great a chance that the accused would for some reason or other be acquitted. Many acquittals were due to a minor slip somewhere in the proceedings. As the preamble to the Criminal Procedure Act[10] put it in 1851, 'Offenders frequently escape Conviction on their Trials by reason of the technical Strictness of Criminal Proceedings in Matters not material to the Merits of the Case.' For example, a prisoner was acquitted in 1845 because the name of one of the magistrates who had formerly convicted him was in one document spelled as 'Dalivon' and in another as 'Dalison'.[11] All these points help to explain the existence in some places of Associations for the Prosecution of Offenders to handle these matters for their members, and it is little wonder that, despite their efforts, reluctance to prosecute was until the 1840s often put forward as a major cause of crime.

Not only was the legal machinery thus inefficient; a further factor in the earlier part of the century was the prevalence of deliberate moves to circumvent justice. There were several stages at which criminals or their friends intervened. First, it was not uncommon in the early part of the century for stolen property to be returned to its owner, through an intermediary (who was often a police officer) and on payment of part of its value. Complaints of this practice were frequent until the end of the 1830s. Collusion of a different type was not unknown, of course. Prosecutors were at times bought off; complaints against disorderly houses were often settled by a payment to the informer, and it was generally believed that many assault cases were cleared up by some monetary payment, often at the insti-

9. s.c. on Police, P.P. 1816, v, p. 240; ibid., P.P. 1828, vi, p. 228; G. L. Chesterton, *Revelations of Prison Life* . . . , 2nd ed., 1856, vol. i, pp. 26–9.
10. See p. 266.
11. E. W. Cox (ed.), *Reports of Cases in Criminal Law* . . . , 1846, vol. i, pp. 148–9. Cf. s.c. on Police, P.P. 1816, v, 65.

gation of the magistrates and with the interests of the watchman or police officers looked after. Prevalent after Waterloo, allegations of this sort continued to be heard until the 1840s.[12]

If efforts of this kind were insufficient to prevent a prosecution being launched, there was always the possibility, in a case being tried on indictment, of breaking bail. The great opportunity, however, in indictable cases came when the bill was presented to the Grand Jury. In the nineteenth century all bills of indictment were submitted to a Grand Jury, a jury of presentment, at the opening of the Sessions or Assizes. The Grand Jury heard the case for the prosecution, and if it considered the evidence sufficient to justify the accused being put on trial it found a 'True Bill'; the case was then heard before a petty jury as it is today. If the Grand Jury found that there was no case to answer, it 'ignored' the bill, in the jargon of the court, and the accused went free. The witnesses went one by one into the Grand Jury room; no one else was allowed to be present, and the case was not 'opened' to the Grand Jury, who had to piece the story together from the accounts of the witnesses. There was throughout the century much dissatisfaction with this system, particularly as it was operated by the tradesmen who made up the London and Middlesex Grand Juries. A major defect was the secrecy of the proceedings, which made it easy to have a bill thrown out. A witness, or the prosecutor himself, could be bribed to introduce a note of doubt or to suppress or falsify a vital detail; it was obviously much easier for this to be done in private than in open court. There were more sophisticated methods of destroying the prosecution's case. A witness might be muddled as to the facts by discussion or badgering beforehand, or a false witness might be introduced into the prosecution's case, one who would in the Grand Jury room contradict the others or in some other way throw doubt

12. L. B. Allen, *Brief Considerations on the Present State of the Police of the Metropolis*, 1821, pp. 41–2; s.c. on Police, P.P. 1828, vi, pp. 9–13; J. Wade, *A Treatise on the Police and Crimes of the Metropolis . . . by the Editor of 'The Cabinet Lawyer'*, 1829, pp. 165–77, 354n.; H. Brandon (ed.) *Poverty, Mendicity and Crime . . .* , 1839, p. 25.

on the matter. It was said that 'regular London thieves' were great supporters of the Grand Jury system; many more disinterested persons felt that the system was a cause of crime.[13]

So widespread was dissatisfaction with the legal machinery that the idea of a public prosecutor and a public defender was being actively canvassed at the time of Waterloo.[14] The latter official of course does not yet exist in this country. The device of a public prosecutor was not adopted until 1879, and then only in a limited form. The Grand Jury lived on until 1933. However, most of the other complaints listed above were remedied during the nineteenth century.

Summary jurisdiction was progressively extended. The process began in 1827–8; magistrates gained considerable powers to deal with larcenies committed by juveniles in 1847 and 1850, and with other larcenies in 1855. The 1861 acts also extended their powers. The stages were:

7 & 8 Geo. IV, c. 29	1827	Stealing deer, hares, dogs, birds, fish, beasts, fruit-trees, etc. (in certain circumstances)
7 & 8 Geo. IV, c. 30	1827	Damage to trees, fences, etc. (in certain circumstances)
9 Geo. IV, c. 31	1828	Common assault and some other assaults
10 & 11 Vict., c. 82 (Juvenile Offenders Act)	1847	Simple larceny by offenders under 14 (who could be whipped or discharged without punishment)
13 & 14 Vict., c. 37	1850	Age-limit for 1847 Act raised to 16.
16 & 17 Vict., c. 30	1853	Aggravated assaults on women and children
18 & 19 Vict., c. 126 (Criminal Justice Act)	1855	Theft under value of 5s., with consent of accused; theft 5s. or over. if plea of guilty

13. *Edinburgh Review*, vol. xlviii, Dec. 1828, pp. 416–17; s.c. on Police, P.P. 1838, xv, pp. 342, 396–7 (qq. 247–55); M. D. Hill and J. E. Eardley-Wilmot, *Papers on Grand Juries*, 1865, *passim*.

14. s.c. on Police, P.P. 1816, v. pp. 130–31, 227; W. Monney, *Considerations on Prisons . . .*, 1812, p. 23.

24 & 25 Vict., cc. 96, 97, 99, 100 (Criminal Law Consolidation Acts)	1861	Various provisions
31 & 32 Vict., c. 116	1868	Embezzlement treated as larceny under 1855 Act
32 & 33 Vict., c. 99 (Habitual Criminals Act)	1869	Various powers relating to released convicts
34 & 35 Vict., c. 112 (Prevention of Crimes Acts)	1871	Various powers relating to released convicts

The jurisdiction of Quarter Sessions was correspondingly increased in 1842 (by 5 & 6 Vict., c. 38), to cover all but the most serious felonies. The Central Criminal Court was established in 1834, and the system of stipendiary magistrates, commenced in London in the eighteenth century, was extended to Manchester in 1813, Liverpool in 1836, Birmingham in 1856 and Leeds in 1869.

Procedure was simplified in 1825–7 (by what became known as 'Mr Peel's Acts'), and at mid century, and the criminal law was consolidated in 1827–32 and 1861. The acts were:

6 Geo. IV, c. 50	1825	Juries Act
7 Geo. IV, c. 64	1826	Criminal Law Act
7 & 8 Geo. IV, cc. 28–31	1827	Criminal Law Act, Larcenies, Malicious Injuries to Property, and Remedies Against the Hundred
9 Geo. IV, c. 31	1828	Offences Against the Person
11 Geo. IV & 1 Will. IV, c. 66	1830	Forgery Act
2 [or 2 & 3] Will. IV, c. 34	1932	Coinage Offences
11 & 12 Vict., cc. 42–3	1848	Indictable Offences Act and Summary Jurisdiction Act
18 & 19 Vict., c. 126	1855	Criminal Justice Act
20 & 21 Vict., c. 43	1857	Summary Jurisdiction Act
24 & 25 Vict., cc. 96–100	1861	Criminal Law Consolidation Acts

Steps were gradually taken to remove the difficulties caused by the undue strictness of criminal procedure. In 1829 (by 9

Geo. IV, c. 15) some courts were given power to make amendments when documents produced at the trial of misdemeanours differed in some non-material detail from the recital of them in the record. The Home Office suggested further relaxation of the rules to the judges in 1842, and received a qualified acceptance of the idea;[15] and by two acts passed in 1848 and 1849 (the Criminal Procedure Act, 1848, 11 & 12 Vict., c. 46, and the Quarter Sessions Act, 1849, 12 & 13 Vict., c. 45) the limited powers of the 1829 act were extended to all offences and to all superior courts. In 1851 a more decisive step was taken (by the Criminal Procedure Act, 14 & 15 Vict., c. 100): courts were empowered to amend mistakes in names and descriptions of people and things and in details of the ownership of property, where the error did not affect the matter in question and where the correction did not prejudice the accused's defence on the merits of the case. The 1848 and 1851 acts made other relaxations in the strictness of the law. Some of these were technical matters, but others covered such points as permitting juries to find someone accused of a substantive offence guilty of an attempt to commit it and allowing alternative counts of stealing and receiving to be included in the same indictment.

Another defect in the law relating to receiving stolen goods had been corrected twenty years earlier. At the beginning of the nineteenth century receiving was only a misdemeanour unless the thief had been convicted or was 'amenable to justice'. By an act passed in 1827 (7 & 8 Geo. IV, c. 29), receiving was made a felony (unless the theft itself had only been a misdemeanour) regardless of the fate of the thief and even if his identity was not known.

A regular system of announcing when cases were to be tried seems only to have become general about 1880. However, there seems to have been something of the sort in London by 1828, for Alderman Wood, when making the comment previously quoted (p. 261), was contrasting the past with what obtained when he spoke. Now, he said, people were more willing to come

15. H.O. 45, O.S. 419, Public Record Office, See also W. O. Russell, *A Treatise on Crimes and Misdemeanours*, 5th ed., 1877, vol. i, pp. 52–6.

forward: 'They will come to the sessions and look at the list that is arranged for that day, and they see that they shall be called that day or the following day, and in consequence of their time being so little occupied they are induced to come and give evidence.' Where such a system existed, it would indeed be an encouragement to the public to play their part in the process of justice.

At least one improvement in the law was said to have had an unexpected outcome. An act of 1836 (6 & 7 Will. IV, c. 114) extended to cases of felony what had always existed in cases of treason and of misdemeanour, the right of prisoners' counsel to address the court; but it was said that this only helped the professional thieves, who could afford counsel, and not the members of the 'honest poor', guilty or innocent, who found themselves before a court. Furthermore, if the prosecutor could not afford to employ a counsel, the want of skilled prosecution gave an additional advantage to the defence counsel.[16]

What were the results of these changes? The improved rules for the payment of expenses, working with the simplification of procedure and the extension of summary jurisdiction, greatly eased the burden on a private prosecutor. The general improvement of communications worked in the same direction. Prosecutions were also encouraged by the greater likelihood of success resulting from the simpler procedure and from the elimination of capital punishment for offences other than murder. The extension of summary jurisdiction must also have done much good by reducing the number of people committed to gaol to await trial and the length of time spent in custody before trial. The new police provided the prosecutor with better protection against vengeful criminals, and of course were taking an increasing part of the burden of prosecution on their shoulders; their more skilful preparation of cases must have helped to

16. G. Stephen, *A Letter to . . . Lord John Russell . . . on the Probable Increase of Rural Crime . . .*, 1836, pp. 22–3; s.c. on Police, P.P. 1837, xii, p. 360 (q. 479), 361 (q. 484); J. Mirehouse, *Crime and its Causes . . .*, 1840, pp. 25–6; s.c. on Juvenile Offenders, P.P. 1847, vii, p. 69 (q. 434–40).

reduce the number of indictments rejected by the Grand Jury and to increase the chance of a verdict of 'guilty'.

We must take account of the views of two experienced judges on this point, however. The Assistant Judge of Middlesex Sessions and the Recorder of Birmingham both recorded the opinion, about mid century, that the increase in the public's willingness to prosecute had had undesirable results, in that people, and especially young people, were being prosecuted more readily for trivial offences and the consequent imprisonment introduced them to a life of crime.[17] There is thus something to put in the other scale, but we can none the less conclude that the general effect of all these changes was beneficial.

Police

One very prominent administrative change in the nineteenth century was the complete transformation of the police. The towns of 1815 were not devoid of law enforcement officers, but major changes in quality and quantity were made during the century; furthermore, the extension of policing to additional areas, until eventually the whole country was covered, introduced a new factor.

London in 1815 was policed by a number of forces. There were detectives attached to each of the police offices; those at Bow Street were known colloquially as the Bow Street Runners but the proper title of all of them was 'police officer'. The Chief Metropolitan Magistrate at Bow Street was also responsible for two night patrol forces, the Foot Patrole (founded in about 1782) in the centre of the town and the Horse Patrole (founded in 1805) in the environs. In 1821 the Foot Patrole was restricted to a narrower area in the centre of the town, and the oddly named Dismounted Horse Patrole was created to cover the gap thus formed between the two older forces. In 1822 the Day Patrole was established to cover the central area of the town

17. J. Adams, *Summary Jurisdiction* . . . , 1849, pp. 12–13; M. D. Hill, *Suggestions for the Repression of Crime*, . . . , 1857, pp. 107–8.

There were in addition the Thames Police (established in 1798) and a bewildering variety of parish watches of different degrees of efficiency. None of these forces operated in the City of London, which had its own system of policing. The Metropolitan Police was formed in 1829; by 1839 it had absorbed or replaced all these forces save that of the City. The City police force was reorganized on the lines of the Metropolitan Police in 1839.[18]

Borough policing was of varying quality, but was fairly effective in the large towns by about 1842, by which date a 'New Police' on the Metropolitan model had been adopted by all of them under the stimulus of the Municipal Corporations Act of 1835 (5 & 6 Will. IV, c. 76). Counties began to acquire police forces in 1839, when justices in Quarter Sessions were given the authority to establish forces if they wished, by the County Police Act (2 & 3 Vict., c. 93). The setting up of a county force was made obligatory by the County and Borough Police Act of 1856 (19 & 20 Vict., c. 69). Both county and borough forces thereafter began to receive visits from Her Majesty's Inspectors of Constabulary, whose appointment was authorized by that act.

Mrs J. M. Hart outlines the general view of the effect of the new police:[19]

It is usually suggested that the new London police was so effective that after 1829 criminals migrated *en masse* to other parts of the country, with the result that the police in the boroughs was reformed in 1835; and, further, that the new watch committees in provincial towns were so active that a fresh migration took place to the rural areas, which in turn stimulated the reform of the rural police in 1839.

But she sets out this proposition only in order to attack it: she

18. See my forthcoming *Policing before Peel*.
19. J. M. Hart, 'Reform of the Borough Police, 1835–1856', *English Historical Review*. vol. lxx, July 1955, p. 411; cf. K. K. Macnab, *Aspects of the History of Crime in England and Wales between 1805–1860*, Ph.D. thesis, University of Sussex, 1965, pp. 273–8.

denies this 'migration thesis'. It is convenient to commence the study of the effect of the new police on crime and criminals by considering Mrs Hart's views.

The migration thesis does indeed postulate a rapidity of legislation in response to changing conditions hardly typical even of the Reformed Parliament. Moreover, the police provisions of the Municipal Corporations Act were not the reason for its being passed. Mrs Hart's attack on the migration thesis may none the less be thought to have carried her too far, for she is sceptical about the migration of criminals as a result of police improvements (though it is fair to say that her interest is only with the migration thesis as an explanation of the reforms of 1835 and 1839). There is a wealth of testimony, however, that this migration did in fact occur.

Mrs Hart suggests that the germ of the migration thesis is to be found in the Report of the Royal Commission on a Constabulary Force in 1839. The Report said:[20]

It is established as a conclusion to our minds, by satisfactory evidence, that in the greater proportion of these cases the migrant habits were formed long anterior to the establishment of any Police in cities and towns. But it is also clearly shown in evidence that these habits of vagrancy have received a considerable impulse from the operation of the new Police established in the provincial towns, on the principle of the Metropolitan Police.

It said also that migrant criminals 'of course prefer the unprotected districts'. An examination of the evidence received by the Commission shows that there was ample justification for the remarks made. Testimony to the way in which a reformed police had driven criminals out of the town came from many parts of the country. The migration thesis itself was enunciated by a Bath clergyman – the London police drove the thieves to the towns, and now the town police is driving them to the country districts. This witness and others emphasized the contrast between Bath and the unpoliced area around it, which had

20. R.C. on Constabulary Force, P.P. 1839, xix, pp. 22 (para. 25), 147–9 (paras, 199–200); cf. p. 21 (para. 22).

been 'inundated' with criminals as a result of the establishment of the Bath police.[21]

However, the migration thesis was not in fact a new idea in 1839. The Chief Metropolitan Magistrate told the Select Committee on Police in 1816 that a drive to eradicate prostitutes from the streets of the City of London had merely driven them into the Bow Street area.[22] The Select Committee of 1828 was told that criminals had been driven out to the environs of London by the activities of the Bow Street patrols and that improvements to the police of towns near London had caused criminals to move to the surrounding districts.[23] The migration thesis was mentioned in the House of Commons; Sir Robert Peel, for example, said in 1829 that the efficient watch of Hackney, St James's and Marylebone drove criminals to other parishes, and that he believed this to be a general rule.[24] The Home Office in 1827 received a complaint from the magistrates of Brentwood that criminals were being driven into their area, and the Leeds Watch Committee in 1836 received a similar complaint from the inhabitants of Headingley.[25] The rules of the magistrates for the Pershore Petty Sessional Division, adopted in 1831, spoke of the increased vigilance of the police in the cities and the large towns and the consequent movement of rogues and vagabonds to the small towns and villages.[26] The Select Committees on Police of 1834, 1837 and 1838, the Select Committee on Criminal Commitments of 1828 and the Royal Commission on County Rates of 1836, the Royal Commission on Municipal Corporations in 1837 – all received

21. Chadwick Papers, box 131 (printed evidence, pp. 6–7, 4), University College, London; H.O. 73/8, Part II (statement of G. Steart), Public Record Office. There is testimony supporting the Commission's views in the Report (loc. cit.) and in these manuscript collections.

22. S.C. on Police, P.P. 1816, v, p. 24.

23. ibid., P.P. 1828, vi, pp. 41, 243, 247–8.

24. *Hansard's Parliamentary Debates*, new ser., vol. xxi, cols. 872–3 (15 April 1829).

25. Letter dated 21 Feb. 1827, H.O. 60/1, p. 270, P.R.O.; *Leeds Police Centenary, 1836–1936*, Leeds 1936, p. 16.

26. Chadwick Papers, box 122 (statement of T. Marriott).

similar evidence, as indeed did the Select Committee on Police of 1852–3.[27]

Sidney and Beatrice Webb appear to have accepted the migration thesis, for they wrote:[28]

The vagrant or the habitual criminal simply dodged the pressure ... by continuing his illicit conduct beyond the police boundary...

The reorganization of the Bristol police was avowedly made 'necessary because the efficiency of the police establishments of London, and some other of the larger provincial towns, has driven hosts of thieves and sharpers of all grades from their former haunts ... to those towns which continue to be guarded (or rather to be left unguarded) by an inefficient and badly regulated constabulary force.' *Bristol Journal*, 5 Feb. 1831.

The outbreak of burglaries in Liverpool in 1834 was attributed 'in a great measure to the efficiency of the London police, which compels the housebreaker to practise his art in the provincial towns ... *Liverpool Mercury*, 24 Jan. 1834.

There is thus much contemporary evidence against Mrs Hart; but it should be recognized that one type of contemporary record favours her case. She uses the statistics of crime to show that the rates of charges and convictions per 100,000 population outside the Metropolitan Police District 'continues to rise after 1829 at roughly the same angle as before'. This argument appears to neglect the significant police improvements, in London and out of it, before 1829. Furthermore, Mrs Hart accepts that her analysis shows only that the statistics do not support the migration thesis, and does not prove it false. The use of nineteenth-century criminal statistics has already been discussed; when they point to a conclusion opposed to that

27. S.C. on Police, P.P. 1834, xvi, p. 181 (qq. 2282–3); ibid., P.P. 1837, xii, p. 390 (q. 806); ibid., P.P. 1838, xv, p. 493 (qq. 1452–3); ibid., P.P. 1852–3, xxxvi, pp. 189 (q. 2813), 331; S.C. on Criminal Commitments, P.P. 1828, vi, pp. 456–7; R.C. on County Rates, P.P. 1836, xxvii, pp. 61 (qq. 78–9), 92 (q. 569); R.C. on Municipal Corporations, P.P. 1837, xxv, p. 201 (section 329).

28. The Webb Local Government Collection, vol. xxxii, London School of Economics.

Some other new laws and new systems

based on contemporary description they can perhaps be dis-
regarded without much anxiety. This is even more the case
when the conclusion to which the statistics point conflicts with
plain common sense. Criminals in the period in question were
constantly on the move around the country, and the distances
involved were not great. What was more likely than that they
should tend to spend longer in the unpoliced or badly policed
parts, that they should move on as quickly as convenient from
places with an efficient police? Criminals resident in areas with
an efficient police force found crime less easy because of increased supervision of property and less safe because of increased detection. Some of them may have abandoned crime,
but it is almost incredible that none of them, or only an insignificant proportion, should have thought of another solution.
Can we accept that criminals deprived of opportunities to steal
or afraid to take advantage of them would not have moved to
places where those difficulties did not arise? The migration
thesis does not rest on the hypothesis that all moved; but to
defeat it one must maintain that only an insignificant minority
moved. It is suggested therefore that that part of the migration
thesis which postulates that the effect of police improvements
was to drive criminals to less well policed districts is substantiated by the evidence and can be accepted.

It is necessary to consider in more general terms the effect of
the establishment of an improved police force. The pre-1829
forces mentioned had their successes, but the decisive step forward was the establishment of the Metropolitan Police. Whatever one's opinion of the migration thesis, the success of the
Metropolitan Police is well attested. A former thief turned publican told a superintendent of the new force that many thieves
were 'so sick through the Police hunting them about day and
night' that they 'would go to work for fifteen shillings a
week'.[29] We need not give full credence to this remark, nor to
the writer who in 1837 claimed that, thanks to the Metropolitan
Police, 'You may walk at any hour, in any part of London,
without the least danger of any outrage being offered to

29. H.O. 73/9, Part II (told to Supt. Peirse by J. Gower), P.R.O.

T–CIS–K   273

you.'[30] It may be accepted that to some extent what was happening was merely a change in method by the criminals: Sir Richard Mayne, one of the Commissioners of the Metropolitan Police, said in 1837 that in the first two or three years of the force many people were arrested in the streets with house-breaking implements, but that the criminals then learnt the need to plant their tools in readiness near the scene of action.[31] We cannot gauge to what extent was fulfilled the hope that thieves would no longer find it so easy to make up to servant girls, since the new police were so active in the same direction.[32] But we can hardly doubt that the Metropolitan Police did do a great deal to make life less easy for the criminals.

The success which attended the new police in London followed in other places as the new method was introduced. It was claimed by the head of the Bristol police that before the new police was established in 1836 shops used to close at dusk, as customers were afraid to be out late, but that a year or two afterwards they stayed open after dark. An impressive tribute came from Bath: someone who had moved his home from four miles outside the town into the area patrolled by the new police said that it was 'as if I were removed from the abodes of savage society to live among a highly civilized and intellectual people'.[33]

However, it must not be thought that the new police was uniformly successful; in the article already discussed Mrs Hart calls attention to the deficiencies of the police of many boroughs between 1835 and 1856, and even when the new police was extended to the whole of England and Wales and a new professionalism imparted by the appointment of Her Majesty' Inspectors of Constabulary it was several years before the whole country was efficiently policed.[34]

30. J. Grant, *The Great Metropolis* . . . , 2nd ed., 1837, vol. i, pp. 10–11; cf. his *Sketches in London*, 1838, pp. 397–9.

31. R.C. on Criminal Laws, P.P. 1837, xxxi, p. 20.

32. *Fraser's Magazine*, vol. vi, Nov. 1832, pp. 463–4.

33. Chadwick Papers, box 126 (statement of J. Bishop, pp. 9, 14–15); H.O. 73/8, Part II (statement of H. Smith), P.R.O.

34. J. M. Hart, 'The County and Borough Police Act, 1856', *Journal of*

So far consideration has been given only to improvements resulting from the establishment of a new force. Obviously, lesser changes than this could have a profound effect. Indeed, the general and progressive improvement as the new organizations settled down and learnt the craft of policing must have had a cumulative effect, though the consequences of each stage cannot be identified.

To sum up, then, improved policing, especially the new police on the model of the Metropolitan Police, was effective in reducing crime in the nineteenth century. It helped to bring about the reduction in the volume of complaints about the working of the legal system in the 1830s and 1840s, though in the period before the County and Borough Police Act of 1856 part of the effect of the new police was to cause criminals to change their habits, and especially to move to different towns. The direct effect of the act of 1856 on the large towns was not as great as elsewhere, in that they all had an efficient police before then; but the bracing effects of regular visits from Her Majesty's Inspectors of Constabulary must not be overlooked. The indirect effect on the large towns resulting from the elimination of unpoliced towns and wide unprotected tracts of countryside was doubtless more important. This indirect effect was probably an unfavourable one for a time, for criminals were likely to confine their activities even more closely to the large towns, with their comforting prospect of anonymity, once the whole of the country was efficiently policed. But after a time – the length of which it would be pointless to speculate about – the benefit from the spread of protection must have outweighed this factor. Improved policing was not the reason for the general reduction of crime in the later part of the nineteenth century, but it was a contributory factor.

Public Administration, vol. xxxiv, winter 1956, pp. 405–17; H. Parris, 'The Home Office and the Provincial Police in England and Wales, 1856–1870', *Public Law*, autumn 1961, pp. 230–55.

The Poor Law

The transformation of the Poor Law during the nineteenth century did not make as much difference to crime and criminals as might have been expected. Before the Poor Law Amendment Act of 1834 (4 & 5 Will. IV, c. 76) poor relief was a matter for the parish, under a system going back to the reign of Elizabeth. After that date, it was the responsibility of the newly established Board of Guardians for each Poor Law Union, who were subject to fairly strict control by the Poor Law Commissioners (and their successors) in London. The basic principle of the New Poor Law of 1834 was that relief to the able-bodied should be given only if they were prepared to enter the workhouse. The main impact of the act was on the rural parishes, with which we are not directly concerned. As far as the large towns are concerned, the prohibition of outdoor relief to the able-bodied proved impracticable, and the 'labour test' was evolved as an alternative: outdoor relief was given only in return for work in the parish stone-yard or similar establishment. A harsher policy was adopted in 1848, when a minute from the Poor Law Board said that 'as a general rule' the Relieving Officer 'would be right in refusing relief to able-bodied and healthy men'. This method was no more successful than its predecessors. It was complained that as a result of the minute private charity increased – and vagrancy also. This policy too had collapsed in London and elsewhere by the 1860s. A system of open admission to casual wards but harsher régimes within them was tried as a substitute first in London and then in the rest of the country; but the tide of vagrancy continued to rise and the new approach, say the Webbs, 'practically legalized vagrancy and professional vaga bondage'. In sum, therefore, Ribton-Turner's comment of 188 that despite various systems in various places the numbers of vagrants continued to rise seems to have been amply justified.[35]

35. S. and B. Webb, *English Poor Law History*, 1st ed., reprinted 196 Part II, vol. i, pp. 364–5, 404–14; C. J. Ribton-Turner, *A History of Vagrant and Vagrancy and Beggars and Begging*, 1887, pp. 290–303, 308, 318–27, 331

Before 1834 the system of poor relief came in for heavy criticism as a cause of crime. Robert Owen denounced it as encouraging idleness and profligacy. Other commentators agreed with him that the system was unsatisfactory, though some were concerned rather to argue that crime arose from inadequate relief than to share Owen's moral scruples about relief at any level.[36] Some parishes were already severely restricting relief to the able-bodied. The Select Committee on Police was told in 1828 that[37]

A man who applies for relief, who is neither blind, lame, impotent or unable to work, has perhaps some temporary relief given to him; but he is told he is not an object of the poor laws, and must not come again; the consequence is, that, if that person is a male, he is driven on the highway; if a female, she is driven upon the town.

It was apparently accepted practice for parishes to refuse to aid children above a certain age, as being able to earn their own bread[38] – which no doubt they did, though in a different way from that intended. The Webbs say that the workhouses had become 'secondhand prisons' before 1834, and that the London workhouses in particular were filled to a considerable extent by a semi-criminal population. They speak too of unwilling parish apprentices committing petty crime in order to get their indentures broken.[39] Someone else recorded in 1831 that the principal class of boys entering Newgate was runaway parish apprentices, especially chimney-sweep apprentices.[40]

After 1834 the complaints of the earlier period continued. The giving of relief demoralizes the poor, we are told on the one hand, whilst on the other we are assured that the strictness of some authorities leads to some unnecessary suffering and to

36. s.c. on Police, P.P. 1816, v, pp. 234–5 (Owen), 33; ibid., P.P. 1817, ii, p. 434.

37. ibid., P.P. 1828, vi, p. 152,

38. ibid., P.P. 1816, v. p. 63.

39. S. and B. Webb, op. cit., Part I, pp. 144, 210, 250–54.

40. s.c. on Secondary Punishments, P.P. 1831, vii, pp. 621–2 (qq. 1469–1).

crime in default of relief. Owen's words were echoed, and it was argued that one effect of the provision of further workhouses and casual wards after 1834 was to aid the progress round the country of the professional vagrant. On the other hand again, the refusal of casual relief, especially to children, was still said to be a cause of crime.[41] One writer drew attention to the impact of the system on those who received 'the legalized pittance at the poor-house. . . . The natural pride and independent feeling of the man are swept away at a blow . . . he feels that as an honest pauper he enjoys little more respect from the rest of the world than if he were a public offender'.[42]

The institutions of the Poor Law also came in for criticism, and the workhouses were regarded as dens of vice. The general wards were regarded as doubly bad. In the first place they were criticized because of the unsystematic habits of work encouraged and the low standards of discipline enforced by the low-grade officials in charge and because nothing was done to fit the inmates for life without supervision. The second complaint was that they were sources of contamination and training-grounds for criminals. As none could be refused admission, the bad characters had perforce to be allowed to share accommodation with those of good character.[43]

The workhouse schools in particular were severely criticized as failing to give adequate training save in crime. These comments were particularly strongly worded in the late 1840s and the early 1850s, and were often coupled with advocacy of the new solution, the gathering of pauper children together in district schools maintained collectively by the unions of a par-

41. Reports received by Poor Law Commissioners, P.P. 1846, xxxvi, pp 342–3; S. P. Day, *Juvenile Crime, its Causes, Character, and Cure*, 1858, pp 20–24, 75–6; W. Tallack, *The Problem of Diminishing Prevalent Destitution and Temptations to Crime*, 1869, pp. 3–5.

42. J. Syme, *Nine Years in Van Diemen's Land . . . an Essay on Prison Discipline . . .*, Dundee 1848, p. 336.

43. M. Carpenter, *Juvenile Delinquents, Their Condition and Treatment* 1853, pp. 190–92, and *Our Convicts*, 1864, vol. i, p. 80; J. W. Horsley, *Jottings from Jail . . .*, 1887, p. 47.

ticular area.[44] Separate workhouse schools and district schools
spread gradually in the second half of the century, and there
was a growth at the same time of certified schools provided by
the religious denominations. After 1861 workhouse children
began to attend ordinary day schools.[45] Perhaps these changes
in Poor Law administration did do something to help reduce
crime. If contemporaries were right – as it seems they were – in
suggesting that children in workhouses and workhouse schools
of the old style were given training in crime, then the improvement in this situation may justly be said to have played its part
in the reduction of juvenile crime in the second half of the
century.

Legal and administrative change in general

Finally, it is necessary to say something about legal and administrative change in general. Changes in the civil law may have
had a desirable effect on crime – for example the changes in the
law regarding debtors.[46] Administrative change was perhaps
even more important. Quite clearly the central government's
machine at the end of the century, with its examination-selected
civil service, its inspectors, and its extended powers, was a vastly
different thing from that available in 1815. The reformed
boroughs, and the new administrative counties with their
equally new county councils, were run in different ways and by
a more professional type of staff. The country, in fact, was
organized much more efficiently; and it was therefore likely to
handle its problems more effectively. The new administrators
would not always be right; but they would on the whole be right
more often than they were wrong. If, as has been suggested,
crime is to some extent responsive to economic and social con-

44. s.c. on Juvenile Offenders, P.P. 1847, vii, pp. 58–9 (q. 345); J. Field,
Prison Discipline; and the Advantages of the Separate System, 2nd ed., 1848,
vol. ii, pp. 144–8; s.c. on Juvenile Offenders, P.P. 1852–3, xxiii, pp. 172
(q. 1634), 239–40 (qq. 2413–18).

45. S. and B. Webb, op. cit., Part II, vol. i, pp. 255–71.

46. W. L. Burn, *The Age of Equipoise*, 1964, pp. 139, 183.

ditions, improved administration must have had a tendency to eliminate the sources of trouble and to reduce crime. That the influx of a great host of country-dwellers into the towns had the effect it did was in part due to a lack of the necessary machinery to tackle the problems which resulted, and when the towns were better organized, when they were better places in which to live, the problems were less likely to lead to crime. The people of the nineteenth century were learning the arts of government, and were consciously studying the problems of running a country or a town and inventing solutions. To the accumulation of minor changes which resulted must go some of the credit for the improvements in the field with which we are concerned.

Part Four

Conclusion

13. Crime and industrial society in the nineteenth century

There seems little doubt that in the earlier part of the nineteenth century crime was at a high level by later standards. However, this was not, as might be expected, to any important extent a consequence of poverty, in the sense of the immediate pressure of want. It was not usually poverty that governed the operations of the criminal class, and the adult honest poor did not, as a general rule, turn to crime however straitened their circumstances. The effect of the trade cycle on the level of crime was confined to special cases. However, two features of crime in the nineteenth century – the large number of juvenile members of the criminal class in the earlier part of the century and the marked reduction in their numbers that began in the 1850s – lead us to think of a relationship between the level of crime and poverty in a broader sense, a relationship which lay fundamentally in the failure of the economic and social system to adjust sufficiently rapidly to the great upsurge of population which was in progress when the century began. The following paragraphs examine this relationship.

The high birth-rates and death-rates of the nineteenth century led inevitably to a high proportion of young people in the population. There were not sufficient jobs for all these youngsters. Their parents were poor, and in some cases worked long hours and in some cases were feckless and drunken. The Poor Law did not – perhaps could not – provide adequate relief for all the children in need. In consequence, many youngsters had to find a living as best they could by begging or stealing. The control of the young, weakened by these circumstances, was further vitiated by the break-up of families which followed from high death-rates; the importance of the wicked step-mother in the

Conclusion

literature of earlier days will not be forgotten, and this was a real part of the problem of crime. Many children, some because of the break-up of their family by death and some for other reasons, had no home and no family and were left to fend for themselves from an early age – the archetype is Dickens's Jo, the crossing-sweeper in *Bleak House* who was always being told to move on but never told where to move to. The problems thus caused were made worse by other factors.

First, there was a considerable amount of internal migration. In the first half of the nineteenth century the towns were growing rapidly, and their people lived in a world of flux where the pressures were often too great to be withstood. This rapid growth had a profound impact both on the original residents of the towns and on the migrants who helped to swell their numbers. It was not only the increase in population that brought about bewildering changes; other factors – improvements in transport, to cite but one example – brought with them a whole host of changes affecting directly or indirectly everybody in the large towns. The people of those towns were jerked out of centuries of certainty into an uncertain world. The effect of the coming of change (rather a different kind of change, and rather later in the century, it is true) on the educated members of the nation has been described by several writers. Professor Burn quotes J. A. Froude:[1]

> The present generation which has grown up in an open spiritual ocean, which has got used to it and has learned to swim for itself, will never know what it is to find the lights all drifting, the compasses all awry, and nothing left to steer by except the stars.

In much the same sort of way, the poor of the towns of the first half of the nineteenth century were living in a world where all the familiar landmarks had gone, where almost insoluble problems abounded, and where to abandon the attempt to live an honest life must have been very tempting.

1. W. L. Burn, *The Age of Equipoise*, 1964, p. 65; the quotation is from J. A. Froude, *Thomas Carlyle: a History of His Life in London*, 1884, vol i, p. 291. cf. W. E. Houghton, *The Victorian Frame of Mind, 1830–1870*, 1957 *passim.*

The feeling of uncertainty thus engendered was all the more important because of the youth of many of the migrants. The unmarried ones living in lodging-houses were especially exposed to bad influences, but the atmosphere of the large towns was potentially dangerous to all young people.

A second factor making the situation worse was the congestion which developed because the supply of housing did not grow sufficiently rapidly to keep pace with the growth of the population. The problem was aggravated by the clearances for street and other improvements in the centres of the towns which reduced the supply of the type of accommodation perforce occupied by the people with whom this book is concerned. Conditions such as Chadwick and Shaftesbury pointed to in the 1840s helped to lower the self-respect of the poor and to reduce the possibilities of the satisfactory control of their children.

Thirdly, there was a lack of adequate educational facilities. Though the provision of schooling increased as the century progressed, action was delayed by the anxious and bitter debates about educational policy. It is clear that in the first half of the nineteenth century such schools as there were had little to offer the children of the poorest classes, those who were most likely to be tempted into crime.

If this analysis is correct, it is necessary to explain how it came about that many of these same youngsters made good when transported to the even more different life of Australia. If it is right to suggest that there was little possibility of reformation in this country, how was it that in many cases those sent overseas became good citizens in their new homelands? W. A. Bonger made substantially the same point when combating the Lombrosian theory of an inborn disposition to crime.)[2] They cannot all have been wrongly convicted; most of them had, like the Artful Dodger, earned their sentence over and over again before they finally received it. We can, too, dismiss out of hand the possibility of a moral transformation having been effected in so many cases. It seems that the answer

2. In the preface to the American edition of his *Criminality and Economic Conditions*, Boston 1916, p. xxvii.

Conclusion

is one which fits in with the diagnosis just made of the ills of English society. These youngsters were criminals in England because of lack of work and because of the pernicious effects of a morally unhealthy urban environment. They were often (but of course not always) honest in Australia because of the very different conditions they found there. Mr R. Ward provides an explanation:[3]

> Judged from the viewpoint of its effect on the people, the greatest single difference between the old environment and the new was that in Australia there was a perennial labour shortage. ... Moreover, the working people enjoyed a vastly higher standard of living than they had known in Britain. ... In Australia three square meals a day, including too often a surfeit of meat, was the unquestioned portion of everyone.

A convict writing home from Western Australia in 1866 said:[4]

> If a ticket-man [a convict who had served the first part of his sentence and had been granted a ticket-of-leave to live as a free labourer] is ever hard up, the hand of every one of his class is open to him. Starvation in a country like this is impossible, except to the man who has his hands tied.

Though conditions in Western Australia were very different from those in New South Wales and Van Diemen's Land in the first half of the century, the quotation emphasizes the camaraderie which modern Australian writers regard as a feature of the convict character, and makes it clear that in one very important respect conditions were better than in England. The transported felons found in Australia an opportunity for honest work and a way of life which, however unfamiliar, however changing, was one with which they could grapple on equal terms with anyone else, where they lived in smaller (and perhaps more cohesive) communities, and where they were not

3. R. Ward, *The Australian Legend*, Melbourne, 1958, p. 31; cf. W. D. Forsyth, *Governor Arthur's Convict System, Van Diemen's Land, 1824–36*, 1935, p. 137.

4. *Cornhill Magazine*, vol. xiii, April 1866, p. 509.

faced with the temptations of an attractive criminal world.

Australian writers have discussed the character of the convicts who played such an important part in the early history of their country. Mr Ward[5] discusses but rejects the notion that 'the greatest English criminals remained in England', and Dr Robson says that:[6]

> There is no evidence that Australia received an element of the British population which was incapable of work or intelligent exertion. A shipload of prisoners who gave every indication in their home land of being desperate men, or persistent criminals at least, were subjected to a profound change in terms of their environment. ... The convicts were neither simply 'village Hampdens' nor merely 'ne'er-do-wells from the city slums'. But if the Hampdens are placed on one side of a scale and ne'er-do-wells on the other, the scale must tip towards the ne'er-do-wells.

There is little doubt that most of the English town-dwellers who were sent to Australia were experienced criminals; it should be realized, however, that, far from being incapable of intelligent exertion, they had to some extent been selected for transportation by intelligence, industry and drive. Contemporaries distinguished two types of juvenile lawbreaker.[7] One type was a vagrant, living mainly by begging and petty crime, but lacking the spirit or the intelligence required for the major crimes. Jo the crossing-sweeper belongs in this category, though Dickens does not let the thought of theft even enter his head. Youngsters of this type seldom qualified themselves for transportation to Australia. Criminals of the other type, the 'grammar-school' stream of this informal 11+, those who by their energy and skill made themselves pickpockets or members of some other superior branch of crime, were as a rule the ones who committed the sort of offence for which judges could pass a sentence of transportation (or a sentence of death which everyone knew really meant transportation). It was youngsters of this second

5. Ward, op. cit., pp. 19–20.

6. L. L. Robson, *The Convict Settlers of Australia* ... , Melbourne 1965, pp. 157–8.

7. See pp. 74 ff.

Conclusion

type who had the sort of record that would lead to their being actually sent to Australia, a step which was by no means an automatic consequence of a sentence of transportation. Of course, as with our own systems of differentiation between children, opportunity and chance circumstance played their part in some cases; but it is not surprising that Mr Ward notes the resourcefulness of the convicts and that he can say:[8] 'The great majority of the convicts became free men and women who at least kept out of prison and performed useful tasks in society.'

An explanation consistent with the earlier analysis of the causes of the high level of crime in the first part of the century can be found for the reduction in the amount of juvenile crime in and after the 1850s. From about the middle of the nineteenth century the great secular boom which lasted until the 1870s saw a marked rise in employment opportunities and a far more general rise in real incomes than had hitherto occurred. Of course, we must not go too far. Charles Booth's survey of the London of the 1890s is there to remind us of the appalling poverty which existed at the end of the century. Furthermore, we are concerned with the lowest-paid workers and with the opportunities offered to their children, and such people were doubtless the last to benefit from the country's prosperity and position in the world. However, we are not concerned to argue that all was well in England after 1850, but that things were a little better than they had been; and this is a generally accepted conclusion.

Not only had the general level of incomes risen; after the great growth of urban settlement of the 1830s, a generation of people accustomed to town life had grown up. The people of the towns were compared earlier to detribalized Africans; and detribalization, in its full intensity at any rate, is a once-and-for-all process. As Froude pointed out in the passage quoted earlier, those who have never known certainty do not miss it as much as those who have once tasted its joys. The populations of the towns increasingly consisted of those who had known no other

8. Ward, op. cit., pp. 29–30.

life than that in a large town. The pace of change was perhaps unabated – though this is, more or less, the period which Professor Burn has labelled the Age of Equipoise – but the impact of the changes was not so great as in the earlier period.

The towns, too, were beginning to cope with their problems. Municipal government had been overhauled in the first part of the century, and it was now beginning to acquire the administrative machinery and the technical knowledge which was required by the new conditions. In general terms it may be said that as society grew richer it was able to devote greater resources to the running of its towns.

One aspect of this movement particularly relevant to the subject under consideration was the reorganization of the police and the prisons. In the eighteenth century and in the early nineteenth century, a high proportion of offenders escaped detection and a higher proportion still escaped punishment; but those who were punished were as a rule punished severely. By the end of the century the proportion of offenders who were detected and were punished had increased, and the punishment inflicted on them had moderated. (In the last quarter of the century the shortening of sentences was to some extent offset by a more severe régime.)[9] These two movements appear to have been connected: the opposition to the moderating of punishment would have been stronger had not the public's feelings been assuaged by the improvement in the proportion of criminals who were punished. It is not argued that the two movements kept pace over the period, so that at any moment we can relate the severity of punishment and the rate of detection. The contrast is between two states of society, one with severe punishments for a small minority of its criminals and the other with more moderate punishments for a higher proportion of its criminals. A period of perhaps sixty years – the period 1815–75, within which England changed in so many ways – saw the transition from the one to the other, and the two movements can be observed within that period even though we cannot relate the stages of one to the stages of the other.

9. See p. 257.

Conclusion

Another movement can in the same manner be linked to the two just described. In the earlier period, the severity of punishment led to the utmost rigidity of interpretation of the doctrine that justice must manifestly be seen to be done: the accused was entitled to an acquittal if the slightest error of procedure was committed. The reduction in the severity of punishment made it possible to reduce the excessive protection against the conviction of an innocent man, though of course the barricades were not, and have not been, entirely demolished.[10]

The Rev. W. D. Morrison saw something of what was going on: 'In proportion as the probability of being punished is augmented, the severity of punishment can be safely diminished. This is one of the paramount advantages to be derived from a highly efficient police system.'[11] In this passage he suggests that the chain of causation ran from increased rates of detection to less severity, but a few years later he put things the other way round: as punishment has 'diminished in severity to a remarkable extent ... there has grown up a corresponding movement to increase its certainty'. He still regarded the improvement in police as important. Whether his earlier or his later view was correct, whether in fact there was any clear-cut distinction between cause and effect, need not detain us. What matters is that improvements in policing and in legal procedures and reduction in the level of punishment went hand in hand and the three movements reinforced one another.

Of course, it was not merely official provision for the needs of the towns which increased in scale and efficiency; the great growth of voluntary charity in the nineteenth century was particularly marked in the 1860s and 1870s, and the improved organization was symbolized by the formation of the Charity Organisation Society in London in 1869. The role of the Evangelicals, the non-conformists and voluntary societies in general

10. See R. Mark, 'The High Cost of Hanging', *The Police Journal*, vol. xxxviii, no. 10, Oct. 1965, pp. 458–61.

11. W. D. Morrison, *Crime and its Causes*, 1891, p. 175; and *Juvenile Offenders*, 1896, pp. 270–71.

is well known. All that concerns us here is to note that the combined effects of all these official and unofficial endeavours must have been beneficial – we may today be critical of some of their diagnoses and solutions, but we must admit that they were usually better than nothing.

One field of official and unofficial action is worthy of more detailed examination. Educational facilities were expanded greatly in the second half of the nineteenth century, and began to have an effect on the level of crime. The general schools began to raise the standards of the main body of the poor and to fit them to take advantage of the increasing opportunities for employment. In both these ways they helped to reduce the inflow into the criminal class. The Poor Law schools were greatly improved, and the Ragged Schools and the reformatory and industrial schools began to do more than had been done before for those who were already in or on the fringes of the criminal class. Indeed, the reformatory and industrial schools appear to have played an important part in reducing the intake of young criminals and thus helping to end a vicious circle and inaugurate a benign circle.

The vicious circle was based on the existence of a criminal class with its own highly organized network of institutions. In London and the other large towns, children saw others living a life of apparent ease and idleness on the proceeds of crime, free from the restraints which hemmed in honest youngsters. They lived in a community whose values were such as to make crime seem normal – a child who chose to remain honest and starve, or even merely to beg but not to steal, was looked down upon. Everything was there to assist the entry into criminal life. It was easy to dispose of the proceeds of crime. Flash-houses provided lodging and companionship. Theatres and books soon acquainted the new entrants with the heroes of the trade, and there were many willing teachers to build on these foundations. A month or two in gaol would further a youngster's education and increase his standing with his fellows. Even the capture and transportation of a prominent thief did not end his influence on the others, for the detailed reports of crimes and criminal trials

Conclusion

were well-known sources of information and ideas – a readiness to imitate others was a familiar trait of criminals.

When improvements came, they were self-reinforcing, for the vicious circle turned to a benign one. Instead of enjoying the glory of frequent appearances at court and a succession of short sentences and triumphant releases, youngsters disappeared for long periods into reformatory schools. They were prevented from committing crimes themselves and were no longer able to draw others into a criminal life by example or by direct encouragement. The low theatres and flash-houses became less numerous. It was not so usual, and hence not so easy, to dispose of stolen goods. Though there were still areas of the town where it was regarded as normal for youngsters to steal, the reduction in the level of crime reduced the size of these areas and hence helped to bring about further reductions. The criminal class was reduced in size, and hence its supporting institutions were less able to attract and assist new recruits. The decline in juvenile crime may also have led to a change in public attitudes to ragged youngsters; the fact that people no longer automatically regarded them as potential criminals may have helped some to remain honest. The reduction of juvenile crime was not, of course, the work of the reformatory and industrial schools alone; but they appear to have made an important contribution. To sum up, then, the result of the various changes outlined was to create a more settled social environment, and this provides the explanation for the qualitative and quantitative change in juvenile crime in and after the middle 1850s.

The present analysis of crime in England in the nineteenth century is broadly consistent with similar surveys of crime in Paris in the nineteenth century and in some American cities in the nineteenth and twentieth centuries.[12] This thought prompts the question: How does it accord with current views of the causation of the crime of the present day? No attempt to

12. L. Chevalier, *Classes laborieuses et classes dangereuses à Paris pendant la première moitié du 19ème siècle*, Paris 1958; E. H. Powell, 'Crime as a Function of Anomie', *Journal of Criminal Law, Criminology and Police Science*, vol. lvii, no. 2, June 1966, pp. 161–71.

answer this question fully will be made here. Such an attempt would have to start with American experience and American views, partly because the American situation is in some respects more similar to that of the England of the nineteenth century than is the present English situation. Dr D. M. Downes[13] has commented on the dangers of too reckless an application of American theories to the present English scene; clearly the danger would be even greater if a mere historian were to seek to apply them to the English scene of a hundred years ago. None the less, it may be of interest to make a few observations and note a few parallels between the past and the present. It will be convenient for this purpose to use the summary of American views made by Dr Downes.

That summary analyses 'the most central American work on delinquent subcultures; that of Cohen and Short, and Cloward and Ohlin'.[14] Both pairs of theorists detect three patterns of delinquent activity, which the latter writers name the 'criminal' subculture – based on rational crimes against property – the 'conflict' subculture – members of which are engaged primarily in fighting amongst themselves – and the 'retreatist' subculture – based on a retreat from society into a world of drugs.[15] Such patterns can perhaps be perceived in the nineteenth century, though only the first has been dealt with at length in this book. The 'conflict' group was represented by the 'Mohocks' and their nineteenth-century descendants the young bloods. The youngsters of the urban poor, however, had little time for the non-utilitarian and malicious activities regarded as typical of American delinquent youth today;[16] they of course did not have access to the society of the bloods. The 'retreatist' group were the inebriates who lived on the fringe of society, criminal and honest alike; but the harsh realities of economic life in the nineteenth century meant that minor crime was generally necessary to support life for members of this group. On the whole, the

13. D. M. Downes, *The Delinquent Solution . . .* , 1966, p. 256.
14. ibid., p. 23.
15. ibid., pp. 28–30.
16. ibid., p. 25.

Conclusion

juveniles of the nineteenth century do not seem to have entered either of these groups on any scale.

The explanation, in part at any rate, appears to lie in their ease of access to the criminal class. American writers have developed the concept of 'opportunity structure', stressing that not every potential criminal has access to those who are already criminal and can in fact adopt the values of the criminal subculture.[17] However, in the earlier part of the nineteenth century this limitation did not exist; contemporary evidence stressed the frequency with which urban youngsters were thrown into contact with the criminal classes, and there was a welcome for all and opportunities for theft galore. It is indeed true that only those who showed some aptitude were selected for higher training and admitted to the superior grades of the criminal class; but recruit training was given freely – and free – in flash-house or gaol. Even the dullest pupils could pick up some sort of a living drifting in and out of gaol.

The theory also has relevance to the concept of a 'criminal class'. Contemporaries regarded entry to the criminal class as normally a permanent step, and did not think that any significant proportion of those who belonged to the class and committed offences as juveniles eventually managed in adult life to live by honest means. It is possible that they were wrong, and that it was principally those to whom the opportunity of entry to the higher grades was given who remained in the criminal class. Some indeed of those who were not selected in this way remained to provide the petty criminals for whose existence there is ample evidence; but contemporaries may have been wrong in thinking that they nearly all did.

The theory of 'opportunity structure' also provides support for the suggestion made in an earlier paragraph that the reduction in the size of the criminal areas and of the criminal class in the latter part of the nineteenth century reduced the number of recruits entering the criminal class. Fewer youngsters would have an opportunity of getting the necessary training.

Subcultural theories examine not only the forms of de-

17. ibid., p. 50.

linquent behaviour but the reasons why youngsters become delinquent. One such theory, that of Dr A. K. Cohen, rests in part
on the individual's need for 'status', his need to feel that others
respect him because he measures up to the standards of their
society. It suggests that youngsters who cannot gain this respect
from respectable society will gravitate towards a group where
they can gain it, a group with standards they can measure up
to.[18] If the contention of this book is correct, in the nineteenth
century youngsters who were rejected and criticized by respectable society found acceptance and even praise in criminal
society, whose standards they could meet by tales of real or
imaginary crimes. Indeed, much of what has been said about
the consequences of rapid population growth and social change
is at least consonant – or so it appears to a non-sociologist –
with the subcultural theories analysed by Dr Downes.

These comments on possible relationships between the present and the past are tentative; and indeed so is the rest of this
book. It is impossible to be sure what really happened, let alone
why it happened. It is impossible to be certain whether the level
of crime increased in the last half of the eighteenth century and
the first half of the nineteenth century. However, it seems
almost certain that the upsurge of population growth in a more
slowly changing economic and social environment provided
greater opportunities for crime and weakened many of the bar-
riers against crime, and that a reverse movement ocurred as
the new form of urban industrial society evolved. In so far as
the evidence bears any conclusions, crime, and especially juvenile crime, in the first half of the nineteenth century was the
crime of a society in violent economic and social transition.

18. ibid., pp. 34–8.

Appendix – The use of statistics[1]

This appendix considers the series of Judicial Statistics which was commenced in 1856. Each annual volume contains three parts, the first of which is known as the police statistics. This part gives, by police districts, the numbers of persons and houses of known bad character; the number of indictable offences known to the police, each offence or group of offences being shown separately; the totals, male and female, of those arrested for indictable offences, their previous character, and their fate; the numbers arrested for each indictable offence or group of offences; the totals, male and female, of those proceeded against summarily, their previous character, and their fate; and the numbers proceeded against for each summary offence or group of offences. The second part, the criminal statistics, gives details by judicial districts of criminal proceedings, and the third part, the prison statistics, gives details by county and gaol, and also figures of committals to reformatory schools and industrial schools.

It is generally accepted today that the nearer the statistics are to the criminal the more likely they are to be correct, and the police statistics are therefore most suitable as a source of information on crime in the nineteenth century. This is true for another reason also: they are the only ones based on the police boundaries, and therefore showing the towns with which this book is primarily concerned separately from the counties in which they are situated.

Most attention is paid today to the number of indictable offences known to the police, i.e. the total of reported offences,

1. Thanks are due to Mr P. Macnaughton Smith, late of the Home Office Research Unit, for advice on the statistical aspect.

egardless of the result of the subsequent investigation. This
otal cannot be used as it stands in the nineteenth century, however, for certain indictable offences could, under the Juvenile
Offenders Acts, 1847–50, and the Criminal Justice Act, 1855, be
dealt with summarily;[2] and offences for which persons were so
dealt with were excluded from the total of indictable offences
known to the police.[3] An attempt has been made later to correct this to some extent by adding to the total of offences known
to the police the number of indictable offences shown in the
tables as having been dealt with summarily. A further source of
error is that certain acts could be charged almost indifferently as
indictable or as summary offences. For example, the line between the summary offence of 'unlawful possession' and the
indictable 'simple larceny' is unlikely to have been drawn in the
same place at all times and by all officers. Thus the destination
of an offence in the statistics depended on the age of the
offender, or in many cases what he chose to declare as his age,
and on the view taken of the matter by the prosecutor, the
police officer and the magistrate. One way to eliminate this
difficulty is to take the sum of arrests for indictable offences and
of proceedings for summary offences. This figure, however,
suffers from the weakness that the total of summary proceedings was swollen by various applications and non-criminal
matters, which may well have varied in a different manner from
the events in which we are interested.

Neither of the totals discussed provides a satisfactory index
of crime, therefore, however we define the term 'crime'. Such
totals are, however, the best available, and as an experiment a
study has been made of the Leeds figures in the police statistics
for the years 1857–75. (Leeds was chosen merely because reliable, but not quantifiable, information about the state of
trade for part of the period in question came fairly readily to
hand.) For the first part of this study, the total of indictable
offences known to the police was added to that of indictable
offences treated summarily under the Juvenile Offenders Acts

2. See p. 264 for details of these and related acts.
3. Departmental Committee on Judicial Statistics, P.P. 1895, cviii, p. 21.

and the Criminal Justice Act, and the combined figure (referred
to as 'indictable crime') was expressed as a rate per mille of the
population. The population of Leeds is, of course, known only
for the census years. Figures for the other years were obtained
by reducing the census figures to logarithms and spreading the
differences equally over the intervening years. Table 3 sets out
the resultant figures, with the rank order and the annual change
also given. A summary indication of the state of trade is added
and certain information about police strength and organization
is shown.

When Table 3 is examined, it appears that changes of chief
constable had more effect on the rate of indictable crime than
had anything else. These changes[4] were:

1859	1 January	—E. Read pensioned off.
	15 March	—S. English took up duties.
1861	21 December	—S. English resigned.
1862	1 January	—W. R. Bell appointed.
1866	15 August	—W. R. Bell died, after having been ill for five months and confined to house most of the time.
	28 September	—J. Wetherall appointed.
1874	26 October	—J. Wetherall died.
1875	4 February	—W. Henderson appointed.

The year for the purpose of the criminal statistics ran from
October to September; the period from October 1857 to September 1858 is thus for this purpose the year 1858, and so on. In
the light of this, the years in which the interregna occurred
(hereafter referred to as 'years of change') were 1859, 1862,
1866 and 1875. The surmise is that the change between one of
these years and the following year will prove to be significantly
larger (regardless of whether it is an increase or a decrease) than
changes between other pairs of years.

The changes in the rate of indictable crime per mille of the
population were:

4. *Leeds Mercury*, 4 Jan. Suppl. 8 Jan. and 10 March 1859, Suppl. 4 Jan.
1862, Suppl. 18 June and 29 Sept. 1866; *Leeds Daily News*, 1 and 2 Jan. and
4 Feb. 1875; Watch Committee minutes.

TABLE 3. Leeds 1858–76: Crime rates per mille of the population, compared with state of trade and changes in police

	INDICTABLE CRIME			'TOTAL CRIME'[5]			'TOTAL NON-DRINK CRIME'[6]			State of Trade[6]	Police[7]
Year	Rate per mille	Rank order	Change	Rate per mille	Rank order	Change	Rate per mille	Rank order	Change		
1858	6·845	3	0·396	21·00	18	1·08	17·56	16	1·18		strength 221 (from 214)
1859	7·241	1	−3·372	22·08	17	−1·59	18·74	13	−2·80		new c.c. in March
1860	3·869	19	2·105	20·49	19	10·24	15·94	19	8·58		
1861	5·974	7	0·118	30·73	3	−1·66	24·52	2	−2·42	good	strength 230
1862	6·092	6	−1·851	29·07	7	0·02	22·10	5	−0·32	good	new c.c. in Jan.
1863	4·241	16	−0·203	29·09	6	0·76	21·78	8	−0·12	good	strength 228
1864	4·038	17	0·251	29·85	4	3·15	21·66	9	3·83	good but strike	strength 257
1865	4·289	14	0·013	33·00	1	−9·41	25·49	1	−8·14	quiet at first, improving	strength 264

Year	Rate per mille	Rank order	Change	Rate per mille	Rank order	Change	Rate per mille	Rank order	Change	State of Trade[6]	Police[7]
1866	4·302	13	2·247	23·59	15	1·32	17·35	18	1·90	good	strength 270
1867	6·549	4	0·322	24·91	13	3·32	19·25	12	3·35	bad – effect of crisis	new c.c. in Sept.
1868	6·871	2	−0·613	28·32	8	−1·02	22·60	4	−0·56	bad	telegraph system strength 307
1869	6·258	5	−1·710	27·21	10	4·88	22·04	6	2·40	slightly better than '67 or '68	divisional system
1870	4·548	11	−0·095	32·09	2	−7·13	24·44	3	−5·71	best since '66	strength 289
1871	4·453	12	0·342	24·96	12	−1·71	18·73	14	−1·33	improving	strength 280
1872	4·795	10	0·769	23·25	16	0·47	17·40	17	0·37	improving	strength 301
1873	4·026	18	1·148	23·72	14	1·89	17·77	15	1·59	improving	strength 315
1874	5·174	9	0·777	25·61	11	4·11	19·36	11	2·44	poorer	
1875	5·951	8	−1·673	29·72	5	−2·49	21·80	7	−1·22	poorer	new c.c. in Feb.
1876	4·278	15		27·21	9		20·58	10		bad	strength 340

5. See definition on p. 306. 6. Derived from *Economist, Commercial History and Review.* 7. See p. 301n. for sources.

Years of change/later years   *Other pairs of years*

		1858–9	0·40	1868–9	0·61
		1860–1	2·11	1869–70	1·71
1859–60	3·37	1861–2	0·12	1870–71	0·10
1862–3	1·85	1863–4	0·20	1871–2	0·34
1866–7	2·25	1864–5	0·25	1872–3	0·77
1875–6	1·67	1865–6	0·01	1873–4	1·15
		1867–8	0·32	1874–5	0·78

Our interest is to see whether those pairs in which a year of change is the first year ('pairs of change') differed from other years. There is of course the possibility that change in police organization might affect the figures, and hence it is best to eliminate pairs in the first year of which a change of organization is known to have taken place. The same possibility exists in relation to changes of police strength, and pairs in the first year of which there appears to have been a change of twenty or more in police strength have been eliminated. From the pairs listed above, the following were hence for safety excluded: 1868–9 and 1869–70 (changes in police organization); 1864–5, 1870–71 and 1872–3 (changes in police strength).[8] (It may be said in passing that in fact the present data would not support the suggestion that changes of organization or strength affect the result; and if the elimination is not made, the figure in the following paragraph becomes 1 in 102, giving even greater strength to the argument.)

When the pairs remaining are placed in rank order of size of change, the four pairs of change occupy the first, second, fourth and fifth positions. This is something which would be expected to occur only once in a series of seventy-two such calculations if it happened purely by chance; the probability of all four pairs of change falling within the top five or bottom five positions by

8. See Table 3; the details are derived from the *Police Almanac* for the years in question and the Force History, *Leeds Police Centenary, 1836–1936*, Leeds 1936. The latter source and the annual police statistics give different figures of police strength for some years, but no significant change in the calculations results if either of them is preferred to the *Police Almanac*.

Appendix

chance is 1 in 71·5. This is a result which is in statistical term significant of a difference between pairs of change and the other pairs. The suggested association is therefore acceptable from a statistical point of view.

It is easy enough to find explanations why the first full year of a chief constable's period of office should differ markedly from the last full year of his predecessor's term. However, it might have been expected that the year of change would reflect the views of the new chief constable rather than those of the old. It seems probable that there was a time-lag before the attitudes and expectations of the new chief constable percolated down to the lower ranks and began to influence their behaviour. Be that as it may, it is reasonable to conclude that changes of chief constable had more effect on the rate of indictable crime per mille of the population than had anything else.

Is it possible at times to see in the figure of indictable crime a reflection also of the state of trade? The years 1867–73 can be arranged in rank order of state of trade, though the relationship of 1867 to 1868 is not known. When this is done, and the rank order of indictable crime set out alongside (Table 4), a pattern

TABLE 4: *Leeds 1867–73: Rank order of indictable crime compared with rank order of state of trade*

Year	1867	1868	1869	1870	1871	1872	1873
Indictable crime per mille – rank order	2	1	3	5	6	4	7
State of trade – rank order	6	6	5	4	3	2	1

of inverse correlation seems discernible. However, there is no statistical significance in what is after all merely a roughly parallel improvement over time in two series, and in any event noting merely the rank order obscures the differences in the size of change. Whatever may be thought of the 1867–73 figures, the earlier and later movements do not follow any particular pattern in relation to what is known about the state of trade (Table

), and we should not be justified in claiming that any correlation between the state of trade and the rate of indictable
crime per mille can be proved to exist.

The tables showing the previous character of those arrested
or proceeded against have been examined. It is not possible,
even if it would be desirable, to treat separately those listed as
of good character, for the fluctuations in the figures show that
the difference between 'good character' and 'unknown character' was uncertain and that interpretation of the terms varied
over time. Thus in 1869 the combined total (males) was 76·8 per
cent of those arrested or proceeded against, and in 1870 76·9 per
cent; but in 1869 this was made up of 71·6 per cent 'good' and
5·2 per cent 'unknown', whilst in 1870 it was made up of 64·9
per cent 'good' and 12 per cent 'unknown'. Therefore, the
numbers of those described as of 'previous good character' or
of 'unknown character' have been added together, and the total
expressed as a rate per cent of those arrested for indictable
offences or proceeded against summarily; these figures are set
out in Table 5. No connection with what is known of the state
of trade can be seen, nor does the percentage of women regarded as of 'good' or 'unknown' character vary inversely with
the number of prostitutes proceeded against under the
Vagrancy Act, as might be expected (Table 6).

There is a rise in the last two or three years examined in this
total of those not known to have a previous record of crime.
This is hardly what one would have expected, for a national
system of recording criminals was commenced in 1869 as a
result of the Habitual Criminals Act (32 & 33 Vict., c. 99), and
though this system collapsed under its own weight and had to be
reorganized on a less comprehensive plan in 1877 it would seem
logical to expect better records to result in a higher proportion
of people with previous criminal records being identified on
rearrest. There was no decisive change in population mobility in
the years in question to make it suddenly more difficult for the
police to keep trace of bad characters. One possible explanation
is that new offences are being included in the totals, offences for
which more respectable people are being proceeded against, or

Appendix

TABLE 5. *Leeds 1857–75: Persons of 'good' or 'unknown' character as percentage of those arrested for indictable offences or proceeded against summarily*

Year	Male	Female	Both
1857	72·85	51·88	68·57
1858	46·49	32·63	43·14
1859	66·31	46·72	61·84
1860	26·13	29·53	26·98
1861	40·09	37·66	39·54
1862	48·68	38·53	46·51
1863	63·61	40·72	58·80
1864	63·00	38·81	58·01
1865	64·72	37·69	59·19
1866	65·98	28·82	59·71
1867	67·72	46·69	63·52
1868	77·84	45·84	72·16
1869	76·84	53·12	72·21
1870	76·94	68·21	75·07
1871	74·81	52·53	70·31
1872	75·76	63·86	73·36
1873	78·92	62·25	75·15
1874	80·70	63·41	76·90
1875	81·88	67·44	78·49

that old offences are being redefined in a way which brings in more people and more respectable people. One such new offence can in fact be recognized, for prosecutions under the Education Act of 1870 had begun in 1873. In Leeds there were 118 prosecutions for offences under the Education Act in 1873, 311 in 1874 and 260 in 1875. (Prosecutions under the act in other towns in 1875 were: Metropolitan Police District and City of London, 5,280; Liverpool, 1,468; Manchester and Salford, 397; Birmingham, 2,603; Bristol, 754.) If it is assumed that all people thus prosecuted would fall into the 'good plus unknown' category, and an allowance made for this, the increase is reduced in size. The figures for the last three years in the last

TABLE 6. *Leeds 1858–75: Percentage of women of 'good' or 'unknown' character compared with proceedings against prostitutes*

Year	1858	1859	1860	1861	1862	1863	1864	1865	1866
Female 'good+ unknown' (Table 5)	32·6	46·7	29·5	37·7	38·5	40·7	38·8	37·7	28·8
Prostitutes proceeded against under Vagrancy Acts	50	62	85	105	82	89	79	106	89

Year	1867	1868	1869	1870	1871	1872	1873	1874	1875
Female 'good+ unknown' (Table 5)	46·7	45·8	53·1	68·2	52·5	63·9	62·3	63·4	67·4
Prostitutes proceeded against under Vagrancy Acts	151	184	118	49	27	5	2	5	5

column of Table 5 become 74·67, 75·84 and 77·78. The differences are not large, but they illustrate the effect of a single new act. The point has been argued at this length because it shows the danger of using the statistics; one cannot always recognize the new offences which are altering the situation in this way.

The discussion thus far has proceeded on the basis that the boundary between 'good plus unknown' and other categories is a real one and that variations in the percentages shown in Table 5 corresponded to a change in the underlying facts. It is possible that this is not the case, and that people who would be classified as of 'good' or 'unknown' character in one year would be placed in another category at another time. There is a hint of confirmation of this, turning once again on a change of chief constable. Bell took up his duties in statistical 1862, in which year the male percentage of 'good plus unknown' rose to 48·68 from the previous 40·09. In 1863 there was a further rise, to

T–CIS–L

Appendix

63·61, and for the rest of Bell's term the figure remained in th
60s. Wetherall commenced duty in statistical 1867, when th
figure was 67·72 per cent, a little above the previous 65·98. I
1868 the figure rose to 77·84, and for the rest of Wetherall'
term remained in the 70s, save for 1874, the last year, when i
just passed 80. Again, in 1862, Bell's first year, the male 'good
figure at 28·1 per cent and the 'unknown' at 20·7 were not out o
line with figures for earlier years. But the 'good' figure droppe
in 1863 to 7·5 and remained below 10 for the rest of his term
the 'unknown' figure rose in 1863 to 51·6 and remained in th
50s for the rest of his term. In 1867, Wetherall's first year, th
'good' figure rose to 42·5 per cent, and in 1868 and his othe
years it was in the 60s or 70s; in 1867 the 'unknown' figure fe
to 25·2 and only in 1868 and 1870 did it again reach doubl
figures (12·1 and 12·0 respectively). The terms of office of Rea
and English do not show a similar pattern, and the figures fo
Henderson's term, commencing in February 1875, have no
been studied beyond 1876. No great weight is placed on wha
may be a mere coincidence; but it is suggested that this series o
figures, like the others, has little to tell us about the criminals.

The year 1870 is worthy of special attention because o
unusual movements in the figures. Indictable crime droppe
sharply, but the total of summary proceedings was high. Th
figure for prosecutions for drunkenness and drunken and dis
orderly conduct was higher than in all other years save 187
and the rate per mille of the population higher than all year
save 1864 and 1875. An unusually high proportion of th
women arrested or proceeded against were listed as of 'good' o
'unknown' character, and the increase in the number proceede
against summarily was due mainly to an increased number o
women. The total increase in summary proceedings in 187
over 1869 was 1,489; this is more than accounted for by th
increases in drunkenness (657), breaches of the peace (200)
offences against local acts (150) and 'other summary offences
(600) – a total of 1,607. The number of prostitutes proceede
against for offences under the Vagrancy Acts dropped, how
ever, from 118 to 49 (Table 6); perhaps some of the offender

gainst local acts were in fact being prosecuted for offences onnected with prostitution. It seems possible that an exceponal police attitude to petty brawls and so forth was responble for the upsurge, and one wonders whether there is any onnection with the introduction of a full divisional system in 369 (the men no longer paraded at headquarters before going 1 duty) or with the reduction in strength which occurred in 369 or 1870.

Other series have been examined, without profitable results. he combined total of arrests for indictable offences and of immary proceedings (referred to as 'total crime' in Table 3, spite the question-begging implicit in the term) was expressed a rate per mille; similar treatment was given to this same gure with the prosecutions for drunkenness and drunken and sorderly conduct deducted ('total non-drink crime' in Table . The association with changes of chief constable is not reated in either case, and no correlation with what is known of e state of trade can be seen. The same negative results were btained from an examination of the figures for drunkenness d drunken and disorderly conduct (Table 7). It is not possible examine the figures for individual indictable offences, such as rceny from the person or house-breaking, or any combination such offences, because of the lumping together in the statics of offenders dealt with summarily for indictable offences. will be remembered that we cannot get round this by studyg the figures for indictable offences known to the police, beuse a deduction (unrecorded in the printed returns at any te) was made in respect of offences for which someone was ealt with summarily. Individual summary offences can only be amined with caution, as detailed examination of local legistion and local records would be needed to identify offenders categories like 'offences against local acts' and 'other sumary offences'.

It only remains to consider whether any good purpose would served by a study of court records or local newspapers in an ideavour to prepare figures classified in a way that satisfies the eeds of a study such as this. This would obviously be an enor-

mous undertaking, but it would be possible to remove some c
the distortions. However, enough of the sources of error mer
tioned earlier would remain for this to be a vain undertaking.

TABLE 7. *Leeds 1858–75: prosecutions for drunkenness and drunken
and disorderly conduct per mille of the population*

Year	1858	1859	1860	1861	1862	1863	1864	1865	186
Prosecutions	3·44	3·33	4·55	6·21	6·96	7·31	8·19	7·51	6·2

Year	1867	1868	1869	1870	1871	1872	1873	1874	187
Prosecutions	5·64	5·63	5·18	7·66	6·22	5·86	5·95	6·23	7·9

Whatever may be thought about the individual speculatio
in this appendix there seem to be adequate grounds on which t
decide that the statistics of crime in the nineteenth century a
of very little use for the purpose of this book.

Bibliography

1. MANUSCRIPT COLLECTIONS

Chadwick Papers, University College, London
Peel Papers, British Museum
Place Papers, British Museum
Booth Collection, London School of Economics
Webb Local Government Collection, London School of Economics
Criminal Register Letter Book, 1827–56, Home Office
Home Office papers (especially Constabulary Force Commission's papers, 1837–9), Public Record Office
I. E. V. Forrester, *The Middlesex Magistrate 1760–1870—Some Social and Economic Aspects of the Work of J.P.s*, thesis, University of London, 1934
K. K. Macnab, *Aspects of the History of Crime in England and Wales between 1805–1860*, thesis, University of Sussex, 1965

2. PARLIAMENTARY PAPERS

a. Reports of Select Committees on:

County Rates	P.P. 1825, vi
	P.P. 1834, xiv
	P.P. 1835, xiv
Criminal Commitments	P.P. 1826–7, vi
	P.P. 1828, vi
Criminal Laws	P.P. 1819, viii
	P.P. 1824, iv
Drunkenness	P.P. 1834, viii
Education	P.P. 1835, vii

Bibliography

Gaols
                                   P.P. 1813–14, iv
- P.P. 1814–15, iv
- P.P. 1818, viii
- P.P. 1819, vii
- P.P. 1835, xi
- P.P. 1835, xii
- P.P. 1836, xxi
- P.P. 1863, ix

Juvenile Offenders
- P.P. 1847, vii
- P.P. 1852, vii
- P.P. 1852–3, xxiii

Mendicity
- P.P. 1814–5, iii
- P.P. 1816, v

Police
- P.P. 1812, ii
- P.P. 1816, v
- P.P. 1817, vii
- P.P. 1818, viii
- P.P. 1822, iv
- P.P. 1828, vi
- P.P. 1833, xiii
- P.P. 1834, xvi
- P.P. 1837, xii
- P.P. 1838, xv
- P.P. 1852–3, xxxvi

Secondary Punishment
- P.P. 1831, vii
- P.P. 1831–2, vii

Transportation
- P.P. 1812, ii
- P.P. 1837, xix
- P.P. 1837–8, xxii
- P.P. 1856, xvii

b. Reports of Royal Commissions on:

Capital Punishment
- P.P. 1866, xxi

Constabulary Force
- P.P. 1839, xix

County Rates
- P.P. 1836, xxvii

Criminal Law

P.P. 1834, xxvi
P.P. 1836, xxxvi
P.P. 1837, xxxi
P.P. 1839, xix
P.P. 1840, xx
P.P. 1841, x
P.P. 1843, xix
P.P. 1845, xiv
P.P. 1846, xxiv
P.P. 1847, xv
P.P. 1847–8, xxvii
P.P. 1849, xxi

Education — P.P. 1861, xxi(i)

Housing of Working Classes — P.P. 1845, xxx

Poor (Ireland) – Report of the State of the
  Irish Poor in Great Britain — P.P. 1836, xxxiv

Reformatories and Industrial Schools — P.P. 1884, xlv

Transportation — P.P. 1863, xxi

. Other papers:

Departmental Committee on Corporal
  Punishment — P.P. 1937–8, ix

Departmental Committee on Judicial
  Statistics — P.P. 1895, cviii

Departmental Committee on Prisons — P.P. 1895, lvi

Reports by Poor Law Inspectors — P.P. 1866, xxxv

Reports received by Poor Law Commissioners on the State of the Macclesfield
  and Bolton Unions — P.P. 1846, xxxvi

Report of Inspector of Reformatory
  Schools — P.P. 1860, xxxv

Statements regarding Criminals — P.P. 1830, xxiii

Return of Executions — P.P. 1846, xxxiv

Home Office Advisory Council on the Treatment of
Offenders, *Report on Preventive Detention,* 1963

Bibliography

Returns of Criminal Offenders, to 1855
Judicial Statistics, 1856 onwards
Reports of Prison Inspectors, 1836 onwards

3. PRINTED BOOKS

a. Contemporary:

J. Adams, *A Letter to Benjamin Hawes, Esq., M.P. . . .* , 1838
Summary Jurisdiction: A Charge to the Grand Jury of the Quarter Sessions of the County of Middlesex . . . at the April Session, 1849 . . . , 1849

C. B. Adderley, *Transportation not Necessary*, 1851
A Few Thoughts on National Education and Punishments, 1874

A. Alison, *The Principles of Population . . .* , 2 vols., Edinburgh 1840

L. B. Allen, *Brief Considerations on the Present State of the Police of the Metropolis . . .* , 1821

R. Anderson, *Criminals and Crime: Some Facts and Suggestions*, 1907

G. A. Anson, *The Fluctuations of Crime*, Stafford 1895

T. Archer, *The Pauper, the Thief and the Convict . . .* , 1865
The Terrible Sights of London, and Labours of Love in the Midst of Them, 1870

R. Armitage, *Penscellwood Papers, comprising Essays on Capital Punishment . . .* , 2 vols. in 1, 2nd ed., 1853

J. Aspinall, *Liverpool A Few Years Since, By an Old Stager* 1852

J. B. Bailey, *Diary of a Resurrectionist 1811–2, with an Account of Resurrection-men in London*, 1896

F. Baker, *The Moral Tone of the Factory System Defended* 3rd ed., 1850

T. B. L. Baker, *War with Crime, being a Selection of Reprinted Papers on Crime, Reformatories, etc.*, 1889

M. I. Tugan-Baranovsky, *Les crises industrielles en Angleterre* French translation, Paris 1913

H. Barclay, *Juvenile Delinquency: Its Causes and Cure* . . . , Edinburgh 1848

Bayly, Mrs, *Ragged Homes and How to Mend Them*, 1859

G. Barrington, *New London Spy for 1805*, 4th ed., ?1805

T. Beames, *The Rookeries of London, Past, Present and Prospective*, 1st ed., 1850; 2nd ed., 1852

J. T. B. Beaumont, *A Letter to . . . Lord Sidmouth . . . shewing the Extreme Injustice to Individuals and Injury to the Public of the Present System of Public House Licencing* . . . , 1817 (*The Pamphleteer*, vol. ix, p. 433)

J. Bee, *A Living Picture of London for 1828, and Stranger's Guide . . . Shewing the Frauds . . . and Wiles of All Descriptions of Rogues* . . . , 1828

T. Beggs, *An Inquiry into the Extent and Causes of Juvenile Depravity*, 1849
Juvenile Delinquency and Reformatory Institutions; A Lecture delivered . . . 23rd of February, 1857, 1857

W. J. E. Bennett, *Crime and Education; The Duty of the State Therein*, 1846
Bill Sykes and the School Board, 1879

W. A. Bonger, *Criminality and Economic Conditions*, ed. U.S., Boston 1916

C. Booth (ed.), *Life and Labour of the People in London*, revised ed., 17 vols., 1902–3

C. B. P. Bosanquet, *London: Some Account of its Growth, Charitable Agencies, and Wants*, 1868

W. L. Bowles, *Thoughts on the Increase of Crimes, the Education of the Poor and the National Schools* . . . , 2nd ed., 1819 (*The Pamphleteer*, vol. xvi, p. 27)

H. Brandon (ed.), *Poverty, Mendicity and Crime, or the Facts, Examinations, etc. upon which the Report was Founded, Presented to the House of Lords by W. A. Miles, Esq* . . . , 1839

C. D. Brereton, *A Refutation of the First Report of the Constabulary Force Commissioners*, 3 parts in I, n.d. (?1839–40)

H. P. Brougham, Baron Brougham and Vaux, *A Letter to Lord*

Bibliography

Lyndhurst . . . on Criminal Police and National Education, 2nd ed., 1847

J. F. Bryan, *A Lecture on Ragged Schools delivered March 11th, 1856, in . . . Ardwick,* 2nd ed., Manchester 1857

J. T. Burt, *Irish Facts and Wakefield Figures in Relation to Convict Discipline in Ireland,* 1863

J. H. Burton, *Narrative from Criminal Trials in Scotland,* 2 vols., 1852

T. F. Buxton, *An Inquiry, Whether Crime and Misery are Produced or Prevented, by Our Present System of Prison Discipline,* 1st ed., 1818

A. McN. Caird, *The Cry of the Children,* 2nd ed., Edinburgh 1849

C. A. de Calonne, *Projet pour obvier aux vols de grand chemin dans les environs de Londres,* 1801

J. Caminada, *Twenty-five Years of Detective Life,* 2 vols., Manchester 1895–1901

E. Carpenter, *Prisons, Police and Punishment . . . ,* 1905

M. Carpenter, *Reformatory Schools for the Children of the Perishing and Dangerous Classes, and for Juvenile Offenders,* 1851
Juvenile Delinquents – Their Condition and Treatment, 1853
The Claims of Ragged Schools to Pecuniary Educational Aid . . . , 1859
What Shall We Do With Our Pauper Children?, 1861
Our Convicts, 2 vols., 1864
Day Industrial Feeding Schools . . . , Bristol 1874

—. Cartwright, *Criminal Management,* 1865

T. A. Cavanagh, *Scotland Yard, Past and Present,* 1893

S. Cave, *Prevention and Reformation: The Duty of the State or of Individuals? . . . ,* 1856

F. N. Charrington, *The Battle of the Music Halls,* n.d. (c. 1885)

G. L. Chesterton, *Revelations of Prison Life, with an Enquiry into Prison Discipline and Secondary Punishments,* 2 vols., 2nd ed., 1856

L. M. Moreau-Christophe, *Du problème de la misère et de sa solution chez les peuples anciens et modernes,* 3 vols., Paris 1851

City of London, *Report from Committee of Aldermen Appointed to Visit Several Gaols in England* ... , 1816

C. T. Clarkson & J. Hall Richardson, *Police!,* 1889

W. L. Clay, *The Prison Chaplain; A Memoir of the Rev. J. Clay, B.D.* ... , Cambridge 1861
Our Convict Systems, Cambridge 1862

G. Combe, *Remarks on the Principles of Criminal Legislation and the Practice of Prison Discipline,* 1854

Committee Appointed to Examine into the State of Juvenile Crime in Newcastle and Gateshead, *Report,* Newcastle 1852

Considerations of the Police Report of the Year 1816, with A Plan for Suppressing Thieving, 1822 (*The Pamphleteer,* vol. xxi, p. 207)

Convict Life, or Revelations Concerning Convicts and Convict Prisons, by a Ticket-of-Leave Man, 1st ed., 1879

C. Cottu, *De l'administration de la justice criminelle en Angleterre* ... , Paris 1820

Criminal Biography: Comprising Trials and Memoirs of the Most Notorious Characters ... *since the Commencement of the 18th Century,* 2 vols., 1829

Criminal Manchester ... , Manchester ?1874

W. Crofton, *The Immunity of 'Habitual Criminals'* ... , 1861
The Criminal Classes and Their Control, 1868
Is Our Treatment of Habitual Criminals Satisfactory?, 1871

Custos, *The Police Force of the Metropolis in 1868,* 1868

S. P. Day, *Juvenile Crime, its Causes, Character, and Cure,* 1858

A. J. B. Defauconpret, *Quinze jours à Londres, à la fin de 1815,* Paris 1816
Dens of London Exposed, 1835

W. Denton, *Observations on the Displacement of the Poor by Metropolitan Railways and by Other Public Improvements,* 1861

Bibliography

J. Devon, *The Criminal and the Community*, 1912

C. Dickens, *Oliver Twist,* 1837–8 (ed. K. Tillotson, Oxford 1966)
Bleak House, 1852
Reprinted Pieces

W. H. Dixon, *The London Prisons* ..., 1850

—. Downing, *A Series of Letters, on Rural Police and the Poor Law Amendment Act* ..., Ipswich 1838

R. Dobie, *The History of the United Parishes of St. Giles in the Fields and St. George Bloomsbury* ..., 1829

E. F. Du Cane, *The Punishment and Prevention of Crime,* 1885

E. Ducpetiaux, *De la justice de prévoyance et particulièrement de l'influence de la misère ... sur le nombre des crimes*, Brussels 1827

T. B. W. Dudley, *The Tocsin: Or, a Review of the London Police Establishments, with Hints for Their Improvement* ..., 1828

J. Dufton, *The Prison and the School: A Letter to Lord John Russell*, 1848

P. Egan, *Life in London* ..., 1821 ed., reprinted 1900

H. L. Elliot, *Causes of Crime, Considered from a Social Point of View*, 1868

W. Ellis, *Where Must We Look for the Further Prevention of Crime?*, 1857

F. Engels, *Condition of the Working Class in England in 1844,* English translation, 1892

D. M. Evans, *Facts, Failures and Frauds – Revelations Financial, Mercantile, Criminal*, 1859

An Exposure of the Various Impositions Daily Practised by Vagrants of Every Description, Birmingham n.d.

L. Faucher, *Études sur l'Angleterre*, 2 vols., 1st ed., Paris 1845

Fidget, *A Letter to the Lord Mayor and Citizens of London Respecting the Introduction of the New Police*, 1838

J. Field, *Prison Discipline; And the Advantages of the Separate System* ..., 2 vols., 2nd ed., 1848

Five Years Penal Servitude, by One Who Has Endured It, 4th ed., 1878

C. R. Ford, *The Boys' Beadle,* 1868

J. B. Freeland, *State of the Police in the Rural Districts, with Some Suggestions for Improvement,* Chichester 1839

H. A. Fregier, *Des classes dangereuses de la population dans les grandes villes et des moyens de les rendre meilleures,* 2 vols., Paris 1840

J. Garwood, *The Million-Peopled City* . . . , 1853

H. Gavin, *Sanitary Ramblings* . . . , 1848

G. Godwin, *London Shadows: A Glance at the 'Homes' of the Thousands,* 1854
Town Swamps and Social Bridges; The Sequel to 'A Glance . . .', 1859

M. Gore, *On the Dwellings of the Poor* . . . , 2nd ed., 1851

J. Grant, *The Great Metropolis* . . . , 2 vols., 2nd ed., 1837
Sketches in London, 1st ed., 1838

J. Greenwood, *The Seven Curses of London,* ?1869
The Wilds of London, 1876
The Policeman's Lantern: Strange Stories of London Life, 1888
The Prisoner in the Dock, 1902

G. N. T. Grenville, Baron Nugent, *On the Punishment of Death by Law* . . . , 1840

J. Gurney, *The Charge* . . . *to the Grand Jury* . . . *of Gloucester* . . . , Gloucester 1832

J. Hanway, *The Defects of Police, the Cause of Immorality, and the Continual Robberies Committed, Particularly in and about the Metropolis* . . . , 1775

G. W. Hastings, *Address on the Repression of Crime* . . . , 1875

Head Constable's Report on the State of the Liverpool Police Force, Liverpool 1857

E. Hill, *Criminal Capitalists,* 1872

F. Hill, *Crime, its Amount, Causes and Remedies,* 1853
The Substitute for Capital Punishment, 1866
Frederic Hill: An Autobiography . . . , 1893

Bibliography

M. Hill & C. F. Cornwallis, *Two Prize Essays on Juvenile Delinquency*, 1853

M. D. Hill, *Report of a Charge ... to the Grand Jury ... of Birmingham ... 1848*, 1848
Suggestions for the Repression of Crime, Contained in Charges Delivered to Grand Juries of Birmingham ..., 1857
Report of a Charge ... to the Grand Jury ... of Birmingham ... 1864, 1864

M. D. Hill & J. E. Eardley-Wilmot, *Papers on Grand Juries*, 1865

R. & F. Davenport-Hill, *The Recorder of Birmingham: A Memoir of Matthew Davenport Hill ...*, 1878

J. Hogg, *London As It Is ... Health, Habits and Amusements of the People*, 1837

J. Hollingshead, *Ragged London in 1861*, 1861

T. Holmes, *Known to the Police*, 1908

J. W. Horsley, *Jottings from Jail: Notes and Papers on Prison Matters*, 1887
Prisons and Prisoners, 1898
'I Remember' – Memories of a 'Sky Pilot' in the Prison and the Slum, 1911
How Criminals are Made and Prevented – a Retrospect of Forty Years, 1913

W. Hoyle, *Crime in England and Wales in the 19th Century ...*, 1876
Crime and Pauperism – A Letter to ... W. E. Gladstone, Manchester 1881

A. Hume, *Missions at Home, or A Clergyman's Account of a Portion of the Town of Liverpool*, 1850
Condition of Liverpool, Liverpool 1858
State and Prospects of the Church in Liverpool, Liverpool 1869

T. Hastings Ingham, *Reformatory Schools: Report of a Speech delivered at the Quarter Sessions of the Peace for the West Riding ... Pontefract, 2nd April 1855*, Skipton 1855

R. Jackson, *Considerations on the Increase of Crime ...*, 1828 (*The Pamphleteer*, vol. xxix, p. 307)

A. O. M. Jay, *Life in Darkest London . . .*, 1891
   The Social Problem and its Possible Solution, 1893

H. S. Joseph, *Memoirs of Convicted Prisoners . . . Remarks on the Causes and Prevention of Crime*, 1853

J. P. Kay, *The Moral and Physical Conditions of the Working classes . . . in Manchester*, 2nd ed., 1832

J. Kingsmill, *Chapters on Prisons and Prisoners, and the Prevention of Crime*, 3rd ed., 1854
   Our Police: Friendly Counsels to the Police, 1860

W. L. Melville Lee, *A History of Police in England*, 1901

Letter to a Member of Parliament on the Police of the Metropolis, by a Barrister, 1821

A Letter to His Grace the Duke of Wellington, containing Practical Suggestions for the Regulating of the Currency . . . and the Preventing, Detecting and Correcting of Crime, by an Englishman, 1828

Liverpool Life, its Pleasures, Practices and Pastimes, 2 series bound in 1, Liverpool 1857

London Committee for Investigating the Causes of the Alarming Increase of Juvenile Delinquency in the Metropolis, *Report*, 1816

T. Wright McDermid, *The Life of Thomas Wright, of Manchester, The Prison Philanthropist*, Manchester 1876

D. H. Macfarlane, *Criminal Contrasts; Property versus Person: Inequality of Sentences*, 1884

G. B. Mainwaring, *Observations on the Present State of Police of the Metropolis*, 1st ed., 1821 (*The Pamphleteer,* vol. xix, p. 531); 2nd ed., 1822 (*The Pamphleteer,* vol. xx, p. 211)

O. C. Malvery, *The Soul Market . . .*, 1906

E. Martin, *The Punishment of Death – A Lecture*, 1849

H. Mayhew, *London Labour and the London Poor . . .*, 4 vols., 1861–2

H. Mayhew & J. Binny, *The Criminal Prisons of London and Scenes of Prison Life*, 1862

H. Mayhew & others, *London Characters . . .*, 1st ed., 1874

G. Melly, *Juvenile Crime and Reformatory Schools: An Address delivered . . . 3rd March, 1858 . . .*, Liverpool 1858

Bibliography

J. E. Mercier, *The Conditions of Life in Angel Meadow*, Manchester ?1897

S. Meredith, *A Book about Criminals*, 1881

W. A. Miles, *Suggestions for the Formation of a General Police . . .*, 1836

A Letter to Lord John Russell Concerning Juvenile Delinquency . . ., Shrewsbury 1837

and see H. Brandon (ed.), *Poverty, Mendicity and Crime . . .*, p. 313, above

Minutes of Evidence . . . Before a Select Committee . . . into the State of the Police of the Metropolis, with Notes . . . by a Magistrate of the County of Middlesex, 1816

J. Mirehouse, *Crime and its Causes . . .*, 1840

W. Monney, *Considerations on Prisons with a Plan for their Regulation . . . and the Prevention of Crimes . . .*, 1812

B. Montagu, *Some Inquiries respecting the Penalty of Death for Crimes without Violence*, 1818 (*The Pamphleteer*, vol. XII, pp. 287, 319)

J. M. Morgan, *Religion and Crime; Or, the Condition of the People*, 1840

A. Morrison, *Tales of Mean Streets*, 1894

A Child of the Jago, 1st ed., 1896; Penguin ed., 1946

The Hole in the Wall, 1902

W. D. Morrison, *Crime and Its Causes*, 1891

Juvenile Offenders, 1896

P. J. Murray, *Reformatory Schools in France and England*, 1854

S. Neal, *Special Report on the State of Juvenile Education and Delinquency in . . . Salford . . .*, 2nd ed., Salford 1851

W. B. Neale, *Juvenile Delinquency in Manchester; Its Causes and History, its Consequences . . .*, Manchester 1840

F. G. P. Neison, *Contributions to Vital Statistics, with . . . an Investigation into the Progress of Crime in England and Wales*, 3rd ed., 1857

Observations on a Letter by J. E. Eardley-Wilmot . . . to the Magistrates of Warwickshire, 1820

Old Bailey Experiences, Criminal Jurisprudence ... by the Author of 'The Schoolmaster's Experiences in Newgate', 1833

W. C. Osborn, *A Lecture on the Prevention of Crime delivered ... Town Hall, Ipswich, November 26th, 1849,* Ipswich n.d.

  The Plea of 'Not Guilty' ... considered in a Letter to ... Sir G. Grey ..., 1847

  The Preservation of Youth from Crime: A Nation's Duty ..., 1860

W. Pare, *A Plan for the Suppression of the Predatory Classes ...,* 1862

C. S. Parker, *Sir Robert Peel from his Private Papers ...,* 3 vols., 1st ed., 1899

W. Parkes, *The Destitute and Criminal Juveniles of Manchester,* Manchester 1854

C. Pearson, *What is to be Done with our Criminals? A Letter to the Rt. Hon. the Lord Mayor,* 1857

C. Phillips, *Vacation Thoughts on Capital Punishment,* 4th ed., 1858

The Philosophy of Ragged Schools, 1851 (Small Books on Great Subjects, no. 18)

Watts Phillips, *The Wild Tribes of London,* 1855

G. H. Pike, *Golden Lane,* 1876

  Pity for the Perishing ..., 1884

L. O. Pike, *A History of Crime in England ...,* 2 vols., 1873–6

J. W. Polidori, *On the Punishment of Death,* 1816 (*The Pamphleteer,* vol. viii, p. 281)

Preface to Minutes of Evidence Taken Before ... Committee ... into the State of Mendicity and Vagrancy, 1815

W. C. Preston, *The Bitter Cry of Outcast London,* 1883

  'Light and Shade', Pictures of London Life, a Sequel to 'The Bitter Cry ...', 1885

A. Pulling, *Crime and Criminals: Is the Gaol the Only Preventive?,* 1863

Bibliography

R. F. Quinton, *Crime and Criminals 1876–1910*, 1910
The Modern Prison Curriculum . . . , 1912

Ragged Schools in Relation to the Government Grants for Education: Authorised Report of the Conference held at Birmingham January 23, 1861, 1861

F. L. G. von Raumer, *England in 1835* . . . , 1836

A Regency Visitor; The English Tour of Prince Pueckler-Muskau described in his Letters, 1826–8, 1957

Remarks on the Present Unconnected State of the Police Authorities of the Metropolis . . . by a Police Magistrate, 1821

Report of the Proceedings of a Conference on the Subject of Preventive and Reformatory Schools held at Birmingham on the 9th and 10th December, 1851, 1851

Report of the Proceedings of the 2nd Conference on the Subject of Juvenile Delinquency . . . Birmingham, Dec. 20th, 1853, 1854

J. M. Rhodes, *Pauperism, Past and Present*, ?1891

R. Ricardo, *Juvenile Vagrancy: Suggestions for its Diminution*, n.d. (?1848)

J. E. Ritchie, *The Night Side of London*, 1st ed., 1857; new, revised and enlarged ed., 1869
Here and There in London, 1859
Days and Nights in London, 1880

J. Robertson *The Progress of Crime and What is Crime* . . . , 1847

F. W. Robinson, *Female Life in Prison, by a Prison Matron*, rev. ed., 1864
Memoirs of Jane Cameron, Female Convict, by a Prison Matron . . . , 1864

S. Romilly, *Observations on the Criminal Law of England* . . . , 1st ed., 1810
The Speeches of Sir Samuel Romilly in the House of Commons, 2 vols., 1820
Life . . . by Himself . . . , 2 vols., 3rd ed., 1842

B. Rotch, *Suggestions for the Prevention of Juvenile Depravity*, 1846

F. Rowton, *The Penalty of Death Reviewed,* 1846

E. Rushton, *Juvenile Delinquency,* 1842
A Letter ... upon Juvenile Crime ..., Liverpool 1850

C. Russell & H. S. Lewis, *The Jew in London ...,* 1900

C. E. B. Russell, *Young Gaol-birds,* 1910
The Problem of Juvenile Crime, Barnett House Papers, no. 1, 1917

W. O. Russell, *A Treatise on Crimes and Misdemeanours,* 2 vols., 1st ed., 1819, and subsequent editions

Sinks of London Laid Open ... with Flash Dictionary, 1848

H. Shimmin, *Liverpool Sketches ...,* 1862

Society for Promoting the Amendment of the Law, *The Treatment of Criminal Children,* 1854

Society for the Abolition of Capital Punishment, *Analysis and Review of the Blue Book of the Royal Commission on Capital Punishment,* 1866

Society for the Improvement of Prison Discipline ..., *Report,* 1818
Sixth Report, 1824

R. J. Statham, *Suggestions for ... an Industrial Association, in Connection with National Schools, as a Preventive of Crime, Vagrancy and Pauperism,* 1851

G. Stephen, *A Letter to ... Lord John Russell ... on the Probable Increase of Rural Crime, in consequence of the Introduction of the new Poor Law and Railroad Systems,* 1836

J. F. Stephen, *History of the Criminal Law of England,* 3 vols., 1883

J. Syme, *Nine Years in Van Diemen's Land ... an Essay on Prison Discipline; and the Results of the Working of the Probation System ...,* Dundee 1848

J. C. Symons, *A Plea for Schools, which sets forth the Dearth of Education and the Growth of Crime ...,* 1847
Tactics for the Times, as regards the Condition and Treatment of the Dangerous Classes, 1849

H. Taine, *Notes on England,* English translation, 1872

Tales of Manchester Life, by a Manchester Minister, Manchester n.d.

Bibliography

W. Tallack, *A General Review of the Subject of Capital Punishment*, n.d.
The Practical Results of the Total or Partial Abolition of Capital Punishment in Various Countries, 1866
The Problem of Diminishing Prevalent Destitution and Temptations to Crime, 1869

H. Taylor, *Crime Considered in a Letter to the Rt. Hon. W. E. Gladstone, M.P.*, 1868

J. S. Taylor, *Selections from the Writings . . .* , 1843

A. Thomson, *Punishment and Prevention,* Edinburgh 1857
Thoughts on Prison Labour . . . , 1824

J. C. Traill, *A Letter to . . . Lord Brougham and Vaux on the Police Reports and the Police Bills*, 1839

C. J. Ribton-Turner, *A History of Vagrants and Vagrancy and Beggars and Begging*, 1887

J. Wade, *A Treatise on the Police and Crimes of the Metropolis . . . by the Editor of the 'Cabinet Lawyer'*, 1829

E. G. Wakefield, *Householders in Danger from the Populace,* n.d. (?1831–2)
Facts Relating to the Punishment of Death in the Metropolis, 2nd ed., 1832

R. S. Watson, *Industrial Schools*, Newcastle 1867

W. Watson, *The Juvenile Vagrant and the Industrial School . . .* , Aberdeen 1851

B. Waugh, *The Gaol Cradle: Who Rocks It? A Plea for the Abolition of Juvenile Imprisonment, by a Member of the School Board for London*, 3rd ed., 1876

E. Webster & others, *Three Papers on Capital Punishment* , 1856

C. C. Western, *Remarks on Prison Discipline . . .* , 1821
Substance of a Letter published in 1821 . . . with a few Remarks on the Criminal Code, 1828

F. Wharton, *Political Economy and Criminal Law,* Jersey City 1882
What is to be Done with Our Convicts? Sketch of a System of Penal State Servitude . . . , Edinburgh 1851

R. Whateley, *Thoughts on Secondary Punishment* ... , 1832
Remarks on Transportation, 1834

A. White (ed.), *The Letters of S.G.O. A Series of Letters* ...
written by the Rev. Lord Sidney Godolphin Osborne ... , 2
vols., 1890

R. Williams, *London Rookeries and Colliers' Slums* ... ,
1893

J. E. Eardley-Wilmot, *A Letter to the Magistrates of War-
wickshire on the Increase of Crime* ... , 1820
*A second Letter to the Magistrates of Warwickshire on the
Increase of Crime* ... *particularly of Juvenile Delinquency
... Causes and Remedies* ... , 1820
*A Letter to the Magistrates of England on the Increase of
Crime* ... , 2nd ed., 1827 (*The Pamphleteer,* vol xxix, p.
1)

R. A. Woods *et al., The Poor in Great Cities* ... , 1896

H. W. Woolrych, *On the Report of the Capital Punishment
Commission of 1866,* no place, 1866

H. Worsley, *Juvenile Depravity,* 1849

T. Wrightson, *On the Punishment of Death,* 1833

b. Modern:

J. V. W. Barry, *Alexander Maconochie of Norfolk Island,* Melbourne 1958

C. Bateson, *The Convict Ships,* Glasgow 1959

E. M. Bell, *Josephine Butler,* 1962

E. Ruggles-Brise, *The English Prison System,* 1921

J. G. Broodbank, *History of the Port of London,* 2 vols., 1921

A. Bryant, *Liquid History: To Commemorate Fifty Years of
the Port of London Authority, 1909–1959,* 1960

W. L. Burn, *The Age of Equipoise,* 1964

G. S. Cadbury, *Young Offenders, Yesterday and Today,* 1938

E. C. G. Cadogan, *The Roots of Evil* ... *the Methods of Dealing with Crime and the Criminal during the 18th and 19th
Centuries* ... , 1937

Bibliography

L. Chevalier, *Classes laborieuses et classes dangereuses à Paris pendant la première moitié du 19ème siècle*, Paris 1958

H. Cole, *Things for the Surgeon*, 1964

P. Collins, *Dickens and Crime*, 1962

S. E. Finer, *The Life and Times of Sir Edwin Chadwick*, 1952

W. D. Forsyth, *Governor Arthur's Convict System, Van Diemen's Land, 1824–36*, 1935

L. Fox, *The English Prison and Borstal System*, 1952

N. Gash, *Mr Secretary Peel*, 1961

M. D. George, *London Life in the Eighteenth Century*, 1925

H. Goddard, *Memoirs of a Bow Street Runner*, 1956

M. Gruenhut, *Penal Reform*, Oxford 1948

A. Hasluck, *Unwilling Emigrants – A Study of the Convict Period in Western Australia*, Melbourne 1959

K. Heasman, *Evangelicals in Action*, 1962

R. S. E. Hinde, *The British Penal System, 1773–1950*, 1951

K. Hollingsworth, *The Newgate Novel, 1830–47 – Bulwer, Ainsworth, Dickens and Thackeray*, Detroit 1963

W. E. Houghton, *The Victorian Frame of Mind, 1830–1870*, 1957

G. Howson, *Thief-Taker General, The Rise and Fall of Jonathan Wild*, 1970

J. A. Jackson, *The Irish in Britain*, 1963

L. James, *Fiction for the Working Man, 1830–50*, 1963

W. Branch-Johnson, *The English Prison Hulks*, 1957

J. van Kan, *Les Causes économiques de la criminalité* ꓤꓤꓤꓤ Paris 1903

J. Kent, *Elizabeth Fry*, 1962

Leeds Police Centenary, 1836–1936, Leeds 1936

D. Marshall, *English People in the Eighteenth Century*, 1956

T. P. Morris, *The Criminal Area*, 1958

J. F. Moylan, *Scotland Yard and the Metropolitan Police*, 1st ed., 1929

C. G. Oakes, *Sir Samuel Romilly, 1757–1818 . . .* , 1935

E. O'Brien, *The Foundation of Australia (1786–1800)*, 2nd ed., Sydney 1950

W. T. O'Dea, *The Social History of Lighting*, 1958

D. Owen, *English Philanthropy, 1660–1960*, Cambridge, Mass. 1965

S. G. Partridge, *Prisoner's Progress*, 1935

P. Pringle, *The Thief-Takers*, 1958

L. Radzinowicz, *History of the English Criminal Law*, 3 vols., 1948–56
    Ideology and Crime: A Study of Crime in its Social and Historical Context, 1966

C. Reith, *The Police Idea*, 1938
    British Police and the Democratic Ideal, 1943
    A New Study of Police History, Edinburgh 1956

L. L. Robson, *The Convict Settlers of Australia*, Melbourne 1965

M. Rose, *The East End of London*, 1951

A. G. L. Shaw, *Convicts and the Colonies; A Study of Penal Transportation . . .*, 1966

D. S. Thomas, *Social Aspects of the Business Cycle*, 1925

E. Tuttle, *The Crusade Against Capital Punishment in Great Britain*, 1961

United Nations Department of Social Affairs, *Probation and Related Measures*, New York 1951

R. B. Ward, *The Australian Legend*, Melbourne 1958

S. & B. Webb, *English Poor Law History*, 3 vols., 1st ed., reprinted 1963
    English Prisons Under Local Government, 1st ed., reprinted 1963
    The History of Liquor Licensing in England, 1st ed., reprinted 1963

B. D. White, *A History of the Corporation of Liverpool 1835–1914*, Liverpool 1951

A. F. Young & E. T. Ashton, *British Social Work in the 19th Century*, 1956

4. PERIODICALS

Anon., 'Injured Innocents', *All the Year Round*, new ser., vol. i, Apr. 1869, p. 414

Bibliography

'How We Make Thieves', ibid., new ser., vol. vii, Feb. 1872, p. 279

'Cautionary Hints to Speculators on the Increase of Crimes', *Blackwood's Magazine*, vol. iii, May 1818, p. 176

'Imprisonment and Transportation', ibid., vol. lv, May 1844, p. 533

'Causes of the Increase of Crime', ibid., vol. lvi, July 1844, p. 1

'On Convict Management', *British Quarterly Review,* vol. xxxvii, Apr. 1863, p. 314

Letter from G.G.G., *Charity Organisation Reporter,* vol. xii, 22 Mar. 1883, p. 94

'Thieves and Thieving', *Cornhill Magazine,* vol. ii, Sept. 1860, p. 326

'Professional Thieves', ibid., vol. vi, Nov. 1862, p. 640

'The Science of Garrotting and Housebreaking', ibid., vol. vii, Jan. 1863, p. 79

'A Day's Pleasure with the Criminal Classes', ibid., vol. ix, May 1864, p. 627

'Letter from a Convict in Australia to his Brother', ibid., vol. xiii, Apr. 1866, p. 489

'Criminal Women', ibid., vol. xiv, Aug. 1866, p. 152

'Our Police System', *Dark Blue,* vol. ii, Feb. 1872, p. 692

'Juvenile Depravity', *Eclectic Review*, new ser., vol. xxvii, Feb. 1850, p. 200

'Juvenile Delinquency', ibid., new ser., vol. vii, Apr. 1854, p. 385

'Police of the Metropolis, Causes and Prevention of Crimes', *Edinburgh Review*, vol. xlvii, Dec. 1828, p. 411

'Police of the Metropolis', ibid., vol. lxvi, Jan. 1838, p. 358

'What Is To Be Done With Our Criminals?', ibid., vol. lxxxvi, July 1847, p. 214

'Young Criminals', ibid., vol. xciv, Oct. 1851, p. 403

'The Police System of London', ibid., vol. xcvi, July 1852, p. 1

'The Management and Disposal of our Criminal Population', ibid., vol. c, Oct. 1854, p. 563

'The Correction of Juvenile Offenders', ibid., vol. ci, Apr. 1855, p. 383

'Life in the Criminal Class', ibid., vol. cxxii, Oct. 1865, p. 337

'Juvenile Offenders', *English Review*, vol. xvii, July 1852, p. 241

'The Schoolmaster's Experience in Newgate', *Fraser's Magazine,* June–Nov. 1832, vol. v, pp. 521, 736; vol. vi, pp. 12, 285, 460

'Principles of Police, and Their Application to the Metropolis', ibid., vol. xvi, Aug. 1837, p. 169

'Some Thoughts on the Connexion of Crime and Punishment', ibid., vol. xx, Dec. 1839, p. 689

'Obituary Notice of John Townsend', *Gentleman's Magazine*, vol. cii, July 1832, p. 91

'Notice on the Death of George Ruthven', ibid., new ser., vol. xxi, May 1844, p. 552

Obituary of T. B. L. Baker, *Gloucestershire Chronicle*, 11 Dec. 1886, p. 5

'Discrepant Criminal Statistics', *Journal of the Statistical Society*, vol. xxxi, Sept. 1868, p. 349

'Transportation', *London Review*, vol. i, Feb. 1829, p. 112

'A Treatise on the Police of the Metropolis', *Monthly Review Enlarged*, vol. xx, Aug. 1796, p. 408

'Report from the Police Committee', ibid., vol. lxxxi, Oct.–Dec. 1816, pp. 198, 311, 418

'Report of the Police Committee, May 1817', ibid., vol. lxxxiv, Oct. 1817, p. 182

'Second Report on Police', ibid, Dec. 1817, p. 384

'Juvenile Criminals', *North British Review,* vol. x, Nov. 1848, p. 1

'Thieves and Thieves' Children', *Once a Week,* vol. iv, May 1861, p. 548

'Forethought for Winter Nights', ibid., vol. vii, Nov. 1862, p. 569

'Thieves in a London Ragged School', ibid., vol. xii, Jan. 1865, p. 62

Bibliography

'The Disposal of Stolen Goods', ibid., vol. xii, Jan. 1865, p. 128

'Suppressing Vice', *Police Review*, vol. lxxi, 30 Aug. 1963, p. 721

'Juvenile Delinquency', *Prospective Review,* vol. ii, 1846, p. 297

'Society in Danger from Children', ibid., vol. ix, 1853, p. 165

'Juvenile Delinquency', ibid., vol. x, Feb. 1854, p. 69

'Amendments of the Criminal Law', *Quarterly Review*, vol. xxxvii, Jan. 1828, p. 147

'The Police and the Thieves', ibid, vol. xcix, June 1856, p. 160

'The Disposal and Control of Our Criminal Classes', *St Paul's Magazine*, vol. iii, Feb. 1869, p. 599

'Crime and its Perpetrators', *Scottish Review,* vol. ii, Jan. 1854, p. 69

Police Report, *The Times*, 28 Jan. 1848, p. 7

Leading Article, ibid., 23 Oct. 1850, p. 4

Leading Article, ibid., 14 Nov. 1856, p. 8

'Capture of 50 Thieves', ibid., 28 Feb. 1861, p. 12

Letter signed 'Australian', ibid., 22 Mar. 1862, p. 5

Leading Article, ibid., 10 Mar. 1869, p. 9

Letter signed N.A.W., ibid., 10 Mar. 1869, p. 4

Letter signed N.A.W., ibid., 12 Mar. 1869, p. 4

Leading Article, ibid., 26 Aug. 1884, p. 3

'Young Criminals', *Westminster Review,* new ser., vol. iv, July 1853, p. 137

R. Anderson, 'Our Absurd System of Punishing Crime', *Nineteenth Century*, vol. xlix, Feb. 1901, p. 268

'The Punishment of Crime', ibid., vol. l, July 1901, p. 77

T. B. L. Baker, 'On the Official Criminal Statistics of England and Wales, 1854–9', *Journal of the Statistical Society,* vol. xxiii, Dec. 1860, p. 427

R. M. Barrett, 'The Treatment of Juvenile Offenders', ibid., vol. lxiii, part 2, June 1900, p. 183

E. Chadwick, 'Preventive Police', *London Review,* vol. i, Feb. 1829, p. 252

'On the Consolidation of Police Forces and Prevention of Crime', *Fraser's Magazine,* vol. lxxvii, Jan. 1868, p. 1

M. Clark, 'The Origins of the Convicts Transported to Eastern Australia, 1787–1852', *Historical Studies Australia and New Zealand,* May and Nov. 1956, vol. vii, pp. 121, 314

J. Clay, 'Criminal Statistics of Preston', *Journal of the Statistical Society,* vol. ii, Mar. 1839, p. 84

'On the Effect of Good or Bad Times on Committals to Prison', ibid., vol. xviii, Mar. 1855, p. 74, and vol. xx, Dec. 1857, p. 378

'On the Relation Between Crime, Population Instruction, etc.,' ibid., vol. xx, Mar. 1857, p. 22

W. Crofton, 'On the Treatment of Our Juvenile Offenders', *Good Words,* vol. xxii, 1881, p. 458

E. F. Du Cane, 'The Decrease of Crime', *Nineteenth Century,* vol. xxxiii, Mar. 1893, p. 480

H. J. Dyos, 'Urban Transformation: A Note on the Objects of Street Improvement in Regency and Early Victorian London', *International Review of Social History,* vol. ii, part 2, 1957, p. 259

J. H. Elliot, 'The Increase of Material Prosperity and of Moral Agents Compared with the State of Crime and Pauperism', *Journal of the Statistical Society,* vol. xxxi, Sept. 1868, p. 299

W. Gilbert, 'A Plea for Criminal Boys', *Good Words,* vol. vii, Apr. 1866, p. 297

'The Thieves' Quarters', ibid., vol. ix, Sept. 1868, p. 552

D. V. Glass, 'A Note on the Under-Registration in Britain in the 19th Century', *Population Studies,* vol. v, July 1951, p. 70

G. Grosvenor, 'Statistics of the Abatement of Crime in England and Wales in the 20 Years ended 1887–88', *Journal of the Statistical Society,* vol. liii, Sept. 1890, p. 377

J. M. Hart, 'Reform of the Borough Police, 1835–56', *English Historical Review,* vol. lxx, July 1955, p. 411

Bibliography

'The County and Borough Police Act, 1856', *Journal of Public Administration*, vol. xxxiv, winter 1956, p. 405

H. W. Holland, 'The Art of Self-Protection against Thieves and Robbers', *Good Words,* vol. vii, Dec. 1866, p. 847

C. H. S. Jayewardine, 'The English Precursors of Lombroso', *British Journal of Criminology*, vol. iv, Oct. 1963, p. 164

A. Lindesmith & Y. Levin, 'The Lombrosan Myth in Criminology', *American Journal of Sociology*, vol. xlii, Mar. 1937 p. 653

J. L. Lyman, 'The Metropolitan Police Act of 1829', *Journal of Criminal Law, Criminology and Police Science,* vol. lv, Mar 1964, p. 141

W. D. Morrison, 'The Increase of Crime', *Nineteenth Century* vol. xxxi, June 1892, p. 950
'The Study of Crime', *Mind*, new ser., vol. i, Oct. 1892, p 489

E. H. Powell, 'Crime as a Function of Anomie', *Journal of Criminal Law, Criminology and Police Science,* vol. lvii, June 1966, p. 161

G. D. Robin, 'Pioneers in Criminology: William Douglas Morrison', ibid., vol. lv, Mar. 1964, p. 48

W. H. Watts, 'Records of an Old Police Court', *St James's Magazine*, 1864–5, vol. x, pp. 353, 458; vol. xi, p. 444; vol. xii pp. 232, 499

G. Weight, 'Statistics of the Parish of St George the Martyr Southwark', *Journal of the Statistical Society,* vol. iii, Apr. 1841, pp. 50–71

Journal of the Statistical Society, 1839 onwards.
Reformatory and Refuge Journal, 1861 onwards.

Subject Index

Subject Index

Index of Persons and Places

(Fictional characters are indexed under the name of their creator)

Index of Persons and Places